Sir Henry Knollys

English Life in China

Sir Henry Knollys

English Life in China

ISBN/EAN: 9783337003999

Printed in Europe, USA, Canada, Australia, Japan

Cover: Foto ©ninafisch / pixelio.de

More available books at **www.hansebooks.com**

ENGLISH LIFE
IN
CHINA

ENGLISH LIFE

IN

CHINA

BY

MAJOR HENRY KNOLLYS

ROYAL ARTILLERY

AUTHOR OF 'FROM SEDAN TO SAARBRUCK'
EDITOR OF 'INCIDENTS IN THE SEPOY WAR' 'INCIDENTS IN THE CHINA WAR'
ETC.

LONDON
SMITH, ELDER, & CO., 15 WATERLOO PLACE
1885

PREFACE.

THE statements contained in this book have, at all events, the advantage of having been recorded on the spot, and at the time when they were originally deduced. Taken down day by day in shorthand, I venture to hope that the opinions may possess the freshness, sometimes so conducive to accuracy, of first impressions; while the authenticity of the facts has been safe-guarded by subsequent careful revision.

HENRY KNOLLYS,
Major, Royal Artillery.

ARTHUR'S CLUB, ST. JAMES', LONDON

CONTENTS.

CHAPTER I.

OUR FARTHEST BRITISH OUTPOST—HONG KONG.
PAGE

Ignorance concerning Hong Kong—Beauty of harbour—Interior of houses—The bank—Shops—Flowers—Means of transport—Shipping—Chinese funeral—Population—Pedlars—The 'Happy Valley'—Precautions against rain—Hourly record of a hot day—Botanical Gardens—Hong Kong healthy or unhealthy?—Dinner-party—Ascent of the 'Peak'—Insect annoyances—Hong Kong Sunday—English mail signalled—Chinese 'boys'—Pidgin-English—The native quarter—Queen's birthday parade—Military funeral—Thomas Atkins' routine—Lascars—Defences—The Birmingham standard of success 1

CHAPTER II.

A MODEL BRITISH REPUBLIC—SHANGHAI.

Shanghai a republic—Yellow Sea—English imperiousness—Busy aspect of town—Frontier territories—Chinese immigration—American settlement—French Concession—Their faulty administration—Gloomy outlook—English Council—Finance—Law—Police court—Adjudications—Social life—'The old folks at home'—Gambling—Racing—Sunday promenades—The incomprehensible English—Agriculture—Graves—A Chinese theatre—Music—Stage—Audience . 65

CHAPTER III.

INSIDE CHINA—THE RIVER YANG-TSZE-KIANG.

PAGE

A China Company's steamer—Mixture of nationalities—Europeans in the power of the Chinese—Natives at meals—French missionary—Chinkiang—Square miles of graveyards—Highways and byways—Railroads—Education—Nankin—The 'Little Orphan'—Wildfowl—Sport—River scenery—Kiukiang—Features of the river Yang-tsze-Kiang—Hankow—The English concession—The small European community—Tea and tea-tasting—Brick tea—The currency—Suburban market gardens 115

CHAPTER IV.

MEDICAL MISSIONS AND THE MISSIONARY QUESTION.

Chinese ignorance of physiology—Principal maladies—Operations—Italian medical mission—Clinical practice—A deformed foot—Nurseries—The process of foot bandaging—School—Religious instruction—Wesleyan medical mission—The service and singing—Secular and religious teaching—Misrepresentation in missionary reports—Unpractical principles—Foochow Mission—Its general superiority—Missionary difficulties — Zic-a-wei — Vespers — Chinese science a fallacy—Deductions from past experience—Charges brought against Protestant missionaries—Failure thus far—Incumbent to persevere—Suggested reforms . . . 163

CHAPTER V.

A CHINESE INLAND METROPOLIS—HANKOW.

Novelty of the experience—Entrance to the native quarter—Pestilential alleys—Revolting inhabitants—Inharmonious voices—Horrible sights—Foul stenches—Chaffering—Absence of machinery—Unfriendly demeanour—Hair-dressing

—Food—Funeral cortège—Expression of the emotions—
Joss houses—Administration of law—Prisons—Torture—
Executions—Mandarin state—Chinese guilds—Their contents and splendour—Gardens—Opium shops—The opium
question—Exaggeration of evils—Experience of opium
smoking—The dragon devouring the moon 215

CHAPTER VI.

CHINESE RIVER AND TOWN LIFE—FOOCHOW.

Magnificent coasting steamers—Forts—Anglo-Chinese hospitality
—Animated aspect of River Min—Boat life—Chinese childhood—Ducks—Panorama of Foochow—English mercantile
community—Chinese dinner-party—Female guests—Small
talk—The food—Singing—Slaves—A journey across country
—Buffaloes—Dogs—House-boat—A night voyage—Scenery
—A rapid-boat—Disembark—Ascent of the Yuen Fuh mountain—Cultivation—The monastery of Yuen Fuh—Toil up
the mountain—The monk's cave—Devils and divinities—
Return rapid-voyage—A garden jungle—'Lead, kindly light'
—Illness—Cross country sights—Kuh Shan Monastery—
Carp—Chinese language—Chinese capacity for learning—
Conclusion 267

INDEX 331

ENGLISH CHINA.

CHAPTER I.

OUR FARTHEST BRITISH OUTPOST—HONG KONG.

Hong Kong—Jericho—Timbuctoo! Are not these names used indifferently to represent the extreme of remoteness? Do not nine out of ten, even among well-informed English gentlemen, consider the first named a place with which we have little in common though it be a British possession, or at all events of little momentous interest? And are they not of opinion that its contingent loss need not, to any material extent, affect our national prosperity? Yet Hong Kong, apart from its military and naval value as our most advanced outpost in the far East, and from its commercial interest represented by an annual average British exchange of about forty-two millions sterling, is marked by characteristic advantages unparalleled in any single one of our other possessions.

The testimony of many who have preceded me in

this subject is frequently puzzling from its contradictory nature. Hong Kong is alternately described as unquestionably healthy and deplorably sickly; as pleasantly cool and intolerably hot; as replete with interest and a desert of dulness; as hospitably sociable and savagely churlish—by the large majority, perhaps, as an odious place of exile, and by the minority as a fascinating residence. These discrepancies are chiefly due to the special circumstances under which the witnesses may have resided there; to the freedom from, or existence of, home ties and anxieties; to the extent to which health has been affected by climate, and, above all, according as hot- or cold-season-life has been selected as the type described.

Now inasmuch as scorching weather prevails over by far the greater part of the year, it is surely most rational to base our judgment on that period. Let us then assume the date of our arrival to be the beginning of July, and by a detail of first experiences—as valuable in a traveller as first thoughts are valuable in a woman—let us endeavour to reconcile discrepancies and to arrive at just and independent conclusions.

As our ship slowly steams into Hong Kong harbour, I defy you to be otherwise than entranced, whatever your previous experience of nature's beauties, with the unsurpassed loveliness of the scene—the brightest sky, and the bluest sea, whereon rest a large fleet of mammoth merchant ships, of men-of-war of every nation, thousands of picturesque junks and myriads of sampans, or native boats.

On our right is the large flourishing town of Victoria, very un-English in its aspect, and in some respects resembling a French or Italian seaboard city. Built along the slope of a steep mountain, the lower part seems to have a constant tendency to be thrust towards the sea; while higher up the houses are large, substantially built edifices, embosomed in the varied green shade of glorious tropical vegetation. Still higher are the steep slopes of the Hong Kong mountains, dotted over with patches of wood, or covered with a darker coloured brushwood, which instantly and vividly brings to the thoughts, ' Scotland, deer, grouse,' were it not for the almost perpendicular rays of the sun, which, in lieu of Scotland's charming alternation of light and shade, result in a uniform fierce glare.

The whole is crowned by a long, sharp, blue crest ridge, the highest point of which (the ' Peak ') is nearly 2,000 feet above the sea level; and which, when rain threatens, loses itself in the white woolly clouds.

Now turn to the other side of the harbour, about a mile broad, to Kowloon, a promontory of the mainland of China. Here we have a changed scenery in the most rugged, bare, and wild of illimitable mountains, streaked over with large patches of brilliant red granite.

As we step on shore, a glow seems to rise from beneath our feet, a very uncomfortable contrast to the ever cool sea surface, and, however leisurely one's movements, in a few minutes we shall lapse into a sticky, clammy condition of body, which I warn you will be your normal state for nearly eight months out of the twelve. Disregarding the importunities of a crowd of three-quarters naked, chattering, pigtailed coolies, we make our way to a hotel, large but terribly stifling—second-rate as regards comfort and equipment, but first-rate in point of cooking, excelling herein nineteen out of twenty of similar palatial European establishments. It is not comfortably bearable for more than a few hours, and we forthwith set to work to search out the addresses of our letters of introduction –passports which in Europe are somewhat disdained, but in Asia are invaluable. Here we are welcomed with a genuine eager hospitality, unparalleled out of China. Our addressee is, we will suppose, a local merchant-prince, a Government employé, a military officer, or a well-to-do agent of a commercial firm. Steer clear of the rank and file of the civilian community, inasmuch as they are not on the whole a favourable set either in their associates or in their ways of life. Our friend does not merely invite us to dinner or reluctantly offer us a bed, in the fashion of grudging home conventional civility; he peremptorily orders you to come and stay with him; he instantly despatches his own coolies to fetch your baggage; he instals you in a suite of luxurious, large, lofty apartments, consisting of bedroom, bath-room, and sitting-room; and, best of all, he avoids that fatal error of hounding you with amusements and occupations. Life indeed would be very agreeable if it were not for its amusements, and he extends to you the immeasurable bliss of leaving you entirely to your own sweet pleasure.

The interior of these houses, indeed, presents an aspect of luxury—I might almost say, of splendour—peculiarly characteristic of the East, and yet attainable at comparatively small expense. The shell, certainly, is exceedingly fragile, but every room and passage is of a magnificent size. Carpets, curtains, hangings, and rugs—those devouring expenses in a cool climate—would here be offensively out of taste, and insufferably uncomfortable. In lieu thereof we have beautifully stained floors, high, wide windows, and folding doors, prettily coloured rattan mattings, large bamboo chairs of every ingenious form to conduce to repose and coolness, feather-weight hand-tables, which can be shifted about almost at a thought, a multiplicity of bright fans scattered conveniently about for use, plenty of handsome lacquer-work, and enough revoltingly ugly china to satisfy the most vitiated taste of a depraved virtuoso. Then there is a profusion of lovely flowers and foliage which can never be out of place, while overhead, solemnly, gracefully, wave the white punkahs—huge oblong fans which stretch completely across the room. They move noiselessly by means of pulleys and ropes worked by a coolie outside, and set up regular waves of cool air, each puff of which gives a feeling of relief. The room is wisely darkened towards the attainment of a lower temperature. A broad, covered verandah lines the entire exterior length of the house, and, in fine, the combination of surroundings produces on a new-comer a strange, Arabian-night sensation. 'Stale trifles,' sneers the military *habitué* of the East. 'Rien si bête qu'un vieux militaire, or a dried-up Anglo-Indian,' is my reply. 'The above minutiæ are striking and even interesting to those who have the luck to stray for a time into a new country, and the good fortune to have been saved from a lifelong expatriation from the civilised centres of experience, and the scenes of the true battles of life.'

Not improbably our first night's slumbers will be broken by a mighty roar of thunder, by blinding flashes of lightning, and by a dashing down of rain. At about six o'clock in the morning we shall be roused by a 'house boy' bringing to our bedside the invariable cup of tea, which will be followed by a nine o'clock breakfast, generally disposed of in solitude, but whereat in some households the whole family is wont to assemble. Afterwards the comparative coolness, due to last night's storm, tempts us to sally forth on a tour of exploration. Why, the slopes of the mountains are covered with alabaster white! Chalk patches? No, only large drying grounds of the native washermen of European linen, the stock of which is of necessity four times more abundant here than in a temperate climate.

All the roads seem to lead straight down hill into the town, and after passing many a handsome bungalow, each with its tract of bright garden, sheltered by clumps of graceful bamboo, we find ourselves in the midst of the Anglo-China metropolis. Here European employés and heads of commercial houses are hastening to their business rendezvous, or bustling about with true English vigour, and a comparative indifference to climate, which we cannot but admire. Their numbers are almost swamped by swarms of coolies and Chinese shopmen, interspersed with specimens of Arabs, Parsees, Sikhs, Madrasses, Negroes, and half-caste, or rather quarter-caste, Portuguese. The streams to a great extent converge towards the Hong Kong and Shanghai Bank, where we get a glimpse of the outside forms of local business. Under the porticoes are sacks of Mexican dollars—the principal current coin—and each coin is being tested one by one by the Chinese servants of the bank. The man, squatted on his hams according to the national attitude, which in five minutes would cause an Englishman to yell with cramp, shovels into his hands a heap of these rough, clumsy pieces from the open sack. Balancing each separately, on two fingers, he instantaneously decides on its fitness for currency. The undoubtedly good he tosses into one heap; the undoubtedly bad into another, and the doubtful coins into a third for future test. These latter comprise the spurious and the light, many of which have had their original weight materially diminished by the 'chop' or trade mark of different firms. Each punch has withdrawn a tiny atom of silver, which the Chinese dealers have, with characteristic economy, carefully preserved for sale in the aggregate. The rapidity and accuracy with which the scrutinisers will detect a slightly depreciated or spurious coin by its mere weight on the finger is truly extraordinary, and can only be acquired after years of practice.

The interior of the bank consists of a large sombre hall, kept fairly cool by the waving of innumerable punkahs, and here are employed a small proportion of European clerks, working in their shirt sleeves, according to the sensible universal custom of the place, and a large proportion of white-clothed natives swiftly ready to do their bidding. As Englishmen we are treated with the utmost civility, and though strangers, with the utmost liberality in the etiquette of business procedure. We wish, suppose, to cash a cheque. 'Schroff!' shouts the clerk, and immediately answering to the above term—not German, but a corruption of the Hindu word Sarraf, Shărrāf, banker's clerk—there glides forward one of the native cashiers with smooth-shaven skull, a four-foot pigtail, and spotlessly white flowing garments. He is silent and rapid in his movements, and though his scanty stock of English is scarcely intelligible to you, he speedily carries out to your satisfaction the transaction in hand, your own pencil and paper complicated conversion of pounds into dollars and cents being easily distanced by the schroff's peculiar method of calculation. Taking up a counting machine, a precise counterpart of the coloured wired balls used in our village schools, his long lithe fingers move over it far more quickly than the eye can follow—he plays on it with the rapidity of lacemaking.

'All right as regards the total—now give me, say, 3*l.* of small change,' for a large supply of five-cent (about $2\frac{1}{4}d.$) pieces is here indispensable.

A means has been devised of avoiding the weariness of counting out one by one the 300 tiny silver coins representing the sum in question. A pile of them is poured on to a small flat wooden tray containing 100 recesses, each of which is just deep enough to lodge one five-cent piece, and just shallow enough to prevent the possibility of two such lurking together. A jerk of the wrist—the 100 recesses are instantly filled, the surplus is swept off, and at a glance you perceive you have your correct tale, which is then funnelled into your hand, the schroff tucking up his enormous sleeves to disarm suspicion that he is playing at legerdemain by concealing stray coins in the folds. The idea is so simple and yet so oddly clever that it never fails to elicit a smile of amusement on first experience.

The streets and the shops in that part of Victoria

which is frequented by Europeans bear a mingled Eastern and Western aspect, which is very striking and by no means displeasing. Order is maintained among the multitudes of nude chattering coolies by the red-turbaned, picturesque-looking, stalwart Sikh policemen, gravely promenading in Regent Street fashion, and there is a general sense of brightness and activity, regularity and cleanliness. British wares, and Chinese and Japanese products, are blended together in amusing confusion, the first named at a robbery price, and the latter to be purchased after a long and humiliating bargaining.

The native shopkeepers are emulative of London fame. One announces himself as 'Hoby, shoesmaker,' another 'Sam Hing Stulz, tailor,' another 'John Bull,' a fourth and fifth bear the suggestive names of 'Old-ah-you,' and 'Wink-kee.' Given a pattern they will produce a copy so exact as to comprise patch, darn and tear, but woe to you if you entrust them with any originality however trifling. I once ventured to direct the variation of about an inch in the position of a button as shown in the pattern coat. In the copy the button was shifted sure enough, but no alteration whatever had been made for the corresponding button-hole.

Do not believe the oft-repeated statements that tropical flowers have little scent, and are in appearance less charming as a mass than the products of an English garden. Squatting under a long stretch of banyan trees, in one of the broad, hilly side streets, are knots of flower-men, making up bouquets of the most beautiful contrasts of green, scarlet, orange, blue, and white, and with the scent of frangipanni, or gardenia, or tuberose, or jessamine predominating according to the season. They arrange their flowers with extreme dexterity, I might almost say taste, according to certain prescribed patterns; and we are importuned to purchase for about 4*d.* a wonder of loveliness and perfume, which in London would cost four guineas, if indeed it could there be procured at any price. 'Beauty and the Beasts' is the parallel mentally suggested by the sight of these hideously repulsive Mongolians and their lovely wares.

On our way we look in at the Club, where our host has inscribed our names as honorary members. This inevitable institution of all Anglo-Chinese communities is not at Hong Kong favourably represented, although the premises and cooking are fair; it contains a few good bedrooms, and the library is remarkably extensive and good. It is, however, the hottest, most stifling Acheron in the town.

How entire and conspicuous is the absence of wheel transport on these wide, well-paved thoroughfares! You may wander about them for days without seeing a single carriage, cart, horse, or even pony. The reasons are that the roads are mountainous inclines except in the lower part of the town; that forage in this small, and for the most part unfertile, island is preposterously dear, and that manual labour is ridiculously cheap. Look at those pairs of coolies, each one supporting on his shoulder the end of a bamboo pole, in the centre of which is slung a heavy weight. If the burden be bulky but light, a single bearer will suffice, supporting his bamboo by the centre and the weights at the extremities; or again, if the object be indivisible, the coolie, with an amusing recognition of the mathematical principle of the lever, will constitute his pole into a long arm to which he fastens his goods, and into a short arm to which he affixes a counterpoising stone. The coolies shuffle along at a hybrid walk-and-trot pace, partly for speed, partly because this jog more easily fits into the regular springing of the bamboo poles. By these agents you can cause your heavy portmanteau to be conveyed nearly two miles for about $4\frac{1}{2}d$. Even five-year old children are sometimes to be seen toddling along carrying light objects of domestic use on little bamboo canes.

As for personal conveyances, we have at an infinitesimally small cost a light, luxurious kind of sedan-chair, or a singular, small, two-wheeled carriage holding one person, and called a 'Jinricksha,' habitually abbreviated into Ricksha, both of which are transported by coolies. The Jinricksha, meaning 'man-power-cart,' was introduced from Japan only a few years ago. We jump into one of them, as possessing the greatest novelty, and smoothly and comfortably are dragged along at a rate of six miles an hour by the one native in the shafts, who labours under this sweltering sun with an unfaltering energy absolutely astounding, and of which no Englishman who ever breathed would be capable under similar circumstances.[1] First along the Praya, a two-mile stretch of marine parade, or rather harbour embankment. The area of the port, almost unsurpassed in anchorage and extent, is ten square miles; its depth admits of the passage of ships of the deepest draught in the world; here are riding men-of-war of every type and nation, in curious intermixture, and the multiplicity of craft which throng it as thick as bees may be estimated from the fact that in 1882, 26,668 vessels, with a total tonnage of nearly five millions, passed into the harbour—a greater amount than entered the port of London during the year Hong Kong was acquired (1842). Moreover, there are five docks for ships of large construction. The boat population of Victoria alone is returned at over 16,000—I have nearly done for the present with these useful but dry numbers—partly living on board those clumsy, typical junks, but chiefly in little sampans, or partly roofed wherries. Each contains an entire family of four or five persons, whose domestic life is entirely restricted to the few square feet enclosed by the few fragile planks. At irregular

[1] In Japan, however, the performances of the 'Ricksha' coolies are even more astonishing.

intervals a fusillade on board of ten or twelve crackers indicates the performance of 'chin-chin,' or worship connected with their idiotic superstitions, to which the term 'religion' can only be metaphorically applied. Yet they are half ashamed of those rites, which nevertheless they will not abandon. 'Boy,' I maliciously ask my Chinese servant, 'what is the meaning of those shots in the harbour?' 'Hum, I no savvy. I tinkee it P. and O. ship makee chin-chin before sailing.'

As we bowl along in our rickshas we may note many a curious feature of Chinese life if we are only watchful to observe. There a funeral procession passes along the quay. Several gaudily gilt cars convey various eatables for the use of the dead in the next world, such as fruit, sweetmeats, and cakes, together with various joss-house paraphernalia, and gilt paper-money. At various intervals in the *cortège* are hired mourners and coolies blowing trumpets, banging cymbals, and letting off crackers. The nearest relations of the deceased, men, women, and children, all dressed entirely in white—the sign of mourning—follow the coffin, which is carried on bamboo poles by twelve coolies. It is indeed a singularly strange, substantial-looking object, carved, ornamented, in general shape like the trunk of a tree, and hermetically sealed up with plaster. The females nearest in kin never cease emitting a kind of tearless howl. Each woman is propped up by two supporters, and it is evidently a point of honour to roll about from side to side as boisterously as possible in a supposed exhaustion of grief. I have observed some of the supporters manifesting much irritation at thus receiving sudden jobs in the side, and clearly muttering to the effect:· 'My word! when will this work be over?' The crowd, so far from showing decent sympathy, grin at my curious watching, and tacitly assent, ' Yes, what fools we are!' The noisy, grotesque procession, sometimes nearly a mile in length, wends its way to some far-off hillside, pronounced favourable for interment by the soothsayers. But let us watch a ceremonial of a humbler nature, where a junk is to convey the remains to the other side of the harbour. The coffin is first deposited on the quay, where a small fire is lighted, and some refreshment burnt whereby the spirit of the deceased is supposed to be invigorated. The so-called mourners stand chattering around, manifesting the utmost indifference, with the exception perhaps of the widow, who grovels down in the mud, and with a howling between that of a jackal and the miauling of a cat, gabbles forth lamentations, but always without tears. Then the coffin is bundled into a boat, which is rowed away, and the formalities of this repulsive, unfeeling ceremonial are brought to a conclusion. The sorrow of the Chinese for their dead and their compassion for the living are apparently about on a par.

The straggling town is about four miles long, and though the houses are chiefly wooden, it contains as many as 6,000 buildings of brick and stone. It must be owned that the streets and population are orderly in the highest degree, and the instinctive submission of the Eastern to the Western races is here very strikingly illustrated. The colony numbers about 160,000 [1] inhabitants, exclusive of the military and foreign ships' population, of which the whites compose the utterly insignificant fraction of about 3,100. Yet that a Chinaman should either by speech or action engage in an open stand-up contest with an Englishman would be an almost inconceivable anomaly. The police it is true number as many as about 650, but not more than 120 are Europeans, the balance being Sikhs and Chinese. Here and there in the most crowded thoroughfares a solitary constable is to be seen, and his somewhat imperious directions are obeyed with the most unhesitating submission.

As to the dress of the fairly well-to-do natives, I can only refer you to the pictures on our nurseries' willow-pattern plates: flowing white or dark blue robes, with sleeves reaching nearly to the knees; loose

---

[1] In 1881 there were :—

Europeans and Americans	3,040
Mixed nationalities	968
Temporary	188
Prisoners	682
Boat population—Victoria	16,687
Boat population elsewhere—in Hong Kong	12,302
Chinese (about)	126,133
Total (about)	160,000

Exclusive of military and naval forces and police.

cotton trousers; the typical turned-up Chinese stuff shoes; and a fan shading the skull, instead of a hat. Several wear spectacles of stupendous size, more for decoration and dignity than for utility. The women's costume differs comparatively little from that of the men, the chief additions being, occasionally, ponderous earrings, jade bracelets, silver anklets, and large pins fastening piled-up rolls of coarse, shiny-looking black hair. They are, however, models of decency. The practice of deforming their feet is now going out of fashion in the south, but a not inconsiderable minority may still be seen, slowly, painfully, waddling along on their poor distorted stumps.

Our first impressions of the population as a whole, so far as externals are concerned, is, to say the least, displeasing; and as, by degrees, we notice their stupid ugly eyes, their air of stolid conceit, their fat, smooth faces, their shaven, pigtailed skulls, and their ceaseless discordant chatter, our feelings deepen into absolute disgust.

What a clatter of small wooden drums! It is caused by peddlers calling attention to their wares, mostly consisting of what they are pleased to call eatables; but, apart from fruit and cigars, of dark, mysterious masses of sweetmeat nastiness, from which the greediest English school boy would turn with loathing. Here we turn down some slums, and, though we choke with close heat and Chinese vapours, English administration has actually prevailed in preserving a fair amount of cleanliness, and in preventing the accumulation of rotting garbage. Really a comparison with the worst districts in Bethnal Green and the Seven Dials would not be unfavourable, a success which speaks volumes to those who, like myself, had subsequent opportunities of exploring the horrors of the large inland China cities.

Emerging from the town, we suddenly arrive at that which is, perhaps, the most beautiful and the saddest acre in the British Empire: the so-called 'Happy Valley,' the English cemetery of Hong Kong. No natives are allowed inside, so, leaving our rickshas at the gate, we pass into the peaceful solitary groves, the silence of which is unbroken, save by the joyful notes of many a singing-bird, and the splashing of a burn down the adjacent overhanging rocks. The term 'cemetery' conveys, perhaps, an erroneous impression of gaudy gardens, crowded and disfigured with monuments which are types of bad taste in construction, and still worst taste in inscription. I would rather describe it as a carefully tended expanse of turf, with a pretty little chapel shaded with magnificent tropical trees, interspersed with beautifully flowering shrubs, and luxuriant foliage of every tint, where are scattered the graves of our countrymen whose sad fate has been to die 'far from the old folks at home.' The inscriptions tell in a few words many a melancholy story, for Hong Kong has been subjected, at intervals, to devastating epidemics. Here we read of whole families swept off in a few days by fever; there is a long record of the losses of a ship's crew, the 'Calcutta.' 'Some men fell while engaged with the enemy, others from the effects of climate.' Here is a hecatomb from the 95th Regiment, 225 deaths from cholera and various causes, between May 1847 and January 1850—a little over two and a half years. Of these, 102 cases were carried off by fever alone in four months, viz. from June 1 to September 30, 1848. Of the 1st Battalion of the 9th Regiment there is even a more terrible record, inasmuch as the destroying angel was smiting them so heavily over the longer period of nine years, viz. from 1849 to 1858. We read that, during that time, the battalion lost by sickness a total number of 658, of whom 107 were children.[1] Are not our soldiers and sailors as deserving of recognition when faithfully carrying out dreary routine duty in a trying, depressing tropical climate at the antipodes, as when engaged in a campaign which may not, in the long run, claim more victims, with the inspiriting anticipations of prospective public honours, promotion, and abundance of medals within a brief space?

[1] The exact numbers were:—

Officers	10
Non-commissioned officers	35
Privates and drummers	470
Women	37
Children	107
Total	659

The picture we are contemplating is, indeed, set in a worthy frame. We are standing in an angle at the base of one of nature's large amphitheatres. Overhead is the unclouded brilliant sky; in front a large green racecourse, bordered in its entire circumference with a fringe of graceful bamboo; through a gap in the hills we catch a glimpse of the harbour, with the red mountains of Kowloon in the far distance, while in our immediate rear rise, almost perpendicularly, dark rugged rocks besprinkled with firs, and losing themselves in the lofty distant main range. Yet, in spite of all my efforts, I am conscious that 'thought hath not colours half so fair' to paint this scene. It is somewhat heightened by the disadvantageous contrast of the neighbouring plot set aside for the Roman Catholics—over-decorated, gaudy, and glaring with untrue sentiment, almost the only adjunct in keeping with the locality being the carved inscription over the portals: 'Hodie mihi, cras tibi' —Your turn next. That little strip reserved for Mahomedan sepulture is surely preferable, for there is, at all events, about it a sort of dismal honesty.

Our ricksha coolies, who, during our absence, have been contentedly resting on their hams, and reinvigorating themselves with chewing sticks of sugar-cane, now resume their journey homewards. Suddenly they stop short with a certain amount of dismayed fuss—a few heavy drops are falling. Well, considering that you have little else on but your 'birthday suits,' I do not see how you can be damaged even if you do get wet to the skin. But they think far otherwise. From below the carriages they detach, hitherto unnoticed, enormous mushroom-shaped bamboo hats, which form admirable umbrellas, and the queerest cloaks of loosely woven mango leaves, in which they envelope their naked hides, at the same time availing themselves of every atom of roof and tree shelter.

In precautions against climate the seasoned aborigines furnish useful lessons to the reckless, raw, newcomers. While careful to guard their skulls from the direct rays of the sun, no matter how high the temperature they revel in it like salamanders, though in a European brain fever would be the result; but the moment December comes, with a breeze a little less hot than the blast of a blow-pipe, all the Chinese who can afford the expense swaddle themselves, from crown to sole, in innumerable folds of thick woollen garments, and the most palpably skinny are transformed apparently into the most conspicuously obese. As for wet, notwithstanding that they are far more clean in their persons than might be expected, they take the precautions of confirmed hypochondriacs against exposing their feet or bodies to the slightest sprinkling of rain.

During a few minutes of downpour, such as is experienced only in the tropics, nearly all the Chinese wayfarers improvise some sort of covering: mats, thermometer may range much higher. This vapour-bath-result exercises a very debilitating effect. A wet deposit covers the entire exposed surface of the body, but especially the hands, which drip, drip, so constantly as to render writing vexatious, a sheet of blotting-paper between the wrist and the paper being absolutely indispensable.

Weary at last of your fruitless efforts to keep cool, perhaps you try the inexperienced new-comer's expedient of a stroll. In the thinnest of white linen garments, with racquet shoes, helmet, and large sun umbrella, you slowly saunter forth. In a quarter of an hour you return; with feverish haste you drag off every stitch of your clothes, so saturated that they fall with a thud on the floor. No—swearing will only make you hotter; you must grin and bear it. You come to the conclusion that there is no escape from this heat —it finds you out in your hiding-places in the shady verandah, or shoots across from the white face of the opposite house. You feel all the better for picking a little bit at luncheon, you succeed in obtaining forty winks afterwards, and you spend the entire afternoon in your room as motionless as possible, for to move into another apartment, even to shift from chair to chair, produces a tendency to renewed soaking. Only, at all hazards, fight against brandy and soda, at any rate until after dinner. The man who dallies with it, like the woman who hesitates, is lost. As for any number of cigars, which, by the way, are here of surpassing cheapness and unsurpassed excellence, in crass defiance of the wisest medical dicta, I have not a word to say against them. I liken their prohibition to withholding chloroform in confinements. Smoke as many as you please. They will do you no good certainly, but it is less hard to boil when soothed with their sweet comfort.

Half-past six o'clock. The 'Victor Emanuel' in harbour fires its evening gun, and the surrounding junks, as though in imitative chaff, pop off their chin-chin crackers. The sun is down; you may get a breath of cooler air out of doors, but make haste, for there is scarcely any twilight in these latitudes, and pitch darkness will quickly and suddenly succeed broad daylight. All the English inhabitants, children and their *amas* (nurses) included, are following suit, and are emerging from their retreats with simultaneous activity. This one hour's walk is the most valuable in the twenty-four; and though on your return you find yourself once more dripping, you feel tranquillised, you can face dinner, and you are consoled with reflecting that after all this pulling down surely bed will be an unmixed enjoyment. Ah, no! Now you are expecting too much. The night season is to be dreaded above all others. You wriggle into your lair through your carefully closed musquito curtains, for this vindictive enemy is ingenious in finding his way through the smallest aperture, and you close your eyes in presumptuous expectation of the death of each day's life. Utterly in vain. You have never felt more thoroughly awake in your life. You are on the coolest, and therefore the hardest, of beds and pillows; in lieu of a mattress you lie on a rattan mat, you kick off even your sheets; the draught of night air sweeps directly across you from the wide open windows to the wide open doors. And yet you break out into a lather, you toss about in intolerably feverish weariness, you hear the endless half-hours solemnly tolled forth across the harbour stillness from the ships' watches—until at last, when matters seem to have reached their worst, you lapse into a broken, unrefreshing slumber. At an early hour in the morning you awake in a debilitated condition of body, suggestive of a previous night of wine and wassail, of riot and debauchery.

Such is a specimen of an average hot day in Hong Kong, and yet the climate is not without a certain charm of variety. After a definite number of days when the sensation of stifling seems to have reached its climax, the clouds suddenly pile up in black masses, sheet lightning glares all over the horizon, the distant thunder growls, heavy raindrops fall, and at last the storm bursts with a fury of which most of us have read, but which none can realise without a personal experience of the tropics. His must be a dull, torpid mind which is not awed by the incessant blinding, almost scorching, flashes, and by the crackling, rolling roar of a thunder which makes heaven and earth quiver. The rain is hurled violently down in thick unbroken sheets, in layers of water so to speak, the fall in half an hour being as much as would represent weeks of wet weather in England.

One of the chief charms of Hong Kong is that which by the inhabitants is most lightly regarded—according to the way of the world—the Botanical Gardens. Outside the town, part of the way up the mountain, with every advantage which natural site and lavish expenditure can render, surely these grounds are without equal in the world. The Pallavicini Gardens of Genoa are in comparison vulgar cockneydom. Take the hothouses of Kew and Chatsworth as marionette imitations; think of acres of green slopes covered with flower beds and flowering shrubs, shaded with giant palms, with towering cocoanut trees, with banyans, magnolias, azaleas, gardenias, frangipanni, and ylang-ylang; picture to yourself enormous ferns and huge-leaved orchids, shrouded beneath a feathery mass of drooping bamboo; add thereto the beauty of art in skilfully disposed shrubberies, in a diverted natural waterfall leaping down the granite steeps, in a winding path cut out of yon crag, in carefully mown lawns, and in neatly kept gravel walks. Here, too, congregate all the bright plumaged birds in the island, while wild doves in hundreds never cease their soft coo. And you can enjoy almost complete solitude in these enchanted grounds during the greater part of the day. Only among certain central broad walks will you sometimes find a queer sprinkling of visitors.

The Chinese, in whom appreciation of nature's beauties is strangely non-existent, admit, in their conceit, admiration of English management in two respects only: our administration of law, and our formation of public gardens. There are a few pigtails pointing out the gardening skill of those 'foreign devils.' More numerous are the groups of children: some repulsive, swarthy little Portuguese; others the pallid, washed-out offspring of English residents. Melancholy indeed is their appearance, as they listlessly, joylessly, creep by the side of their *amas*, who, I should mention, are universally represented as proud of and devotedly kind to their charges. Where is the healthy shouting, romping, dirt-pie-making, without which childhood seems so unnatural? English mothers, do not bring out your children, whatever their age, to Hong Kong except under dire necessity. They will not drop off suddenly, but they will inevitably droop and pine, and drift into weakly health, which not improbably may permanently affect them.

Then is the station so very unhealthy? Yes—very unhealthy for a prolonged residence, though not deadly, and not subjected to the devastating epidemics of cholera and fever except at long intervals. Only that minority whose constitutions apparently defy all unfavourable conditions escapes scathless. The majority of the men, nearly all the women and the children without exception, succumb more or less, sooner or later, to the enervating effects of severe heat combined with extreme steamy humidity. Dysentery, fever, liver, or a general break down ensues, and it is out of the question to re-establish health thoroughly here after such attacks—a voyage to other climes is inevitable.

The most favourable admission I could extort from impartial and experienced witnesses was that Hong Kong is not unfavourable to asthmatic, bronchial, and other pulmonary complaints, provided the health of the patient be maintained unimpaired in every other respect. Truly this is damning with faint praise. In indignant refutation of the above verdict, the remarkably low death rate is frequently quoted as being actually lower than that of temperate and admittedly healthy regions. An illusory argument. All whose circumstances admit fly to other climes as soon as they sicken, for the only question then is whether they will be carried away *from* the island or *on* the island. During the first years indeed of English occupancy, Hong Kong was little better than a charnel house, in proof whereof we have only to quote the records of the 'Happy Valley.' The necessity for climatic precautions was not recognised; the appalling system of Chinese drainage, or rather the entire absence of all drainage, exercised to the full its pestilential effects; and, moreover, it was only discovered by degrees that the wholesale turning up of the ground for building purposes involved a disintegration of the red granite, and the consequent emanation of fatal mephitic vapours. This last evil has now subsided with diminished building, but even now old stagers are careful to avoid loitering about recently excavated ground, as fraught with more or less risk of an attack of fever. Sanitary measures have done much to obviate the other sources of sickness. To sum up I would say: fairly strong people encounter only an average amount of risk, provided their stay is not to extend over a considerable length of time, and provided, above all, they are prepared to quit the island on the first clearly marked development of ill health. I must, however, warn you of the probable ungenerous treatment of your friends when you first return as an invalid. They will make no allowances for the invigorating sea voyage, change of air and scene, and unless you are carried on shore on a stretcher or hobble about on crutches, you will be regarded as a rank impostor.

To pass from the locality to the English inhabitants thereof, to the general composition of the society. Here we find a small number of heads of banks or of wealthy mercantile houses, whose energy and ability have so largely contributed to raise the colony to its present condition of prosperity. Pleasing in manner, of enlarged ideas, and the essence of liberality, their presence is a credit to Hong Kong—would be an honour to any community in the world. Then we have a small sprinkling of able administrators from the mother country, a larger proportion of Anglo-Chinese officials whose views scarcely range beyond the town of Victoria, and a number of clerks whose thoughts are engrossed with dollars, and who are seeking their fortunes, which probably will be ultimately largely swallowed up in drink, play, and rowdyism. There is, however, a corrective leaven in the shape of the military element, which represents by far the greater proportion of the educated and gentlemanlike stratum. As to the Hong Kong women, born and bred there, the most charitable criticism is that their attractions are on a par with their scanty numbers, and that those with whom an English gentleman would care to exchange two words of conversation are *rari nantes in gurgite vasto.*

Let me detail the ordinary experience of a local dinner-party. You are carried to your destination in a sedan-chair, like a Guy Fawkes, by a couple of coolies struggling with native energy under your English weight—an average Chinese rarely exceeds nine stone. You find the guests—men in black alpaca evening dress or in white jackets and trousers —assembled in lofty spacious rooms furnished with every luxury compatible with a maximum of coolness. The dinner table is a beautiful mass of flowers and foliage arranged by the native servants with native care and skill, and with a taste which they have covered by degrees that the wholesale turning up of the ground for building purposes involved a disintegration of the red granite, and the consequent emanation of fatal mephitic vapours. This last evil has now subsided with diminished building, but even now old stagers are careful to avoid loitering about recently excavated ground, as fraught with more or less risk of an attack of fever. Sanitary measures have done much to obviate the other sources of sickness. To sum up I would say: fairly strong people encounter only an average amount of risk, provided their stay is not to extend over a considerable length of time, and provided, above all, they are prepared to quit the island on the first clearly marked development of ill health. I must, however, warn you of the probable ungenerous treatment of your friends when you first return as an invalid. They will make no allowances for the invigorating sea voyage, change of air and scene, and unless you are carried on shore on a stretcher or hobble about on crutches, you will be regarded as a rank impostor.

To pass from the locality to the English inhabitants thereof, to the general composition of the society. Here we find a small number of heads of banks or of wealthy mercantile houses, whose energy and ability have so largely contributed to raise the colony to its present condition of prosperity. Pleasing in manner, of enlarged ideas, and the essence of liberality, their presence is a credit to Hong Kong—would be an honour to any community in the world. Then we have a small sprinkling of able administrators from the mother country, a larger proportion of Anglo-Chinese officials whose views scarcely range beyond the town of Victoria, and a number of clerks whose thoughts are engrossed with dollars, and who are seeking their fortunes, which probably will be ultimately largely swallowed up in drink, play, and rowdyism. There is, however, a corrective leaven in the shape of the military element, which represents by far the greater proportion of the educated and gentlemanlike stratum. As to the Hong Kong women, born and bred there, the most charitable criticism is that their attractions are on a par with their scanty numbers, and that those with whom an English gentleman would care to exchange two words of conversation are *rari nantes in gurgite vasto.*

Let me detail the ordinary experience of a local dinner-party. You are carried to your destination in a sedan-chair, like a Guy Fawkes, by a couple of coolies struggling with native energy under your English weight—an average Chinese rarely exceeds nine stone. You find the guests—men in black alpaca evening dress or in white jackets and trousers —assembled in lofty spacious rooms furnished with every luxury compatible with a maximum of coolness. The dinner table is a beautiful mass of flowers and foliage arranged by the native servants with native care and skill, and with a taste which they have borrowed from their masters. The Chinese attendants with their pigtails and white, fresh-looking, flowing robes, glide noiselessly, rapidly about, the perfection of waiters whom no European can match. You have, however, according to custom, brought with you your 'boy,' whose special function it is to attend to your wants.

The cool puffs from the waving punkahs give a slight spur to your moribund appetite. The cooking is excellent in spite of the difficulty that the meat having been killed the same day, the tissues are apt to be as hard as death stiffened them; the wines even better. So far good; but the dinner, which ought to lubricate conversation, soon turns out a dreary affair, and hangs fire terribly. The current momentous incidents of the world, including those of the vast adjacent Chinese Empire, politics, literature, and even educated small talk, are almost ignored, save in a few exceptionally favourable houses, and the topics are limited to inquiries as to how you like the colony, to sordid matters of dollars, to racing speculations, and to spiteful petty scandal. Nor can you take a greedy refuge in the enjoyment of your food. Your appetite allows you little more than to trifle with it, at least until dessert time arrives, when your spirits are raised by the wealth of mangoes, pineapples, leichees, pummelows and bananas, which amply compensate, I maintain in opposition to general received opinions, for the absence of English strawberries and peaches.

Cigars, more sleepy talk in the drawing-room, and at an early hour you escape from this house of entertainment as from a prison. Outside, the carriage equipage certainly amuses you. There are clustered knots of patient squatting coolies with their sedan-chairs. The ladies and gentlemen emerge, each one steps into his or her own vehicle, which is then hoisted on to the bearers' shoulders, and in strings, or side by side, according as the occupants wish to converse, they are borne off at a rapid jog, two large coloured Chinese lanterns swinging from each set of poles, and gradually disappearing in the darkness of the steep, winding road.

Let us avail ourselves of this comparatively cool opportunity and make our way home on foot. The thoroughfares are solitary and silent as the grave, for the Chinese are forbidden, with a Russian sort of despotism, to wander abroad after 9 P.M. unless provided with a special police permit. We only meet with an occasional red-turbaned, white-clothed Sikh policeman, swarthy, stealthy, and stalwart, provided with a dark lantern and a loaded carbine which he handles somewhat ostentatiously at the approach of footsteps. 'Easy, my friend, with that weapon of yours,' with a slightly jumpy sensation. Nevertheless this guardianship is expedient, and was absolutely necessary a short time ago, when knots of Chinese footpads would, without a moment's hesitation, have robbed and made away with any belated

D

Englishman. It is still the practice for a policeman at the wharf invariably to take down the number of any sampan hired to convey a diner-out to one of the men-of-war, lest the rowers should revert to their former favourite practice of suddenly lowering the awning, scragging the passenger beneath, rifling him, and then pitching his body overboard.

Our experience of Hong Kong society at this season of the year will, however, be comparatively limited, inasmuch as nine-tenths of those who can afford the expense take refuge from the heat at the cooler 'Peak,' a sharply defined range of mountains overhanging the town, and nearly 2,000 feet high. There they betake themselves with their families about the end of May, and do not return to their town residences until October, making the journey backwards and forwards daily to their hongs, or places of business.

We have been asked to dine and sleep at one of these mountain châlets, and at 5 o'clock one sweltering afternoon we make a start in a sedan-chair, wherein also is stored our baggage, and which is borne by four coolies, for the ordinary team of two would here be quite insufficient for the tremendous work in hand. The path is so steep that it can only attain its objective point by incessant turns and returns, and so narrow that during a considerable portion of the time we are half-swinging over giddy precipices. Our coolies struggle on valiantly, the two rear bearers being careful to keep out of step with the two leaders, and thus converting the movement of our chair from a tiring tilting into a pleasant swing. How horny must be the soles of their feet, which are either entirely unprotected from these sharp rocks and flints, or at most are shod with thin open-work grass slippers. The sun beats down on their tanned carcases, the poles press heavily on their poor protruding shoulder-blades, which are sometimes kneaded into black and blue, and we almost feel a sensation of shameful sloth at thus taking our ease, while four human beings are slaving under our weight. But they themselves, totally indifferent to heat and fatigue, are jubilant over their remunerative task, and are quite content if we will occasionally wait for a few minutes while the relative positions of the bearers are changed, or while they regain their breath squatting on their hams at one of the broadened angles of the path.

After nearly an hour's toil we are at the summit of the range, whence the bird's-eye view certainly is incomparable. On one side and at our very feet is Kowloon, with its encircling framework of mainland mountains; the harbour swarming with gigantic vessels, whereof I have often counted as many as fifty, exclusive of myriads of junks; the town and its beautiful slopes. Still higher are the web-like tracings of the mountain tracks, the splashing burns, and the alternate shades of green ferns and scrub, and bright azaleas glowing in wild profusion. Creeping up the hills are innumerable specks showing the merchants returning in their chairs from their daily labours. As we peer over the reverse side of the range we see the blue expanse of the China Sea, dotted with numerous rugged volcanic islets. Closer in are isthmuses, bays, and villages, which are exceedingly picturesque provided you keep at a distance, and unutterably filthy if you approach them closely. Scattered all over the jagged summit are low, straggling bungalows, *simplex munditiis*, which English taste and coolie labour have rendered gems of picturesqueness among the rough mountainous beauties of nature. Then how delightful is the eight or ten degrees of cooler temperature! We are no longer stifled and depressed; we pluck up spirits, vigour and appetite; we actually welcome a single blanket at night.

The Peak is the sanatorium of Hong Kong. Its drawback is the damp, the effects of which are astonishing and vexatious. In a week's time books and clothing are ruined, papers and bindings are transformed into pulp, linen is hopelessly mildewed, and the only alternative to the complete ruin of all such property is a perpetual drying at a large glowing stove.

Our return journey will be most comfortably performed by a start at 9 o'clock the next morning. Plenty of society on the way, for strings of business men are streaming down in their chairs in single file.

Some carry on a shouting bothering conversation with those in front or in rear, some con their business papers, and some are immersed in books. The transformation from the mountain coolness to the valley heat is like stepping into the kitchen boiler, and hence many consider that the advantages of cool nights at the Peak are more than counterbalanced by the contrasts of temperature, and by various other attendant inconveniences.

There is one serious subject of annoyance connected with the island which I cannot pass over in silence: the insect life. The inexperienced will pronounce the place an elysium if its troubles are to be measured by such a standard of comparison, which he will liken to the advertiser's warning, that the only drawbacks to his country place are the littering of the rose leaves and the hubbub of the nightingales. But the experienced stager will burst forth with the eager declaration that this evil, though infinitesimally small in its single instance, when incessantly repeated, involves a disgust and a bodily discomfort which cannot be ignored. The butterflies are undoubtedly of surprisingly varied and beautiful hues; the myriad swarms of dragon-flies, which so mysteriously portend the approach of a typhoon, are local and can be 'dodged;' but the cockroaches, enormous brown creatures twice the size of an English black beetle, twice as nimble, alternately flying and running, here, there, and everywhere; eating up bodily the bindings of your books and all leather work, rummaging through and devastating your clothes, and, worse than all, intruding their huge loathsome bodies on to the tablecloth, up your sleeves or down your neck. I have seen an assemblage of middle-aged officers, some of whom had faced shot and shell, rise in simultaneous dismay at dinner, angrily shout for coolies, and decline to resume their seats until a pigtailed myrmidon, pursuing the agile disgusting insect monster like a terrier pursuing a rat, has triumphantly proclaimed, 'Hab kill 'um!' Then the nasty fat-stomached spiders are of Brobdingnag proportions, and surely one may shudder at centipedes without affectation.

Of snakes, there are some cobras and other scarcely less venomous sorts in the island, but we are not often brought face to face with them. The Chinese have a terror of reptiles which is almost morbid. One twilight evening I narrowly escaped treading on one in the prettiest of the Botanical Garden walks. 'Snek!' screamed a solitary Chinaman standing by, springing into the air with affright, and excitedly dancing about at a cautious distance, while I performed the easy task of dispatching it. The frogs are more noisy in their croaking than even a chorus of their congeners called 'Canadian Nightingales.' During the daily few minutes of twilight they set up a series of short barks so loud that it would seem almost impossible such a noise could be emitted by so small a creature. Really it resembles the yapping of a Skye terrier, yet herein their powers are far exceeded by the tree-cricket, a single one of which will worry one past endurance with its never-ceasing chirp, so like the rasp of a grindstone that they are locally termed scissors grinders. The noise is produced by the vibration of a horny spring affixed to the stomach. It has been calculated that if a human being in London could shout as loudly in proportion to his size as an English cricket, he would be audible at St. Petersburg. It is certain that with a similar comparison of magnitude with these brown Hong Kong creatures, which are about as large as a black beetle, the voice could be heard at the antipodes. Crickets are often kept in jars by the Chinese for fighting purposes, wherein they are considered superior even to the pugnacious quail. At Canton I saw a man tending a collection of these insect captives on which large sums are habitually staked.

Sometimes a gigantic green grasshopper, with hind legs serrated like a saw and capable of inflicting a nasty scratch, will come in banging with enormous jumps against the lamp, startling the guests as he falls with a thud on the dinner-table. Foremost, too, in nastiness are the ants. At a certain season they develop wings and are attracted in myriads by the gleam of a light—to perform suttee? Nothing half so convenient. A moment or two after alighting they convulsively wriggle their legs and bodies, ending by stripping themselves of their large wings which instinct prompts them to cast. Thus we have platefuls of their filthy old clothes, while the original owners scamper off on their own hind legs into every possible corner. Purely an ideal sentiment of disgust? Well, at all events you cannot say as much for the musquitoes. A naturalist has discovered that these ubiquitous and indefatigable assassins have their jaws furnished with seven miniature working implements, whereof one is a gimlet, two are lancets, and two saws, by which means they can with the greatest ease stab through thin drawers or silk stockings. Stifled with your musquito curtains, you throw aside their protecting ægis, or drop off in the daytime in your chair for five minutes, or engrossed in writing, ignore the heralding hum of their sinister intentions. Forthwith you are aware of a number of tiny red spots on your body: twelve hours after you begin to scratch unless, indeed, you are possessed of heroic fortitude; big lumps, as though from hornets' stings, make their appearance; again you scratch like a madman, fingers are of no use, nothing but a rusty nail will serve your turn. Most people prefer positive pain to extreme irritation, and if you are one of them, pour a little ammonia into the torn-open bite. It is true you will dance about the room for ten minutes afterwards, but this pain is less severe than, say, the extraction of a tooth, and the intolerable itching will have ceased. I have known soldiers incapacitated from duty and admitted into hospital owing to a musquito bite. But my fullest sympathy is reserved for the poor women. I have noticed them at dinner-parties, first their eyes wandering aggravatingly in the midst of one's most eager sentences, then almost perspiring with unrelieved itching, and at last, desperately casting to the winds all conventionality, set to work scratching with might and main arm or—ankle, like the veriest coolie.

The Sunday aspect of Hong Kong is represented almost exclusively by service at the cathedral, practically the sole parish church, although divine service is habitually held in other buildings improvised for the purpose. The home sound of the church-going bells falls pleasantly on our ears; a concourse of English people are wending their way thither, a few in rickshas but more in chairs, especially women. Inside and outside the building is all that could be reasonably wished; architecturally handsome, fitted up with good taste, comfortable, large and roomy; almost sadly roomy indeed, since the space available for about 2,000 is only occupied by a scanty congregation of four or five hundred. The majority of our countrymen seem to have left their religion behind them in England. In every point of view, practical and theoretical, it is but coldly regarded here, and it is a poor plea to retort that a large proportion of the shepherds are idle and inferior.

At first we are bewildered at the novelty of the scene, chiefly due to oriental expedients for obviating the heat and discomfort which otherwise would render attention to the service impracticable. Each seat in the wide spacious pews is partitioned off to prevent neighbours crushing on to each other. Men and women are dressed in the lightest, whitest, and airiest of costumes; there some ten or twelve natives, forming a strange contrast in their national costumes, have been persuaded thither by the missionaries. Rows of gigantic punkahs, extending completely across the interior, wave aloft with solemn graceful movement, and with each wave send forth streams of fresh air which render the cathedral the coolest place in Hong Kong; the heathen Chinee, pigtailed, barefooted, and only just saved from nakedness by a light robe thrown loosely across his shoulders, is monotonously tugging at the punkah ropes throughout the entire service, occasionally refreshing himself by a supplementary flourish of his own hand-fan. He is stolid, unobservant, and unwondering, in the midst of music which he considers harsh, and worship which he considers fetish. The place seems in externals to resemble a Moorish mosque as much as an English church. And yet in these antipodes the familiar hymns and the incomparably beautiful prayers of our simple service stir up many a thought of our own far-off village churches.

Once a week there sounds in Hong Kong a note which thrills with the effect of magic. We will suppose ourselves at a large luncheon-party, a substantial mid-day meal, here ranking almost first in eating proportions. Suddenly there is a roar from a cannon which makes the windows rattle and re-echoes over the distant mountains. In an instant the party is spell-bound in profound silence. 'What is it?' we whisper interrogatively to our next-door neighbour, and he answers in an undertone, 'The gun at the Peak is signalling that the English mail is in sight.' Ah! that sound is indeed a harbinger of joy or a knell of grief. Perhaps that girl's face brightens with eager expectation, or that young fellow's mouth is twitching with the sorrow of the recollection that his nearest and dearest no longer exist to cheer him with a sight of their handwriting. Perhaps that middle-aged man's face grows anxious and overcast in dread anticipation lest he should be about to learn of some calamity which has befallen absent wife or children; at all events, everyone is stricken with silence, and though after a few minutes the conversation resumes its course, it is forced and 'abstracted. Each is anxious to get away, to receive and read in solitude the letters of weal or woe which will be shortly delivered to him, and which will darkly or brightly tinge his existence for at least the next week.

To enter into some further details of social life. Among the natural productions of the country, the very best and foremost is the race of Chinese servants, or 'boys' as they are invariably called, whether their age be sixteen or sixty: very quick in learning their business, sharp all round, clean, attentive, and for the most part singularly honest, so far that they will suffer no one but themselves to pilfer their masters, and that their own depredations are limited to certain recognised 'squeezing' or extortion in commission. Each one makes the general and particular character of his master his special study—sometimes to a very amusing extent. The first day I engaged my 'boy,' I had carelessly tossed my hat into one corner of the room, gloves on the bed, a stump of pencil at an acute angle with one corner of the mantelpiece, and a pipe at the other corner. For many successive days I found hat, gloves, stump of pencil and pipe carefully deposited in exactly the same spot and at precisely the same angle. He has a proper idea of his own dignity derived from a carefully considered estimate of the status of his master. For instance, he holds a lieutenant in contempt in comparison with a major, and while he will condescend to do no rough work himself, he takes care that the coolie hired as slavey fulfils every imaginable requirement to render his master comfortable. He is never by any chance drunk; he is never in the way or never out of the way; and in fact is so admirable as to render subsequent experience of the average English man-servant odious. Again, in the transaction of minor matters of business with which they may be entrusted, they show a great deal of zeal and aptitude—indeed it is necessary to beware lest they exceed instructions, as in the case of the following local Joe Miller.

The Chinese being totally unable to pronounce our English names with any proximity to accuracy, it is customary for a visitor, even though well known, to send up his card in advance, and it is quite allowable during the hot siesta hours for the 'boy' to bring back the message 'no can see.' 'Here is that stupid Mr. Smith,' says the lady to her husband. 'Oh, do not let the snob in,' is the drowsy reply. Accordingly the 'boy' thus delivers himself to the self-complacent Smith : ' No can see. Master say you snob. Missus-ee say you plenty too much fool-o.'

In travelling, the value of the Chinese servant becomes still more apparent. In most steamers the native 'boy' of an Englishman is conveyed free, and whether on board ship, in a hotel, or as a guest in a private residence, you never have a moment's trouble about his food, lodging, or comfort. You may be quite sure he will turn up at exactly the right moment, encumbered only with a small handbox and a large pile of bedding, on which latter, however, he bestows extreme care. After he has attended to your comfort, off he marches with the above bedding to the servants' domain, where he at once makes himself at home. An occasional few friendly words will establish your mutual relations on the most pleasant footing, though as for gratitude, do not delude yourself with any such futile expectation, however constant and prolonged may have been your kindness. Gratitude is a plant which does not exist for twenty-four hours in the mental flora of the Chinese. A hairs' breadth of advantage will instantly counterbalance the friendship and obligations of years, and he will throw you over without a grain of regret.

The mistress of an English household, tormented for years with the worries of legs of mutton, soap, and candles, enters on a period of holiday in these details when she lands in China. A few directions in the morning to the comprador or native family agent will provide for the whole of the daily requirements of the dining-room. This sleek long-tailed major-domo has a sort of secret freemasonry tie with every native tradesman in the place, but he suffers no one but himself to cheat his employer. The servants cater for their own food, and stow themselves away in mysterious multiplicity in sleeping nooks according to their own fashion. Apparently they altogether ignore our own exigencies in the matter of space.

There is, however, one shady side to the above picture—the language. It is exceedingly vexatious to be compelled to deal with that miserable substitute Pidgin [1] English—not, remember, the imperfect broken jargon of foreigners, but a hybrid gibberish interspersed with a variety of bastard Chinese or Portuguese terms concocted by our nation when we first took possession, on a supposition about as reasonable as would be the

[1] The Chinese pronunciation of 'business.'

idea of an Auvergnat patois being more comprehensible to a stranger than Parisian French. That dreadful pidgin is almost a new language, the basis of which is the conversion of every *r* into an *l*, adding final vowels to each word, and the constant use of certain argot expressions. An 'American' is rendered 'Mellican man'; 'savvy' means 'to know,' from the Portuguese 'sabe.' 'Speak' is 'talkee'; 'piece' 'piecee'; exalted 'rank' or 'excellent,' 'number one'; 'do you understand' and 'that will answer the purpose' are both translated 'can do.' 'Pidgin' means business in the most varied and illimitable extent of the word; 'joss' means 'religion.' Their periphrases are certainly sometimes rather ingenious. A paddle steamer is 'outside-walkee-can-see,' a screw, 'inside-walkee-no-can-see.' The Chinese designate the officer commanding the Royal Artillery as 'number-one-big-gun-man,' the commanding Engineer as 'number-one-bricklayer-man,' the Bishop of Hong Kong as 'number-one-topside-heaven-pidgin-man,' and really there is no burlesque in the rendering of

by
>My name is Norval. On the Grampian hills
>My father feeds his flock ...
>
>My name belong Norval, topside that Glampian hillee
>My father he chow-chow he sheep-ee.

The jargon has now taken a firm root and constitutes an indispensable acquirement, for until you can fluently speak, and, far more difficult, understand it readily when rapidly slurred over in a monotonous tone of voice, all communication with the servants is a source of constant vexation and misunderstanding. It is urged that if we ourselves were to persist in grammatical English, our employés would soon fall into the way of it. I tried the experiment individually, and it was a dead failure. To be successful, it must be unanimous throughout the community, and to expect this is clearly out of the question. No; the language is a small thorn in one's side. To attempt to pick up Chinese would, in nineteen cases out of twenty, be a deplorable waste of time, as I will endeavour to show in a subsequent chapter. Even the pidgin is confined to a small fraction who are in direct communication with Europeans; the street multitudes of the Treaty Ports do not know a single sentence. French, very rarely spoken even in the French settlements, though broken, is not pidgin; German, Italian, and Spanish are totally unknown to the Chinese.

Let us not fall into the frequent English error of dismissing with a mere allusion the native population. True, their submission to the behests of our authorities is of a spaniel nature, but inasmuch as for every European resident there are about forty-five Chinese, it is evident that on the latter must largely depend the commercial prosperity and social order of the colony. We set out on a tour of exploration of that part of Victoria which is exclusively occupied by the natives, and is known as 'China Town.' On our way we traverse a sort of intervening neutral territory, the Portuguese quarter—'Geese,' as they are called in the abbreviation of contempt—a little nucleus of a singularly effete and deteriorated Iberian population. The women, with traces of mantilla and national costume, missal in hand, are dawdling and gossiping on their return from vespers. The mother-tongue has been maintained fairly unimpaired. The men are modern Portuguese, worn-out descendants of valiant ancestors; the Senhoritas have bartered part of their national beauty, so entrancing at sixteen years of age, for a Chinese cast of countenance which has ruined the original; the crones are more haggish than in Pyrenean Spain; and the muddy-complexioned children, many of whom are the hybrid offspring of effete Portuguese fathers and half caste native mothers, arouse a disgust not entertained towards the pure-blooded Chinese children.

Farther on, and we are in the native quarter, quite unlike any of the Chinese cities which I subsequently visited in the interior, still more unlike any European town, and perhaps the best specimen extant of the possible amelioration of the aborigines under a wise and energetic civilisation. The front part of the houses is entirely open, the upper stories are built with inconsistently handsome balconies, and the exteriors are decorated with oriental colour and gilding which produce rather an imposing effect. Nowhere is there a trace of a chimney or a glass window. There is the usual 'bouquet de Chinois,' chatter, and nakedness, but the wares are abundant and of fairly substantial value, and throughout there is an evidence of prosperity and order for which we may search in vain in Canton, Foochow, or Hankow. A large open area, half market, half recreation ground, is thronged with natives, some hucksters, some conjurors, and some fat old fellows simply taking their pleasure fanning themselves in unclothed indolence. The skinny coolie is a queer sight; the obese idler is a marvel, with roll upon roll of layers of fat upon his portentous stomach thicker than would be revealed by incision in a sleek oily seal. Englishmen so seldom penetrate into China Town that we are looked at with surprise, but are treated with perfect civility. One street, 'Kum Lung,' illustrates by its nomenclature the curious transformation of words by the mere lapse of time. It was much frequented during the early years of the colony by English sailors, and 'Come along, Jack,' was the persuasive greeting addressed to them by the female denizens. This phrase became modified into 'Kum lung,' which in Chinese happens also to signify 'Red Dragon,' and when names were painted in both languages on the corners of the thoroughfares, the place was designated as 'Kum Lung' and 'Red Dragon' Street, by which term it is now known.

Thus far we have been dealing with normal Hong Kong—with its resident European and native population. But it contains in addition an important elément, that of the military, without which the colony would lapse into an aggregate of traders at the mercy of the adjacent, ill-governed, overwhelmingly numerous brutish Chinese nation. Not only does the garrison serve to safeguard English interests in a constant condition of a contingent crisis where extraneous aid is too remote to be available; not only does it give the character of a slice of our empire to this farthest advanced British outpost; but by its mere presence it establishes a nucleus of administration and order, of civilisation and educated society. The normal strength is a battalion of infantry, one and sometimes two batteries of artillery, and a section of the military departmental adjuncts. We have no reason to be ashamed of the general appearance of our soldiers here, for the immature weeds have been left behind in England, and the chosen residue look very striking in their clean well-ordered array, of course enormously favoured by their contrast with the rabble rout around them.

The Queen's birthday parade presented a so strongly mixed oriental and occidental aspect that I am tempted to describe it in detail. The site is a slope of bright green turf in the middle of the town, stretching down to the water's edge, shaded with rows of banyan trees, and overshadowed by the cathedral and lofty, eastern-looking public buildings, with an adjacent background of rugged mountains. Here is drawn up the single line of British soldiers, white in feature and still more white in their snowy tunics and helmets. Their bayonets glitter in the bright clear light, though eventide is now approaching; their carefully dressed, serried ranks are motionless, their mere silence and immobility in the midst of the noisy crowd imparting to them an imposing and masterful air. For patches of colour we have the red-turbaned swarthy Sikhs scattered along the margin and keeping the ground. A few English ladies and their sickly stalky olive-branches gather languidly round the saluting flag, while on every advantageous spot in the neighbourhood, level ground, mounds, walls, windows, verandahs, and housetops, are clustered in hive-like swarms a multitude composed of numerous nationalities. The black-coated, respectable Parsee gentlemen, who, but for their foolscap-shaped head-dresses, might be mistaken for Europeans with a dab of the tar-brush; the solemn-looking Arabs with their beards dyed red, such as were the associates of Haroun al Raschid; mongrel Portuguese; here and there a Hindoo or a negro, and an overwhelming multitude of Chinese, unanimous in their pigtails, but in every descending stage of *déshabillé*, or rather nakedness. The General (Lt.-Gen. J. Sargent) comes on the ground, and forthwith is carried out a ceremonial which bears with it a strange aspect under such novel circumstances. A salute of twenty-one guns from the volunteer field-battery echoes over the mountains; the crack of the *feu de joie* rolls up and down the ranks, and the magnificent 'God save the Queen' almost justifies the legendary remark of the Indian potentate, 'Is your sovereign a divinity that you worship her with such music?' The native population, which has hitherto been jabbering like talking machines, is instantly hushed into wondering silence which lasts throughout the operations. Then comes the trooping of the colours, when 'Meet me by moonlight,' and ''Tis my delight of a shiny night,' played by the band marching down the line, arouses curious mixed emotions, half smiles and half sighs. Finally, the march past in the now rapidly deepening twilight by the mathematically dressed companies, with their regular tramp and their resolute warlike demeanour, convince us that this 'thin white line,' notwithstanding its tenuity, would without difficulty cut through and through like a razor any aggregate thousands of Chinese soldiery in the open. While guarding against the folly of despising an enemy, it is not, surely, too much to say that the idea of these miserable wretches offering any serious resistance in a fair stand-up fight, seems preposterous beyond measure. Nor is this view confuted by the recent ill success of the French. They were baffled by sun, swamp, sickness, and maladministration, certainly not by the fighting powers of their antagonists.

Once more let us turn to a military display, but of an exactly converse nature—a soldier's funeral. Most of us are acquainted with its impressive simplicity at home, and here too is the 'Dead March' with its funeral cadence, the firing party with reversed arms, the lengthened files of the deceased's comrades, the coffin borne on the gun-carriage with the Union Jack, the dead soldier's helmet and bayonet. But the white clothing of our men, the red-turbaned Lascar gunners dragging the carriage in default of horses through the grotesquely built native streets, the crowd of ugly chattering Chinese, unmoved in their grinning materialism by the saddest strains of music and the most touching form of ceremonial, present additional features which almost make us feel as if we were taking part in some dream pageant. We reach the 'Happy Valley,' and here we can shake off these vermin. The coffin is borne on soldiers' shoulders through those beauteous groves of which I have already spoken; the long white procession winds slowly up the mountain side, standing out clear against the varied green and red dazzling tropical foliage; the three volleys are fired with an effect augmented by the echo; the drums beat the Point of War, 'Fall in, Quick March,' and homewards to a lively tune. For aught I know, technicalities may render the scene unsuitable for a painter's delineation, but as an episode in real life no human ingenuity could devise a more extraordinarily impressive combination of sight, sound, and circumstance.

Are deaths among the soldiers frequent? No—although the hospital returns are startlingly high, and I have had as many as 20 per cent. of my battery on the sick list, during part of a season by no means exceptionally unhealthy, and with every conceivable precaution for the preservation of health. The patients are sent off to the roomy hospital ship, 'Meanee,' a teak-built three-decker, which formerly belonged to the East India Company; should they continue to droop in spite of the sea air, they are transferred to the cool sanatorium high up on the 'Peak;' and should this fail, they are unhesitatingly invalided home.

The precautions taken by the military combatant authorities to avert sickness are wisely minute and incessant, inasmuch as the conveyance of each soldier to China costs the Imperial Government about 100*l.*; but they involve such apparent though necessary pampering that a new comer will in his inexperience bristle with horror. The men are strictly prohibited stirring out of barracks between 9 A.M. and 5 P.M. during the hot season; or if some emergency renders the despatch of a European orderly necessary, he is provided with an immense sun-parasol, a certain number of which are furnished by the commissariat. To wear a forage cap instead of a helmet before sunset is a punishable offence, and inspections are held to ascertain that each man has on a cholera belt. Barrack accommodation is luxuriously spacious—commissariat coolies are told off to work punkahs in orderly rooms, schools, workshops, and guard-rooms during the day, and during the night in the barrack-rooms—though, as an old gunner explained to me in one pregnant sentence, 'Them punkah coolies are not of much count, sir, unless you keep a boot handy by your bedside'—*i.e.* to use as a missile.

The following may be taken as a fair sample of Gunner Thomas Atkins' daily routine during the hot months. At 5 A.M. he awakes with a soft punkah breeze fanning him. 5.15. Cup of cocoa and a biscuit brought to his bedside by a coolie. (N.B. A silver salver is dispensed with.) 5.30. The barber coolie shaves him, still in bed. 6. Bathing parade. 7.30. Breakfast, of which $\frac{1}{2}$lb. of beef-steak forms an invariable component. 8 to 11. Nothing whatever to do, and plenty to help him to do it—the everlasting coolies perform nearly all the cooking, sweeping, and cleaning up in barracks. 11. A short spell of school and theoretical instruction in gunnery. After dinner unanimous repose on bamboo matting, as being cooler than a mattress. 5 P.M. One hour's easy gun-drill. 6 to 10. Sally forth to chaff the Chinese folk, try a trifle of 'samshu,' and practically ascertain that this potent rice spirit will prostrate with splitting headache the seasoned old soaker to whom a tumbler of brandy would be but as a glass of water. In fact during the hot weather he merely mounts guard, and is available for emergencies; in the cool season he is of course made to rub up his drill. His idle life is not a happy one, destitute as it is to him of interest and active amusements, and in a very short time he becomes listless, depressed and pulled down, contrasting painfully with his newly landed, fresh-looking comrades. This unfavourable condition seems to extend to the officers. I have known it asserted that no efforts of a commanding officer can keep European troops permanently stationed at Hong Kong in a state of military efficiency.

As a supplement to the British force, two companies of gun-Lascars have been brought from India, and they form most useful adjuncts for duties such as orderly and fatigue, involving an exposure to the sun, which they can face with impunity, but which would surely entail sickness on Europeans. Both companies are dressed like gunners, except that the Sikhs wear turbans. The Madras company is, however, in most respects, miserably inferior to the Sikhs. Undersized, feebly built, contemptible in cast of features, they approximate to the usual type of the cringing eastern. Those splendid Punjaubees, on the other hand, of powerful physique, handsome features, grave and dignified, are fine specimens of orientals. In the bygone period of the Sikh war they put forth all their powers to try conclusions with us, and after a valiant struggle were defeated. Since then they have accepted their fate with dignity, and, without self-abasement, have acknowledged us as their masters. They rely with implicit faith on the justice of their British officers, and are confident in the efficacy of an appeal for redress in any of their little grievances. I can imagine few prouder positions than the command of such a splendid body of men on active service. Owing, however, to the general ignorance of any language but Hindustani, and to the consequent necessity of the services of half-instructed native interpreters, adjudication and administration are frequently attended with difficulties. Their diction, both written and verbal, is of an amusing grandiloquence. 'Sahib,' was the translated peroration of a proud, swarthy, turbaned Sikh—nobleman, shall I call him—who considered that he had been both defrauded and insulted: 'I no care for dollar, I care only for shameful disgrace how I treated before all peoples.' Another, presenting a written petition for discharge, explains that he 'had the determined resolution to pass my life as a soldier. But the Almighty's decision cannot be rescinded. I try to satisfy you that this is true.' Another, reporting on a drain, says: 'It (the drain) had a great, disagreeable, and bad smell, quite impure, causing the men to be in unhealthy state . . . according to the rules of sanatory.' They entertain a most exaggerated idea of the far-reaching authority of the British officer. One man draws up a petition setting forth that a girl in India to whom he had been engaged was about to be bestowed by her avaricious father on a more wealthy suitor, and praying the commanding officer to issue an injunction which would restrain the father from such a measure for two years.

Hong Kong harbour is well adapted for defence, and the expense of the small garrison stationed there, to which the colony annually contributes 20,000*l.*, is money well spent. It is urged that under any circumstances a landing could be easily effected on the opposite side of the island, but it must be first assumed that our fleet would be either absent or perfectly inactive; and, secondly, granted the landing, the invaders would be compelled to fight their way against the defenders along a single road easily broken up, or to toil up to the crest of the main range of mountains. Restricted in either case to field-pieces, they could, after a considerable expenditure of time and ammunition, effect a great deal of damage on the open town below; but they could not hold it: the merchant ships would be well under the shelter of the detached forts, and if the latter were strengthened and more efficiently armed, their guns could both effectually hold the harbour and checkmate any further operations on the part of the enemy by land. These forts and batteries, six in number, even now command the narrow eastern or Lye-moon sea-pass, only a quarter-mile broad, the western entrance, which to a great extent is blocked by shoal water, and, in fact, the entire area of this incomparably splendid harbour. It is, however, greatly to be desired that the Imperial Government should resolve upon the expenditure of some small additional sum in strengthening the defences according to some resolutely carried out scheme, and thus take full advantage of the natural capacities for rendering this important post absolutely impregnable.[1]

It is worth while to cross over to the promontory of Kowloon on the Chinese mainland, acquired at the conclusion of the war of 1860 so successfully conducted by Sir Hope Grant, on the indisputable ground that its possession is tactically indispensable for the efficient defence of the harbour. On this strip of ground, about two miles in length and an average of three-quarters of a mile in breadth, commercial enterprise has been so busy as to imperil the attainment of the proposed military objects. Forts and barracks have, it is true, been erected on a stunted scale, and a small detachment of infantry is habitually stationed here for rifle practice; but docks, wharves, godowns, hongs, and villa residences have sprung up with flourishing rapidity, and every year tend more and more to elbow the military out of the field.

Kowloon is occasionally resorted to during hot afternoons, as a more breezy spot where lawn tennis may be played, with the pleasant sequence of a cool return voyage in the evening across the harbour. Steam ferries ply constantly to and fro.

The barren, uncultivated red ground presents a curious feature in the large patches of the sensitive

---

[1] Since this was written the Home Government has taken measures of a practical and comprehensive nature for rapidly putting Hong Kong in a far more efficient state of defence.

plant so well known in English hothouses. The waving of a stick over them seems to produce a withering curse as in the case of the wand of a malignant necromancer. The green plants simultaneously quiver, shiver, shrivel, and close, showing streaks of leafless, dry, withered stalks.

A steam-launch voyage round the island—the extreme length of which is eleven miles, maximum breadth five miles, and area, including Kowloon, thirty-two miles—gives us a good epitome of our survey of details. Throughout, the coast scenery is of that rugged, towering nature characteristic of igneous formations, but the back part of the island differs from the harbour side in its wide, unlandlocked expanse of the China Sea, in the rougher nature of its waters, in its precipitous little islets dotted about in every direction, and in its solitude and entire absence of all shipping save for a few piratical-looking junks, which, sallying forth from semi-hidden inlets, perpetrate abominable crimes for wretchedly small game. These wasps are, however, fairly cleared out from their former Hong-Kong haunts. Here we arrive at the little village of Stanley, in the bend of a bright, quiet, yet breezy little bay. It is now occupied by a few Chinese, in their usual tumble-down pigsties. It once formed a sanatorium, and here are the officers' quarters, the barracks, now utilised by the police, hospital, surgery, and the various accompaniments of a military establishment. But, for some occult reason, it was not found to answer its purpose; and, indeed, the justice of this conclusion is justified by the terrible extent to which its unduly large cemetery was in a very short time filled. English officials have cared for these sepulchres, first whitening, then crumbling, and finally blackening under the full glare of a tropical sun, with an unfailing solicitude. The ground is trim, even as an English village churchyard, and the renovated records still tell their tale of how, say, Sergeant Smith, died of fever on 3rd Aug^t, his wife on 5th, and their 2 children on 7th, and so on. A large proportion of the tombstones are in memory of officers who died in China as far back as forty years ago, and whose bodies were apparently brought here for interment.

Let us now apply to Hong Kong the Birmingham standard of £. s. d.—the inexorable test of receipts and expenditure. Its estimated revenue for 1884 was 1,200,000*l.*; its expenditure, 1,190,000*l.*; its exports to the United Kingdom in 1882 were of the value of 1,429,000*l.*, and its imports 3,143,000*l.*; and it is the only one of our colonies which, so far from being burdened with a public debt, has for many successive years been accumulating a surplus for unforeseen emergencies. In 1845 it cost the British taxpayers 50,000*l.* plus its military expenses. Now, it draws not a farthing from the home exchequer, and actually contributes 20,000*l.* a year towards defraying the expenses of the troops quartered in the garrison, the total strength of which, all told, is about 1,200 men. Its shipping, trade, and wealth are annually increasing, and, as already pointed out, have now assumed enormous proportions. Its local government, which is of an admirable simplicity, is smoothly and prosperously administered by a Governor and an Executive Council of six members, aided by a Legislative Council of eleven—one of whom is a Chinese—nominated by the Crown.

Well—have I succeeded in persuading you, even by this sketchy account, that Hong Kong is one of the most singular spots in the world ? Other localities possess their own special characteristics and as great beauties—superior of their kind they can hardly be. But this island, owing to its extreme remoteness from all centres of European civilisation, and to its strange population, which only resembles ourselves—apart from the theological point of view—in being two-footed, unfeathered, grinning mammals, possesses a novelty unequalled elsewhere. In addition to the advantages which I have already endeavoured to set forth, it is conspicuous by the fact that during the past thirty years its opulence has been increasing without a substantial check, and that, of all our vast colonial possessions, it may be considered, on the whole, as the most prosperous. Ceded in January 1841, and confirmed to us by the Treaty of Nankin, August 1842, its retention has never cost a drop of blood, or involved a single diplomatic difficulty, and there has never been a breath of allegation against a harsh or unjust sway. Indeed, its large native population, far from resisting our rule, flies to us from their own misgoverned country as to a haven of rest, justice, and security. As a nation, we are in the habit of contrasting our public measures unfavourably with those of other European countries, of proclaiming our shortcomings, of minimizing our successes. Here, at all events, we may point proudly to results, and quote Hong Kong as an instance of what may be achieved by English rule, English industry, and English integrity of administration.

CHAPTER II.

A MODEL BRITISH REPUBLIC—SHANGHAI.

BRITISH REPUBLIC! The very title sounds like a parody. Is this chapter a mere repetition of those numerous prophetic fables which endeavour to delineate the supposed conditions of existence, when England shall have learned antiquity of usage is not identical with excellence, and America that innovation is not *per se* amelioration? No. I seek to draw a picture of a small British community, over 10,000 miles distant from England—a nucleus which contains the elements of importance and aggrandisement in a future when, according to modern Chinese philosophers, the history of China will be the history of the governing world, while the annals of the British Empire will be comprised in a marginal note, to the effect that this active, intelligent race started into a sudden and ephemeral existence for a couple of thousand years, or so, and then vanished from the face of the earth. Even now, our fellow-countrymen in the Shanghai settlement, though theoretically English subjects, practically owe no allegiance to the Foreign Office,

Colonial Office, or Horse Guards; the settlement administers its own government with an independence little short of that exercised by Switzerland, and, in fact, the tiny Republic realises the supposition of an English tribe without a sovereign.

In 1884 British Republican Shanghai having requested British Imperial Hong Kong to send an officer to inspect their volunteers, horse, foot, and artillery, I was selected for this duty. Our stormy four-days' voyage between the two places resembled a prolonged Dover and Calais crossing, the discomfort of which no size of ship or luxury of accommodation could obviate.

As we enter the Yellow Sea, the hitherto blue water assumes the colour and consistency of pea-soup; we steam a short distance up the Yang-tsze-Kiang River, the mere pronunciation of which brings on a sore throat, and arriving at its confluent the Hwangpoo, are transferred to a tug to enable us to cross the rapidly silting-up Woosung bar, which subsequently assumed importance as a tactical obstacle to French operations. We paddle through slime, amidst darkness and bitter cold, for about ten miles to Shanghai. Here some dozen brilliant meteors, the last efforts of that electric light which here, as elsewhere, succeeded in enriching the directors and impoverishing the shareholders, reveal some large English buildings standing out in weird distinctness through the surrounding darkness, and the scene is rendered still more striking by the sudden influx of swarms of hideous chattering Chinese coolies springing on board from the adjacent wharf, like a flock of sheep through a gap.

The master of the tug, thinking this influx inopportune, quietly knocks down the foremost coolie, and intimates his intention of bestowing similar marks of favour on the others. Were there cries of ' Shame! ' or threats of vengeance from the mob of his outraged comrades? Oh dear no. The knocked-down coolie submissively slips away, and his outraged comrades fall back like frightened partridges. A few minutes afterwards, when the master's attention is diverted, they again swarm on board and handle the luggage with such dangerous freedom that I interpose. Merely stretching my leg across the gangway, I shout out in the ridiculous pidgin-English: 'Plenty too many coolie'; and these men, about 120 in number, keen for hire and shrouded in darkness, who could have brushed me aside like a fly, never dream of disputing the self-assumed authority of the single Englishman, but submissively and instinctively fall back until, in my good pleasure, I graciously permit one or two of their number to pass. Why do I dwell on this triviality? Because I want to illustrate the fact, so incomprehensible to those who have never dwelt in the East, that a solitary resolute Englishman can cow into spaniel submissiveness, under certain circumstances, an almost unlimited number of Asiatics.

Herein, too, lies a tendency to grievous oppression, against which it behoves us to be on strict guard—that tendency on the part of Anglo-Indians to strike and ill-use those who, they well know, will never lift a finger in their defence.

At Shanghai I was once rowed by some taciturn, quiet, respectable blue-jackets to a jetty crowded with native boatmen, who did not show sufficient alacrity in getting out of our way. Whereupon the blue-jackets, quite as a matter of course, methodically banged their heavy oars about the heads and the shoulders of the unfortunate Chinese, shoved the sampans right and left into the swiftly running river, and then the coxswain respectfully touching his hat, 'Beg pardon, sir, but them Chinamen are very slow in getting out of the way unless you hurry them a bit.'

Sallying forth in broad daylight, the first impression on my mind is that the English part of the settlement is a collection of small palaces. No alternation of houses and hovels, of neatness and filth, of luxury and squalor characteristic of most Anglo-Eastern towns. The private residences, the public banks, the wholesale warehouses, and even the retail shops, are large substantial stone buildings, constructed on a scale of absolute grandeur, externally handsomely decorated, internally equally handsomely fitted up. Along the whole frontage a broad marine parade called the 'Bund'—I presume from the Indian term Bunder—with an expanse of beautifully mown turf, slopes down to the water's edge and marks the European highway where commercial activity is at its highest. On the adjacent river, Hwangpoo, huge European ocean steamers are loading or discharging, while Chinese junks, Chinese sampans, and even Chinese steam-launches are fussing about in every direction. Their business-like appearance is enhanced by the six or seven foreign ironclads showing their teeth in the shape of monstrous guns, but riding in dignified repose at anchor, and by some large unwieldy opium hulks freighted with a burden which many pronounce to be somewhat more deadly, and infinitely more disastrous, than 25-ton guns and 400-lb. projectiles. Then the streets are as busy as a swarm of bees. Innumerable rickshas dash along at a sustained speed which would soon distance the whole tribe of Westons and pedestrian competitors. Innumerable pairs of coolies, with burdens suspended on bamboo poles which they bear on their shoulders, shuffle eagerly along. Their weights seem perfectly back-breaking, a contingency which they recognise by the most absurd rhythmical groans which apparently solace their minds and ease their bodies. Innumerable 'chit'-carriers, with that useful contrivance a chit book, wherein the recipient of the letter signs his name, hurry to and fro, imitating the businesslike anxiety of the English which foreigners pronounce to be our uncomfortable characteristic, but which perhaps is merely an incident due to the fact that that which we do, we do with all our might.

But where are the master minds, the irresistible potentates, in whose service these ricksha-men, these coolie labourers, these factory agents are working with an unwearied striving energy which only these pig-tailed Chinese can exercise? There are numerous tangible signs of them, from the street lamp-post, the invariable concomitant of English settlers in the most remote regions, to the vast storehouses of wealth which line the river frontage; but their presence in the body is comparatively rare. They are but as single salmon in a river teeming with myriads of smelts. Yet here and there the imperious subduer is seen striding through the crowds of the subdued, who carefully avoid jostling the Saxon potentate, intuitively fall back from his path, and obey his behests with the docility of well-broken spaniels towards their stern but not unkindly masters.

Let us now walk round the frontier territories of our republic, which we must remember is outside, and completely separated from, the enormous adjacent native city of Shanghai. Its strict limits, indeed, comprise an area of not more than one square mile, yet within this narrow space are assembled upwards of 250,000 human beings. One side is bounded by the river, two sides by brooks, and the fourth by a dry ditch. The top of the local Piccadilly is marked by its corresponding Hyde Park under the jurisdiction of the Republic Woods and Forests. About an acre of neatly turfed, prettily planted garden is railed in with handsome iron palings which no turbulent Reform mob has ever yet carried away. For nearly a mile the main road runs in a straight direction, then turning to the right we find ourselves in the Chinese section of the European settlement. Here a vast number of natives have established themselves, rejoicingly submitting to our taxation and incomprehensible cranks respecting sanitary laws. Some seeking that security of person and property for which they vainly search elsewhere; some hoping to escape from the spite and tyranny of their own rulers, and others, women, about 13,000 in number, concerning whom the least said the better. Yet these immigrants under such unfavourable auspices are a thoroughly law-abiding, orderly community on the whole. Under the restrictions of the Board of Works, even the poorest streets contrast most favourably with the back slums of Bethnal Green, and in general aspect are far handsomer and wider than the handsomest and widest in the native capitals of Foochow and Canton. The walls are, it is true, the thinnest possible shells—merely the three-inch thickness of a single brick—but a brick shell must surely be deemed superior to a thick mud and dirt crust. Most wonderful of all, there is not a garbage heap within nose-shot. The thoroughfares are a marvel to all Celestials; amply broad and well paved, and lighted sometimes with gas and sometimes with electricity, and strikingly supplemented by the painted paper lanterns swinging in front of the windowless tenements, under the provisions of the Defence Committee they are patrolled by policemen in dress and appearance the very dittos of the London Cerberus, and differing only in being more stalwart, more useful, and less meddlesome.

The densely thronged thoroughfares at first produce an impression of market day, instead of a normal condition of business. The dwellings of narrow frontage but of wonderful horizontal depth—I still insist on their comparative salubrity—are packed as closely as corpses in a speculator's cemetery. The disgorging process never comes to an end; the stream of human beings is incessantly pouring out of the doors into the streets and *vice versâ*, and we can now more readily understand how in China vast seething masses are compressed into minute areas, and why the ordinary European rules for estimating population are in this country entirely fallacious. Here we are outside the pale of the luxurious ricksha conveyance, but the thrifty Chinaman still finds a little opening for swagger according to his notions, by means of a double-seated wheelbarrow, whereon I have seen as many as three specimens of flesh, fat, and pigtail conveyed by a single coolie, struggling, staggering, sweltering, and inwardly groaning. A few years ago, indeed, these wheelbarrows were the sole means of conveyance for diners out. Now they are largely used at a fare of one cash—about twenty-five cash make a penny—by the Chinese women, and for a very sufficient reason. The practice of forcing their miserable feet into a shapeless mass, which is becoming less universal in Southern China, here prevails with unabated unanimity. The push of a little finger will cause a pedestrian thus deformed to topple on one side, and the accomplishment of a few yards on their own hind legs is more formidable and tedious to them than to the traditional tortoise. It may interest Darwinites to learn that this disuse of the feet muscles has called into play those of, shall I say, the dorsal vertebræ, thus developing enormous curves which, according to Chinese taste, constitute a line of beauty, and are held in far higher estimation than mere facial attractions.

Dear to the heart of the Chinese are the pursuits of bargaining, buying, and selling, but they despise any ostentatious display of their wares. Nastier, dirtier, more trumpery, and, in fact, more loathsome shops I have never seen in Whitechapel or the Seven Dials. Here is a display of cakes, of sweetmeats, and of black quivering jellies; they remind me of childhood's dirt pies. Here is a butcher's shop. Oh the horrors of the dangling fragments of fish, flesh, and fowl, carrion which they call food! they would be beneath the notice of a London cat's-meat-man, while the street is ornamented with extraordinary frequency with the strange, artistic, cheerful productions of the coffin makers.

Next crossing a bridge over a creek, I find myself in the American settlement Honkiew, a long straggling strip fairly busy and prosperous, and yet, according to the fashion of American locations, only half occupied. Indeed it bears in every lineament the stamp of its imported nationality, which, mixed up with local aboriginal features, forms an amusing mongrel medley. Large pretentious mansions, but without any features of details; embryo factories and incipient storehouses, not unlike a mushroom town in a Colorado clearing, indicate commercial enterprises which may result in enormous wealth or wholesale bankruptcy, for there will be no medium. The one long unfinished-looking street ambitiously called Broadway contains an excellent hotel and a few flourishing shops. The majority are, however, Chinese, and have accumulated their trumpery wares in true Yankee 'store' fashion, the principal dealer proclaiming his name as 'chop-dollar-Jack,' *anglice* 'Honest John.'

In the course of my exploration of the British settlement, I pass abstractedly over a narrow stream and bridge, and in an instant am roused into consciousness that the scene has changed. Why, where is the business activity, where the handsome mansions, where the throng of populace? All is languid and unenterprising. I stare in surprise. 'Rue Montauban' and 'Quai des Fossés' meet my eyes, while 'voulez-vous croire' and 'sapristi' strike my ears. Oh, I see, I have wandered into the French concession, spiritless, unprosperous, an instance supporting Mr. Forster's assertion in his 'Manual of Political Economy,' that of all nations who have had recourse to colonisation the English and the Chinese alone have been conspicuously successful; a warning to other settlers 'how not to do it.' The two settlements are side by side with every possible identity of circumstances and equality of advantages. Yet our success could scarcely be surpassed, their failure scarcely exceeded. Why this remarkable contrast? I suggest because the French national character is innately antagonistic to successful colonisation; and this in spite of Algeria glorious as a conquest, invaluable as a military school, and disastrous as a £. s. d. transaction.

At Shanghai, for example, they seem to be unable to modify their system of administration and business, suitable in Normandy and Auvergne, to meet the altered and inexorable requirements of the far East; they have tried to introduce a fraction of France and have failed. Their administration is imperious, autocratic, and at the same time injudiciously paternal. Enterprise and independence are strangled; wealth and the producers of wealth drift into another habitat —unwilling to be encumbered with the vexations of official cross-questionings, official permits, official stamps and official blotting sand. Neither Europeans nor Chinese can endure that their private transactions should be supervised by public functionaries, and consequently there is a steady flow from this atrophied district, the French population of which does not at the utmost exceed 200, across a few feet of planking into the English settlement, where an exactly converse state of affairs results in an expanding prosperity.

Still more gloomy is their outlook. Erst flourishing firms are now deplorably consumptive, the population is actually diminishing, and there is little or no young blood, fresh money, or enterprise flowing in to recuperate the ravages of a premature decay caused by over-fostering. Why, the very *sergents de ville* are absurdly fish out of water. The 'il est défendu,' the ozone of municipal atmosphere in France, is here amusingly out of place. The Chinese chatter and cannot comprehend; the English mockingly grin and will not obey; the officers of state look outraged and woe-begone, but are perforce silent. Their language scarcely finds a place in China generally; it is rarely employed in international commerce, nor have the coolies manufactured a pidgin-French corresponding to pidgin-English. Address these officials, with a redundancy of *galons* and a scantiness of clean linen, in their own tongue, and the floodgates of their national garrulity will be opened; they will feelingly expatiate on their sensation of isolation, on their aversion to a country so dissimilar to la belle France, and on their longings—fatal feature in a colonist—to return to the home of their fathers.

Again, at long intervals native rowdyism breaks out into a feeble spasmodic ebullition, which we English consider is best quelled by a body of police dealing whacks all round on the heads of the most noisy. But the French, with a vast amount of turmoil, turn out all their employés with rifles—unlike ourselves, they have no volunteer corps—and fire with wanton precipitancy on the mob, entailing a deplorable sacrifice of human life, and engendering much bad blood against the European community generally. An instance of the above occurred some years ago, when a new road having been marked out to run through a Joss house, the Chinese populace became turbulent. A little timely concession in slightly deviating from the original track, even a few conciliatory words, would have calmed them down. Instead of which the French rushed to arms, and with little semblance of leadership—for they failed in dragging their consul from his refuge under the bed—they charged down the street, bayoneting on their way innocent wayfarers, and finishing up with a rain of bullets.

Quitting the sombre, unprosperous-looking main thoroughfare, gardenless and Bundless, lining the river, I strike into some squalid side streets, with their names engraved Paris fashion at the corners in white porcelain on a blue ground, a trace, however slight, of an imported practice. Every external is strongly suggestive of an effete provincial French town. Here and there is a hairdresser, a pastry-cook, a *marchand de modes*, with a shadow of their habitual taste in their window displays. But there are few shops, and those few have scarcely any customers. Dinginess, dulness, and depression of trade reign throughout. There is indeed one oasis. The 'Hôtel des Colonies' is a very fair counterpart of the 'Hôtel des Deux Mondes' in Paris. A French landlord, French waiters, or Chinese, who for a marvel speak the language excellently, French floors, French furniture, French cooking and French atmosphere; in fact, thoroughly French, inside and out.

And now that we have surveyed the domains of our model British Republic—have scanned its outward appearance, its size, its population, and its wealth— avoiding indeed the bare statement of facts which in Colonial reports are habitually only less deceptive than the bare statement of figures, our next logical step is to investigate how so successful a system of administration has been attained, now is maintained, and will be sustained. Happy the country whose previous constitutional history may be summarised in such few words.

In 1842, during the first China war, Shanghai was captured by the British, but was not subsequently claimed as an appanage of our crown. Foreign commercial residents, among whom the English from the very outset immensely preponderated, began to settle down—first of all in the native city. But in 1850, finding the horrible purlieus intolerable to civilisation, they shifted their habitat to the present adjacent open area. 'Veni, vidi, vici,' but in this instance with little or no physical violence. Gradually, peacefully, they elbowed out of the way the native administration, and the native administration, philosophically admitting the inexorable logic of facts, tacitly recognised three settlements: one English, one American, and one French. The two former, wisely content with the substance without the shadow, accept the term 'settlement,' and lay no formal claim to the privileges of British territory. The French, on the other hand, persists, in season and out of season, in designating itself a 'concession,' a portion of France, and struggling to obtain its individuality merely succeeds in prolonging a struggling and somewhat contemptible existence.

Since 1843 the English settlement has steadily and without a material check been increasing in population, wealth, and prosperity, threatened, it is true, by dangers from Chinese rebels, especially by the Taepings, who held the native city from 1853 to 1855, and desolated the province up to 1862, and by the hostile operations carried on by the English and French in 1860, but always successful in dealing with those perils through the resolution and courage of the settlers.

Here I must explain that the American concessionists have dealt with certain difficulties arising out of their inferiority of numbers by merging their administration into that of the English. Smoothly and harmoniously does the plan work at present, our cousins are excellent neighbours and valuable mercantile coadjutors. But we are on delicate ground, perhaps the Sleswick Holstein of the Shanghai future; and it is a question whether, with increasing prosperity and numbers, there may not be a development of friction.

The Government at the present moment (1884) is carried on by a council of nine, which comprise a chairman, who to all intents and purposes is President of the Republic, a vice-chairman, and seven members, four of whom are English, two German, and one Frenchman who formerly was actually President of the council for his own settlement. The absence of any special American representative is an eloquent index of the extent to which the two tribes of cousins have merged their interests into one. The Parliament is annual, but the members are eligible for re-election, and the propriety of the substitution of a biennial or triennial one has been actively mooted. The franchise is extended to every European adult in the English and American settlement who is rated to the extent of 100*l.* a year. They number about 300 persons. Subjects of Great Britain pay a poll-tax of $5 a month, $1 for artisans, which entitles them to registry in their consulate, and to be heard as plaintiffs in their own court. The council assembles in conclave once a week, and the minutes of its proceedings are published. At the end of each financial year a sitting is held, which is freely open to the general public, and on which occasion are stated the various measures, executive and financial, which have been adopted during the past year, the existing state of the treasury, and the Budget for the coming twelve months.

The absence of an organised opposition is clearly a great evil; but this is, to some extent, counterbalanced by healthy internal bickering and spite, a tolerable substitute for the clap-trap, stump-oratory of certain sections of English politicians, whose first thought is the acquisition of place or power, and whose last thought is the public welfare.

The council is, moreover, subdivided into three working committees: one for finance, one for public works, and one for watch and police, who, of course, render accounts of their stewardships to the main conclave. The following is an epitome of the printed Budget, dated, I think, January 1883 :—

RECEIPTS (IN ROUND NUMBERS).

	Taels.
Land taxes	31,300
Municipal rates	112,400
Licences	72,100
Loan	60,000
Miscellaneous	44,000
Total	319,800 = £80,000

Expenditure.

	Taels.
Police	49,000
Sanitary	22,800
Public works	73,200
Volunteers	5,300
Municipal expenses, such as lighting, cemeteries, surveyor's office	38,700
Secretariat and collection of taxes	19,400
Public buildings and land and stores	49,700
Previous deficit and interest	18,900
Various	42,800
Total	319,800 = £80,000

There is in addition a funded public debt of about £60,000.

Thus we see that the bulk of the revenue is derived from a tax on houses and land, and from licences. It is collected with astonishing ease and regularity, albeit in a somewhat high-handed manner. The English, recognising the necessity of adequate supplies for the support of the administration, magnificently and as a matter of course accept their heavy assessment; while the natives cheerfully contribute their quota, which secures for them a treatment of justice and humanity, instead of a treatment of robbery and cruelty—a boon for which, by the way, they entertain the customary gratitude of recipients towards benefactors.

Finally, as an evidence of the commercial prosperity of Shanghai, I quote the following few statistics for 1882, in fear and trembling all the time for their unutterable dulness:—

Entered port, steamers (over)	2,000
Entered port, sailing vessels	500
Tonnage	3,850,000

Of these, the percentage was—

English	54·8
Chinese	42·5
Other nations	2·7

Gross value of trade of port nearly 31,000,000*l.*, of which the English percentage was ·67.

There are four splendid dry docks.

The Shanghai Republic has framed its laws on the principle of the deflagration of gunpowder—not instantaneously whereby the agents and the machine would be simultaneously shivered, but progressively rapid. The Statute Book has been codified from the regulations drawn up from time to time by the residents themselves, assisted in legal and international technicalities by the foreign consuls; and here we stumble upon an element of protectorate similar to that exercised in behalf of Belgium by the great European Powers. Laws and transactions affecting the relations of Shanghai with the external world are transmitted, through the combined consular body at Shanghai, to the ambassadors at the Pekin Court for final ratification.

The police is composed of 54 European and 240 native constables. After a little experience these latter appeared to be such nonentities that for a time they were entirely suppressed. Whereupon a sudden accession of street offences occurred at night, and it then became evident that the mere sight of the functionaries of the law, even though they were Chinese dummies, exercised a deterrent effect on Chinese malefactors. They were consequently re-established.

The administration of justice in a community composed of such heterogeneous materials as English, Americans, Germans, Portuguese—of whom there are a considerable number,[1] many of them descendants of the settlers in Macao in 1550—French wanderers from their own settlement, Chinese, a few Italians, Danes and Russians, is a matter requiring the very nicest management, and has been skilfully dealt with. The principle is that every case shall be adjudicated by a tribunal which represents the nationality of the defendant. If, for instance, an Englishman were assaulted by a German, the offence would be disposed of by a court presided over by the German consul, while a Chinaman robbed by an American would seek redress in the Consular Court of the United States. Some modification is, however, necessary in the frequent cases of the Chinese being involved as defendants, for to relegate them to their country's tribunal in the adjacent native city would indeed be to involve the unfortunate offender and not less unfortunate plaintiff in the meshes of systematic extortion and prolonged cruelty. Therefore a 'Mixed Court' has been organised, presided over by a Chinese

[1] I conjecture about 300.

mandarin, who generally plays the part of a puppet with the wires out of order, while the English, American, and German consuls act theoretically as 'assessors,' but practically as judge, jury, prosecutor, and counsel for the defence. For the trial of important civil suits, and as a supervisor of the general administration of justice, a member of the English bar, Sir Henry Rennie, has been nominated, or rather lent, by the British Government, furnishing almost the only faint trace of imperial authority over the settlement.

So simply and so efficiently is the police administered that a single court-house and machinery suffices for the enormous Chinese population of about 200,000 souls. I admit that it is chiefly composed of industrious law-abiders, who have taken refuge in European equity from mandarin rascality. Yet, of course, there is a leaven of scoundrelism both among the natives and in the shape of some stray cosmopolitan black sheep, of whom the most conspicuous are seventy 'she' black sheep, chiefly Americans.

Chaperoned by an English police superintendent, I proceed to the local Bow Street, in the outside courts of which are collected a large motley crowd of loungers, witnesses, plaintiffs, and prisoners. Here the contrast of silence, so far as silence can be enforced on these everlasting chatterers, order, the absence of smells, and the presence of the traditionally-garbed British policeman, attest European administration. The prisoners are tied together in twos by their pigtails, looking very much like captured hares, and so shrinking and unintelligent that one would suppose them to be equally incapable of an active deed either of good or evil. The native bystanders, in awe of all European 'casuals' as representatives more or less of the majesty of the law, awful in its mysterious far-reaching and inflexibility, make way for me with ostentatious deference, and I am conducted to the centre of the judgment hall, where, with the strange-looking surroundings of English official tables, chairs, and writing apparatus, is seated the mandarin, who in pigtail and Chinese robes appears an absurd burlesque of 'his worship.' A nonentity and full of effete national self-importance, he holds the scales of justice *de jure*, but by his side is the Thetis *de facto*, the European assessor, Mr. Giles, the vice-consul, full of English acumen and activity. He introduces me to his mandarin worship, Mr. Huang, and in response to the latter's obsequious obeisances I instinctively shake his slender snaky hand with a hearty national grip, by which unaccustomed proceeding he seems totally disconcerted.

The first case is called, and a Chinese policeman, dressed exactly like a fair-weather-man in the cardboard toy barometer, drives into the open dock, at the magistrate's feet, a prisoner as though he were vermin. Down he flops on his knees, and the picture of oppressed spiritless misery retains his grovelling attitude during the whole of the evidence. 'But perhaps he may establish his innocence,' I whisper to my cicerone, in scandalised compassion at this enforced demeanour of guilt. 'No matter, old-o custom invariably prescribes that attitude for a prisoner;' which rather reminds one of the American lynch law system of first the execution, then the verdict, and finally the trial. The natives do not seem to have the courage of great crime, and offences against the person are rare, resort to the knife being almost unknown. Hence the great majority of the charges are of the lightest possible nature. Number one case is, we will say, for gambling in the streets. The evidence, to be worth much, must be supported by a European, for both Chinese police and Chinese populace are incurably venal as witnesses, and are quite prepared to exculpate the guilty or to inculpate the innocent for a consideration of a few farthings. One or two pertinent searching questions from the assessor; fair play for the defendant's defence, but no legal quibbling. 'Fined 20 cents (10d.),' says the Vice-Consul in a low tone of voice to the mandarin. 'Fined 20 cents,' echoes the nonentity in a loud tone of voice to the Chinese public. Away scuttles the prisoner with every appearance of relief at the short and decisive nature of the investigation, and number two case is brought forward, a theft at the same time ludicrously trivial and disgusting. 'Three days' imprisonment,' repeats the cuckoo mandarin at the dictation of the Vice-Consul, who, however, treats the

Chinese cypher with affability personified compared with the browbeating of the German or American assessors. 'I should have thought three minutes ample,' was my whispered remark. 'Not at Shanghai,' is the reply, the case here affects the whole question of agricultural prosperity.

Next appear three Chinamen lashed together by their pigtails, and charged with burglary, which in point of fact amounts, perhaps, to prowling at night about an outhouse and absconding with property of the value of about three half-pence. The Chinese witnesses set to work in 'independent file firing' in a breathless chorus of gabble, supplemented by the Chinese policeman. There is a certain amount of conflicting evidence, and gradually the case becomes amusingly typical of the people, and the administration of justice in China. Notwithstanding the energetic endeavours of the English functionaries to preserve silence, they are not even moderately successful. Not only the Chinese official underlings, but the witnesses, the prosecutors, and the general public, at uncertain intervals suddenly shove themselves forward, utter in loud simultaneous chatter their opinions and remarks, and—scandal of scandals—even proffer eager advice to the magistrates! Perhaps in a certain way they perform the functions of a jury, and thus, in a country where even truth is a lie, they assist by this expression of public opinion in the equitable administration of justice. At all events the assessor seems to deduce sufficient therefrom to enable him to form his own opinion, for with sudden decision he says, 'Not proven; released,' and after a moment's dumb amazement on the part of the prisoners, that anyone accused should thus be dismissed scotfree, away they shuffle voluble in their delight. But even after the verdict has been pronounced, fresh comments are volunteered from the public, and it certainly may be laid down as a general rule that, the less justice is tempered with mercy, the greater the advantage to the community at large. It sometimes actually happens that, after sentence has been passed, the accused and his friends will harangue the magistrates on the iniquity of the judgment, and will bring forward new facts to show that the verdict was all wrong.

The next captive is charged with unlawful possession, and is led off by the tail to imprisonment for forty-two days. The next, a crafty old offender, has been arrested for returning to his settlement after having been deported, as a penalty for previous offences, to his own city. Cat-like, he will not be driven away; he prefers an English prison to liberty in his native dens, and is condemned to a further period of incarceration, which appears rather to gratify him than otherwise. The next case is suggestive. The prosecutor, an inhabitant of the French settlement, with a mean opinion of the executive of his own countrymen, has so adroitly managed the point of venue as to have transferred the adjudication to the English court. The offence is one of pilfering, and the sentence, I think, ten days' imprisonment. 'Won't you order him the cangue?' (public exposure in a wooden collar) asks the plaintiff entreatingly, and the peremptory 'No' of the Vice-Consul conveys to me the satisfactory reluctance of our officials to inflict a form of punishment which, though when carried out by us is merely a form of discomfort, has nevertheless been borrowed from the severely torturing infliction of the cruel Chinese.

I could not but remark that, on passing sentence in each case, there was a general air of exhilaration and surprise among the culprits. Subsequent experience confirmed the explanation thereof which was given me. Chinese offenders subjected to their own tribunals invariably suffer petty extortion, cruelty and suspense, so that our prompt, clear, and disinterested awards appear to them in the light of positive benefits. The above-described mixed court, unique among modern tribunals of justice, was established by the late Sir H. Parkes in 1864, and, in defiance of its theoretical imperfections, its practical working is undoubtedly admirable.

The Anglo-Shanghai prisons would perhaps barely satisfy finicking humanitarianism in England, but they fully meet the requirements of wise humanity in China; indeed, in comparison with native dungeons they are so little punitive as to be barely deterrent.

The prisoners are confined in what I may describe as Brobdingnagian windowless cages, one side of which is barred by bamboo poles at wide intervals, admitting an unrestricted view into the interior, and the passage of extra food, opium, and tobacco to the incarcerated from their outside friends. The normal temperature obviates suffering from cold, as a rule; the atmosphere, the unrestricted air of heaven, is untainted, save by the inevitable civet-cat-like accompaniments of all natives, the Bouquet de Chinois. Here let me be pardoned for adding one word in all seriousness on this unsavoury subject, not so much on the score of interest, but as an admonition to practical forbearance all the world over. There is no living creature whose presence is not accompanied by emanations utterly loathsome to those not of its own species or even tribe. Let the cleanest woman-finger touch a bait and no rat will look at it. Enter a room occupied by four or five young Chinese who have daily been scrubbed in hot water from childhood, and you cannot abstain from grimaces of disgust. 'Why,' asked an Englishman of a highly educated, refined native gentleman, 'do your countrymen evince such reluctance to hold with us occasional intimate social intercourse?' 'Well,' was the embarrassed reply, 'we are many of us fully aware in our hearts that you are very wise, humane, learned, clever, and often very friendly disposed towards us. But, to tell you the truth, there is one feature about all you English which we are totally unable to endure. We cannot at any price stand your *esprit de corps*.' The actual term used would of course strike the reader very disagreeably in print.

To revert to our prisoners. Thirty or forty are incarcerated in each cage, which in our eyes amounts to overcrowding; but they are clearly of another opinion owing to their unmistakable appreciation of a large gathering. I walk along the rows of lock-ups, scrutinising at my leisure the scene within. The occupants are gleefully chattering with their fellow inmates inside, or through the bamboo bars are holding unrestricted converse with their clustering acquaintances outside. They have no sense of shame at this public exposure, because Chinamen have no sense of distinction between virtue and vice otherwise than as it affects profit and loss; they would consider as pure gibberish the classical invocation, 'Disguise thyself as thou wilt, Slavery, still, still, thou art a bitter draught;' and so they sit happily on their hams—Easternlike they always prefer nature's portable chair—congratulating themselves on this repose from their everlasting toil, toil, toil, and on this chance for healing afforded to their shoulders and neck muscles, habitually bruised and strained by the burden-bearing bamboo poles. A few of the worst offenders are, it is true, subjected to a somewhat more strict form of imprisonment, and a fewer still to the cangue, a wooden collar encircling the neck. The Chinese implement is so ponderous as to cause torture, and so broad that the hands below cannot reach the face above, either for purposes of eating, or for brushing away the clouds of persecuting stinging insects which settle on their perspiring skins. But that used by the English is so small and light that it inflicts inconvenience rather than pain, and its chief object is to attract the attention of the public to the special crime of which the prisoner has been guilty. Strokes with the bamboo are in rare instances applied to persistent offenders, but in a very mild form.

In the social life of Shanghai, where each numerically small nationality maintains a resolute exclusiveness, the prominent features, especially among the English, are unstinted luxury and open-handed hospitality, mingled withal with a considerable amount of formality, and the casual 'Globe Trotter' (i.e. amateur traveller) and the sportsman will find their objects furthered with friendly zeal. Invitations to dinner and to 'tiffin' are incessant—and at the latter midday meal you will not be spared a single item of a luxurious artistically cooked dinner, from which you will rise with a sense that your digestion, brain faculties, and afternoon's leisure have been equally impaired. Indeed, a week's experience of these double daily dinners will make you crave for the simplicity of gruel and parched peas. As regards the company, the element of Englishwoman is very scantily represented; the men are usually of the successful merchant class—for Shanghai, offering almost a certainty of ultimate wealth, at all events of competence, to the diligent and able, is no place for the bankrupt loafer or the disreputable fool. And the conversation? Well, perhaps it would be improved were there less mercantile and dollar and tael talk, but at all events the outsider gains thereby a faint idea of the world-wide magnitude of English commerce, a dim insight into the real meaning of the term 'merchant-princes.' After dinner it is customary, especially on Saturdays and Sundays, to drink one of three toasts. 'Sweethearts and Wives,' says the host—received with the usual levity considered appropriate to the strongest ties by which mankind can be bound. Or, more gravely, 'Absent Friends,' and 'Absent Friends' is warmly repeated, perhaps with a sigh of regret, perhaps with a chuckle at the recollection of former larks carried on with those absent friends. But there is one health, usually given at the Sunday luncheon, which is invariably received with the gravest earnestness : 'The Old Folks at Home,' and in a subdued tone, which bespeaks softened feelings, even the spendthrift, the ne'er-do-weel, or the callous materialist will re-echo the words : 'The Old Folks at Home.'

And now that I have alluded to kindly influences which have originated probably in childhood's religion, and which more than aught else distinguish us from the Chinese—unkindly hearted, their fetish of ancestral worship notwithstanding—I am led to speak a word of the Shanghai Protestant Cathedral. The only fault I can find with the building is that it is of a size and internal splendour absurdly in excess of the requirements of the English Protestant residents, and the money thus spent might have been far more usefully applied in improving the local clerical administration. Outside, a Chinese heathen coolie is summoning Christian worshippers by banging with a bludgeon a huge tongueless bell; inside, the tiny congregation looks even more tiny in contrast with the dreary array of empty seats—though this again is somewhat relieved by the presence of the pleasant-looking, decent blue-jackets from the adjacent British 'Champion.' In addition to the cathedral there is a Wesleyan place of worship, the frequenters whereof set a conspicuous example of humble sincerity, while their affiliated temperance society effects immense good amongst those who can abstain, but cannot be moderate. Perhaps a China Sunday rather jars upon the old notions of an English Sunday, but perhaps, too, the hard-working, money-making merchants will reply that they are so busy during the week that on this day alone have they leisure to start on shooting expeditions, to play at rackets and lawn-tennis, to look after their racing ponies; and that, after all, church-going is in many cases a mere form. Well, is it wise to acquiesce in the abandonment of a form which yet establishes a link with duty, and in which may be recognised the shadow of a forsaken good?

An invariable concomitant of all English settlements in the East, large or small, flourishing or impecunious, is the Club. That at Shanghai, to which casual visitors are made welcome with generous hospitality, is an excellent specimen of its kind. A large, handsomely furnished building, a first-rate library, innumerable European newspapers and periodicals, a good coffee-room, and infrequent rowdyism—it surpasses a considerable number of London clubs in its presence of comforts and absence of scandals. Unfortunately it tends to become a focus for gambling both in the stockbroking and pony-racing line—evils of serious dimensions, especially among the younger members of the community. There is no written or unwritten code among the brokers, whose over-crowded ranks are largely recruited from the Shanghai failures in other avocations; there is no regular Stock Exchange, and immoderate gambling in shares has blasted, not only in Shanghai but in China generally, the fortunes of a number of young men to an extent out of proportion to the total residents. A good deal of money is lost at cards, the whist stakes being portentously high, though the Australian standard of 'sheep points, and a bullock the rubber,' has not yet been introduced.

Then the pony racing—what a boyishly harmless, wisely to be encouraged, pastime does it sound! But in the majority of cases it is a mere subterfuge for all the evils and none of the advantages of horse racing—little of the plain sailing of the '4 to 1 bar one' element, but an elaborate system of selling lotteries, of squaring races, of roping, and of most of the ingredients of racing blackguardism. Its best feature is the racecourse itself, which here, as at Hong Kong, Amoy, Foochow, and even at the far inland settlement of Hankow, is the principal natural characteristic of the place—a large, carefully turfed space, just outside the town—fair, fresh, and free from the native throng which elsewhere seems to choke one. Here I see strings of racing ponies being exercised, sometimes thirty or forty belonging to one stables. They are small, rough, wild-looking Mongolian 'Griffins,' as fresh importations are called, well-shaped, singularly strong and enduring, but with no turn of speed, and with a sour temper evinced by their habitual knack of catching hold of an unsuspecting bystander, and with a simultaneous craunch shaking him as a dog would a rat. They are wonderful proficients in the art of bucking. If once the aggravating little beast stops short, and arches its back like a spitting cat, it is all over with the best rider who ever sat in saddle. The mafoos, or native grooms, who habitually stick like leeches, the moment they recognise in an apparently placid animal the

H

first signals of an intention to set to bucking, roll off to the ground with grotesque agility.

A walk about Shanghai environs on Sunday afternoon will throw on the daily life of the inhabitants fresh lights which we might seek in vain elsewhere. Starting, let us assume, from the Bund or Marine Parade, we pass through the Anglo-Chinese portion of the settlement, and emerge into the country, where a continuous combination of sight and sound never ceases to remind us of England, and yet, at the same time, never suffers us to forget that we are 10,000 miles off, amongst a race almost as divergent from ourselves as Gulliver's Houyhnhnms. The one admirable, metalled, high road would alone mark the presence of Europeans—it has no parallel throughout the whole gigantic empire, for the Chinese routes, for thousands of miles in the interior, are literally wheelbarrow paths.

The English have obtained from the Fuhtai, or governor of the district, a concession of this road for a distance of three miles into the imperial territory. Here flock the Europeans of all, and the Chinese of the *élite*, classes; and here, too, the amount of gossip would imply that everybody knows a great deal more of his neighbour's affairs than his neighbour knows about his own affairs. Here are merchants bent on a brisk constitutional during the cool season, bearing that aspect of earnest intent which foreigners declare render even our pleasures melancholy and laborious.

A few family couples are strolling about rather spiritlessly; you may depend upon it that the wife has been leading up to the never-ceasing subject: 'Let us go home,' and that the husband has replied: 'Let us first accomplish the object for which we came out.' Amas (Chinese nurses), in charge of two or three English children, most of whom are so pale—here, as elsewhere in China, the climate is sadly unkind to them—so languid, so joyless, and with an idealised thoughtful expression approaching to beauty, only to be seen when the faint rustle of the angel of death has been heard. The amas are usually excellent nurses, very fond of, kind to, and liked by, the children; but their grotesque ugliness reminds one of a baboon taking care of kittens.

There are but few representatives of the eager 'he' making a rendezvous with the bashful, modest, English 'she,' for all these garden plants are transplanted at an early age to home nurseries, and their would-be usurpers are large numbers of brazen Americans, with the most ragged of reputations, driving faultless turnsout, usually Victorias or basket carriages. In their vehicles they have found a host of imitators, in the shape of wealthy Chinese merchants, who come to Shanghai as the Americans go to Paris, to spend their money and acquire an illusory veneer. They are an amusing burlesque as they bowl along in a rickety antiquated landau, equipped with tawdry, furbished-up harness, and driven by a Chinese coachman bedizened in national rags. Their equipage is calculated to hold four, but into it perhaps six fat old mandarins have wedged themselves, conspicuous with their six pendent pigtails lying coiled up in each other's laps, with six flabby parchment physiognomies, and six loud cackling voices.

Here, again, are merchants' broughams, which only differ from the best-appointed London ones in that their back panels are of splendid movable plate glass, ensuring a current of air in hot weather, and imparting a pleasing appearance of lightness. I may observe that, except at Shanghai, carriages are almost unknown to the English in China, so impossible are the routes for this species of conveyance.

The handsome villas with pretty gardens which line this English road really smack of Peckham and Balham, except that here they are comfortably habitable, while the illusion is heightened by a pillar-post, and a reproduction of Policeman X patrolling, apparently more for ornament than for use, inasmuch as, in this ignorant, semi-civilised country, there is neither drunkenness, rowdyism, nor brawling. There, too, is the Country Club, charming inside and out, well furnished with literature and available for ladies, who resort to it in large numbers. And yet a woman in a club somehow always seems out of place, and is generally sour, masculine, and long in the tooth—a pleasant rosebud is rarely to be found there. But Englishwomen in China are wont to fall away terribly. Habitually they abominate the country, and not unnaturally, for there is little to accord with their tastes, or to enlist their interests—they grow languid, listless, out of health, and out of temper. They are in a bad plight, indeed, unless they are wise enough and good enough to find happiness in the consciousness that they can safeguard the health and happiness, the material and moral welfare of their husbands, who, but for this influence, have here a tendency to go to rack and ruin in the above respects—prosperous, perhaps, in their business avocations, but deteriorating in almost every other point of view.

We pass numerous lawn-tennis grounds, of which game almost everyone here, male or female, who is not a cripple owing to avowed infirmity or dissimulated age, is wisely a devotee; then the racket court and cricket ground, and above all the pack of drag hounds, about nine couple in number, the Chinese never resenting their trespassing. The country is perfectly flat and open, and is sufficiently intersected with big water jumps to ensure a keen pleasure in watching for the calamities of others. The sight of the apparently purposeless, exhausting, and dangerous run quite confirms the natives in their opinion that these 'Fung Yang' (foreign devils), who hold over them such a mysterious and lordly sway, are the maddest lunatics the world ever produced. Their general line of argument is as follows:—

'You will spend hours, you will face cold and

heat, wet and fatigue, in the pursuit of a few snipe or wild duck, which you could obtain far more easily in the shops, and at a mere fraction of the enormous sums you spend on your houseboat and other shooting arrangements. Then a number of you, to whom every hour may mean hundreds of taels, will, after toiling in your offices all day, drill every evening for a month without the slightest compulsion, and without receiving one cash in payment. (Alluding to the Shanghai Volunteers.) Can you maintain that your hunting is a reasonable occupation? Wherein consists the pleasure or the profit in riding behind a quantity of barking dogs, risking your lives in jumping over broad wet ditches, when you had much better remain on the safe side? But of all your insane occupations that which you call athletics is surely the most insane. Coolies stagger under heavy burdens, and toil at other severe manual labour, because it is their sole means of earning a few cash. But you rich Englishmen will actually reduce yourselves to an exhausted condition of perspiration in purposeless lifting of weights, in wearing your muscles, in running at full speed, in fact, in performing coolies' work without even coolies' pay—sometimes indeed at a positive expense. Are these the pursuits of reasoning beings, or of hare-brained madmen?'

My long strolls after spring snipe answered the additional purpose of studying the Chinese farming system and agricultural labourers. Hideously flat and naturally marshy—for water may always be found here three feet below the surface—the country had yet a sort of pleasing aspect of its own from its extraordinary fertility and careful cultivation. Every square yard, almost every square inch, is tilled to the highest point, and in the main by that hand industry in which the Chinese have no equals on the face of the earth. An inefficient buffalo plough is to be seen on rare occasions—a horse plough never. Fertilising agents, which we in England consider too trumpery or too disgusting, are here utilised with miserly econony; the results charm the eye of the practical farmer—the emanations insult the nostrils of the sentimental wayfarer, and this impression is not counteracted even by the vast expanse of sweet smelling beanfields, or by the acres of peach trees spread all over the plains, and in all the beauty of their spring blossom.

Such importance do the inhabitants attach to putting plenty into the land, by which system indeed they get three full cereal crops annually out of it, that they yearly plough in as manure many a sack of good sound beans, and many an acre of half-grown bean crop, to which plant they attribute specially enriching qualities. Indeed the bean crop is the staple Shanghai product, varied with a considerable area of paddy fields (rice), corn, cotton, and roots. Conspicuous by their absence are flocks and herds—not an ox or a cow not a sheep or a goat, not even a pig, except as a refined member of their hovel society, is to be seen over the entire landscape. There are no products of milk, butter, cheese, mutton or beef. We have little to learn from China in the way of agriculture.

In search of further details, tramp with me reader, gun in hand, and coolie at heels, over the fields. The ground must be left entirely to your own selection, for the coolie, useful as a creature of burden, cannot speak a syllable of English, and will not exert himself an ounce to further the game-seeking objects of his lunatic employer. Strangely enough the agriculturists, with all their minute care and industry, let me wander at my own sweet will through their standing crops, eagerly beckoning me to come on when my farmer instincts would be scandalised at such trampling down, and when a British yeoman would pitchfork me for less than half the amount of trespass.

The beanfields, knee-high with their white flecked stalks, are the dearly-loved resort of spring snipe, innumerable, mysteriously fat, and resting here for about a fortnight in their flight from Mongolia to Cochin China. Now and again a pleasant gets up with the same fuss and under the same circumstances as his English brother, with whom indeed he is identical in shape, size, and plumage. Of course he gets off scotfree at this season of the year, being 'père de famille,' as Alphonse would say—though, alas! in these climes Alphonse does not usually spare him even under these sacred circumstances.

Two or three shots, and up start in every direction Chinese urchins in keen competition for the prize of an empty cartridge case, which the inscrutable natives turn to some use. They accumulate in numbers such that to fire in almost any direction would produce the same results as to fire into the 'brown' of a dame's school. It is critical work, for it is hardly possible to point your gun without finding a Chinese child at the end of your barrel. 'Masquie'—pidgin-English 'Never mind'—says my coolie encouragingly. I know better. Humanity apart, I am fully aware that the parents would rejoice were a couple of pellets to lodge in the eye of one of their offspring, provided I would pay a few dollars indemnity. I must seek for fresh pastures—a vexatious task, because the entire country is intersected, at widths sometimes only four or five hundred yards apart, with narrow, seethingly stagnant canals, deep enough to float small junks, broad enough to deter a jump, and muddy enough to entail on failure a mass of execrably smelling nastiness. Sometimes it is necessary to tramp many hundreds of yards in search of a foot-bridge.

By far the most astonishing objects in these large, flat, hedgeless fields—for Shanghai stands on a plain without a hillock for twenty miles—are the innumerable graves. It has been estimated that the area of ground thus withdrawn from cultivation in this locality is equivalent to about one-tenth of the total arable space, and I can quite believe it. Single circular graves, or large grave heaps containing ten or twelve coffins, stand out in bare ugliness in the midst of every beanfield and cornfield, in every roadside patch and thicket. The sites seem to have been chosen in defiance of all convenience to the living, the sole requirement being a thoroughly dry, well-drained spot. The areas thus occupied are held sacred to an extent attained only where bigotry or superstitious folly are rampant. Should the land change hands, the grave mounds still remain the property of those who there interred their relatives; they remain undisturbed from generation to generation, and to level them, or to cultivate the superficies of the most insignificant or the least known, would be held not only a criminal offence but an outrage shocking to humanity; yet there is no attempt to decorate them or even to trim them, not a sign of ·that would-be-prettiness over a grave which, prompted by sorrow for the dead, saves it from the sneers applied to mere sentiment.

I was once puzzled by observing an English-made bye-road twisting like a snake, apparently in the most stupid purposeless fashion, over a perfectly level sound country. At last I discovered that these expensive deviations were absolutely necessary in order to avoid disturbing the adjacent places of sepulture. Here we have an illustration of the strength of their tenets of ancestral worship—tenets which at first appear to pivot on some of the better and softer feelings of our nature, but which on further examination prove to be merely another feature of that fetish superstition which is so strangely mingled with their repelling scepticism.

Even more repugnant than their gaunt graves are their ghastly coffins, standing on the surface of the ground in the ratio, say, of about one to every ten acres. Originally they were constructed with remarkable solidity, were lutened up and made carefully airtight, and were bound round with thick straw plaits. But time has more or less rotted all away, and the revelation of a weird outline of corpse shocks our sense of decency, still further outraged, by the way, by the unceasing inquisitiveness of our English Ponto.

Next we come to a flimsy bamboo fence, impenetrable to eyesight, but so fragile that a puff of wind would overthrow it. It encloses a collection of some twenty or thirty low, tumble-down-looking sheds. Pigsties? No, only in the sense that they are the habitat of the Chinese human. Mud and wattle, often mud without the wattle, windowless, chimneyless, doorless, filthy outside and curiously loathsome inside, they can only be paralleled with the worst of those hovels for the retention of which the Irish shoot their landlords, who desire to clear away such eyesores; only the Irish miscreant with national hypocrisy whitens his den-sepulchre. Here are a few of the typically ugly, featherless, indecent Shanghai fowls which some years ago a perverted English taste valued at nearly their weight in gold; here some English-looking magpies and sparrows with more than English pertness; and here, numerous above all, the everlasting crow, less of a garbage eater than the Shanghai human. There is a conspicuous absence of trees, gardens, and inside or outside ornament.

The approach of a European stranger rouses that aggravating chorus of the jackal-like dogs, which in turn evokes the presence of a population, young and old, so numerous in comparison with the numbers of dwellings that a hive of bees might herefrom pick up a hint in economising space. They all watch the Englishmen with some dislike and contempt, but with still more curiosity. One glance at the interior, one sniff at the atmosphere, causes me to hurry away with unfaltering haste.

Strange, striking, other-world like, as are the impressions produced on Europeans by Chinese surroundings, these sensations are never so thoroughly developed as in a native theatre. Thither I one evening betook myself, accompanied by my Hong Kong 'boy' as cicerone, on one of those expeditions of personal experience which casual visitors seek and residents shirk. The coolie trots my ricksha through darkness and rain as quickly as a pony, and as comfortably as a brougham, down the broad, well-lighted English Bund into the narrow, dim, French settlement, where the principal Chinese theatre is situated in close proximity to the native city. As we draw near, the crowd becomes too thick to be parted asunder by the mere cry 'Hyah!' which habitually announces the approach of a European and ensures the immediate removal of all obstacles. Slowly we thread our way, and finally pull up at an unusually broad entrance, bright with many-coloured paper lanterns, and redolent with that odour peculiar even to clean Chinese atmosphere—a sickly, mingled smell of sandal-wood, joss-sticks, camphor, and opium.

The custodian, at the sight of European prey, shuffles obsequiously forward and demands a price of admission which would probably be equivalent to a charge of four guineas for a box at the 'Victoria.' He would gladly have accepted one-fourth of the sum, but I am growing sick of the atmosphere of everlasting chaffering in which I have been living, and prefer to allow the robber to pick my pocket. He ceremoniously conducts me through a throng of natives, who stare at the isolated intruding foreigner with the stare of suspicious *feræ naturæ*, to the parterre where innumerable chairs and tables are scattered about. Here he assigns to me a seat of honour, kicking out, to create a vacancy, a fat Chinaman who had probably paid the lawful sum for possession, but, unlike me, had not submissively permitted himself to be fleeced.

The dispossessed man angrily chatters, expostulates and abuses, but there his spirit of resistance, according to the wont of his countrymen, stops short, and I am at leisure to realise the scene, which however at first bewilders me owing to its extraordinary novelty.

The theatre is luridly lit up with a few lanterns and miserable oil lamps, which gradually reveal to me a house of the average size of a London theatre, filled exclusively with the long blue robes and pigtails of males, with the glazed rolls of black horsehair and with the deformed feet of females, and with the hideous, opaque, demon-looking faces, from whence arises a diabolically ugly clatter of voices which almost drowns the stage dialogue. Dialogue, do I say? I use the term in sheer despair of accurately qualifying the yelling falsetto of the actors—not a civilised falsetto, but a loud discordant monotone between an eldritch yell and a wooden howl, and in it every single word of the play from beginning to end is uttered. Still I should have pooh-poohed the notion of its being unendurable to a strong-nerved man, but for three fiends who, seated at the back of the stage, smote, with the ceaseless regularity of machinery, a wooden drum, clashed cymbals which would have disgusted a Punch and Judy audience, and so manipulated some tightened strings of catgut that they emitted shrieks which would form a suitable accompaniment to Dante's refrain: 'Abandon hope, all ye who enter here.' In all sober seriousness I declare that I, a matter-of-fact middle-aged man, after having been subjected to the above combination of sounds, the description of which is miserably inadequate, felt overpowered by the hysterical sensations of a miss of seventeen, and that eighteen hours afterwards those sensations of the 'horrors' still remained in the ears. But that 'One dog's meat is another dog's poison' is more true in China than in any other part of the world, and the opinion of native gentlemen whose appreciation of the fine arts has, after their own fashion, been cultivated is as follows:—

'In all the sciences and in most departments of civilisation you greatly surpass us. But in one respect we are undoubtedly far ahead. We alone understand true harmony: you are ignorant of its very first principles.'

Of course I was entirely dependent on my 'boy's' interpretation for a complete comprehension of the plot; it was apparently the essence of dulness, it was unquestionably grossly indecent. Happily in the interests of morality the women's parts were represented by men, and indeed they were almost undistinguishable from females so perfect was their feminine get-up. The piece continued until about one or two A.M. every day, and to follow out the whole story it would be necessary to attend on six or seven consecutive occasions. There is no division of acts and no scenery, the normal dim lighting being supplemented by an attendant bearing a long pole with a candle fixed at the end, and waved about according to the direction where its rays are required. The players from time to time explain to the audience the situation of affairs very much after the manner of Pyramus and Thisbe in 'Midsummer Night's Dream.' Let me make the most of one note of admiration. The costumes, if sometimes a little ridiculous owing to the peacocks' feathers quivering about six feet above the heads of the wearers, were most beautiful, and must have cost enormous sums. The actors were covered with paint, red, black and white, thickly laid on and highly polished.

So much for the stage. Now I am beginning gradually to realise the surroundings. The audience is certainly enjoying the play in their way, though that way assumes the form of a universal chatter which at times almost rises above the recitative. That man dispossessed of his seat in my favour is loudly holding forth on his wrongs, and now and again there surges what I assume to be roars of execration, imperfectly represented by 'Hoo-gh,' 'Boo-oo,' 'Y-ah,' and which every moment I expect will be followed by 'Turn him out!' But my boy explains that these are national interjections of applause, corresponding to our 'bravo,' and are directed to the actors. A shuffling waiter puts before me a little pile of melon seeds which the Chinese consider delicious. My untrained taste likens them to beech-nuts without kernels. Tea, in the form of an infusion from a pinch of leaves at the bottom of each cup is likewise provided. It is sugarless and milkless, but somehow is better than any I have ever tasted in England. More refreshment in the shape of little flour paste-balls swimming in hot water-bath substances taste equally of dirt. Then some glutinous nastiness of the nature of sweetmeats, but which would be efficacious as an emetic. I continue to shake my head in negative. There is no pleasing these foreign devils, thinks the waiter. So at last he brings a huge trayful of smoking hot, wet cloths, and insists on my taking one. 'Very happy to gratify you, but what on earth am I to do with this dripping rag?' Then I observe that my neighbours, greasy, fat, perspiring, and in fact Chinese in olfactory details, snatch hold of some, and therewith dabble, pat, and mop their unlovely countenances with every expression of luxurious enjoyment, and then pass them on to their sweltering neighbours. I master my own emotion, and do not hurl my own rag at the head of the attendant who has just presented it to me.

The gallery is crammed with a well-to-do, poorer class of native, obviously delighted; the boxes barely filled with gaudily bedizened, childishly vain-looking mandarins, ostentatiously indifferent; the basement with the overwhelmingly prevalent type of the upper middle classes, perhaps the truest type of the average Chinese. The men largely predominate, and are of sedate middle age—vicious youth and satyr-like

I

dotage being entirely absent. The women, a minority though a numerous one, are decent both in demeanour and dress. Indeed were they what we term *décolletées*, i.e. as bare as far as they dare, they would be considered by their countrymen as half mad and wholly brazen. The reputation of most of them is tattered according to our standard, but according to their own they are not held in the same disrepute, and are quiet and orderly under the jurisdiction of their attendant duennas.

But I feel that my powers of endurance are rapidly coming to an end. The inharmonious gabble, the jarring sounds of the orchestra, the ear-cracking falsetto of the actors, the flickering lurid lights, the peculiar Chinese odours so strange and so distasteful to European nostrils; above all, the concentration of so many unfriendly pairs of eyes on one's every movement, produce at last a sensation of discomfort and daze closely akin to indisposition. I elbow my way out, jump into a ricksha forming one of a string as long as a line of carriages on a London opera night, and splash at a rapid trot through the driving rain and wind. I rejoice, having witnessed a sight, unparalleled in any other part of the world, once; I should regard it as a hardship to be compelled to be present a second time at such a jarring, displeasing, unlovely display.

CHAPTER III.

INSIDE CHINA.—THE RIVER YANG-TSZE-KIANG.

NOTWITHSTANDING the modern thirst for exploring, we are almost entirely without knowledge concerning one-fourth of the population of the globe—the enormous Chinese Empire, numbering at a moderate estimate 350,000,000.[1] We have, it is true, nibbled at the Treaty Ports, but they differ from the normal country almost as much as the rind of a Cheshire cheese differs from the inside. So perhaps I may be able to say somewhat interesting concerning a journey I have recently made 600 miles into the interior, as far as Hankow on the mighty river Yang-tsze-kiang.

Provided with an amount of baggage so small as to be scarcely consistent with respectability, I embark on board the 'Kung-wo,' one of the ex-China Merchants Company's steamers recently handed over to an American firm. A regular type of her class, she is adapted for carrying a large cargo of tea and several hundreds of coolie passengers, and is moreover provided with a little niche where three or four Europeans can be accommodated, with a comfort and

---

[1] Various authorities differ to a most puzzling extent in their computations.

cleanliness on which Englishmen will insist, as we have taught the Chinese, at whatever trouble and cost. We screw along through a river broad as the arm of a sea, and more yellow and thick than the Thames at London Bridge, and yet not half so dirty, the extraordinary colour being due to the clay washed from the banks of the ever-shifting current and held in suspension. The distant country looming through the plain of dreary waters is as flat as though it had been planed and spirit-levelled. There is for the present no interest to be gathered out of that, but there is abundant novelty in the circumstances of the steamer.

What a curious mixture of nationalities we have on board! The captain, a sharp, civil little American, as amusing and worldly-wise as most of his country are, and as quiet in his demeanour as most of his countrymen are not; two or three English ship's-officers; a Manila Spaniard; a couple of 'Geese,' i.e. Macao Portuguese; fifty Chinese crew; about 200 Chinese and three European passengers, viz. a French Jesuit, a Danish tea agent, and an English artillery officer. The Chinese consider that to be jammed into an individual contact of carcasses, and to breathe the same atmosphere several times over, is essential to comfort, and hence the rest of the community was by no means crowded. Diverse as are the above nationalities, they may nearly all be blended into two great divisions: European and Asiatic. The Europeans regard all who are not of their own continent as half intelligent and wholly strange baboons, with a strain of man-nature in them; the Asiatics here consider all who are not Chinese as 'Fung Yang' (foreign devils)—nearly all, not quite.

The original Portuguese settlers in Macao of the sixteenth century, the fellow-countrymen of Vasco de Gama and Camoëns, have so degenerated from their original nationality, have so deteriorated from climate and intermarriage with the aborigines, are so completely changed in physical aspect and mental characteristics, that they can only be regarded as displeasing hybrids, viewed with contempt by Europeans and with mistrust by Chinamen.

Peering down hatchways and wandering aft, where are congregated the natives, three-parts naked, crafty and diabolical, wizened and skinny, with none of the dignity of the human race, the sensation of one's own isolation, of being one amongst a tribe with whom we cannot have the most remote affinity, gradually becomes very strong. Why should not these 250 wretches, whose sole principle is that of gain, without the common tie of civilisation which is the common tie of brotherhood, select one day or night out of the three we are to spend on board with them, far from other human aid, cut the throats of the five or six Europeans, plunder the ship at leisure, and disappear into the wide adjacent country? I really feel grateful to them for their forbearance. They could crush us by mere numbers as easily as they could a few flies, and such deeds have from time to time been perpetrated. Indeed, to enable Europeans to fight at all events with the same chance as rats at bay, it is the almost invariable practice to range rifles and ammunition in handy spots about the cabin. Why is this omitted in the present instance? 'Oh,' says the American captain, with that ignoring of danger which is the surest way of inviting it, 'there is nothing to fear from outrage. There is not a Christian within 100 miles of us.' Nevertheless I am not sorry I brought my revolver with me.

In the middle of one of the following nights, a din of compound noises in an instant roused me to the keenest, startled, attention. Intense darkness was emphasised by incessant flashes of lightning, the thunder cracked rather than rolled, and the rain splashed down with a violence which resembled blows, yet high above the riot rose the shouts and yells of many voices in tones both of anger and entreaty, and the trampling of many feet. Have the hundreds of Chinese passengers risen upon the half-dozen Europeans, and is the 'last scene' being enacted? The swift course of the ship is suddenly stopped, and there is a profound stillness; then an imperative order to go ahead; then hark! the splash of rapidly dipped oars, boats are approaching; louder and closer grow the angry shouts and yells, once more the ship is suddenly arrested, junks are grating against the side, swarms of men are clambering on board

.... pirates perhaps ... my revolver ... not much use ... and ... 'I hope you were not roused last night opposite that village,' says the captain next morning. 'We took on board a wonderful number of passengers who thought we were not going to wait for them. What a row they did make to be sure!' The evils we suffer from most are those which never occur.

Look at those Chinese at meals, or 'Chow-chow' as they call it, on deck, squatting in knots with true Eastern preference for their own hams over chairs, an attitude which draws an invariable but sharp line of demarcation between civilisation and barbarism. Why, their very method of eating would disgrace a well-bred jackal. With a large caldron of rice, and, on a separate dish in the centre, a fearful mess of salad and pickled fish or flesh carrion, each eater plunges his basin into the rice pot, holds it close to his widely stretched open mouth, and, with his two chopsticks in one hand, shovels the contents down his gullet with extraordinary rapidity. During the process he apparently neither masticates nor breathes—his eyes start from his head—he perspires—his cheeks and another department of his interior economy swell almost visibly, but he never ceases from his shovelling and his gulping, save for a second or two when he turns to his pickled garbage for a relish. 'Graceful chopsticks, dexterity, skill, neatness.' Traditional nonsense. The transaction is nasty beyond measure, and its sole palliation is that it is performed only twice a day—at about ten and five—though if in the intervals an odd snack comes in their way it is never regarded as amiss.

Then, although the bulk they consume is considerable, Europeans certainly would not consider an almost exclusively rice diet sufficiently nutritious on which to perform so astonishing an amount of hard work. Yes, literally, 'almost exclusively.' Milk is only consumed under circumstances too filthy for publication, and the small coarse fish like Thames dace or tench, the little lumps of fat pork or reeking semi-putrid viscera of their unhealthy swine, can only be regarded as subsidiary adjuncts to impart flavour to the staple bulk. It is only natural they should consider our consumption of steaks and chops as indicating the propensities of ravenous ogres, and they can only account for our powers of assimilating such large quantities of animal food by the assumption that all Englishmen possess, in their interior economy, two grindstones which, gizzard-like, reduce to a pulp all they swallow.

While sitting quietly in the little cabin, inditing the notes from which this acccunt is taken—the hypothetical value of which is chiefly due to the fact of their being recorded day by day on the spot while impression and memory still retain that vividness which must inevitably be weakened with every twenty-four hours—I notice with surprise a tall Chinese figure seat himself at the table, very humbly, very quietly. Yet I cast about in my mind for an explanation, inasmuch as only under very exceptional circumstances does a Chinaman, however well-to-do, seek to introduce himself into the society of Englishmen. A tall, middle-aged, grave fellow, in Chinese hat, blue robe and shoes, with every detail of native costume, including, of course, the inevitable pigtail. And yet—and yet, what is there about you which puzzles me? Your movements are not like the shambling furtive movements of the Chinese; your expression of countenance is simple and straightforward, instead of shifty and crooked; the few sentences you mutter in pidgin-English possess not the genuine aboriginal clack. Come, my friend, this won't do, you are no more Chinese than I am. So I hazard, 'Monsieur, parle-t-il Français?' 'Ah, oui, Monsieur, bien mieux qu'Anglais,' he answers, brightening at the sudden and unexpected sound of his native language, and in a very short time we are talking with all the confidence of intimate friends.

Père Gannier is a Jesuit priest who has devoted himself to a missionary life in China—not merely come to China for a short time to do a 'spell of mission-arising,' as is the wont with so many of our Protestant workers. Six months ago he had never quitted France in his life; then at forty, suddenly feeling himself called on to a new work, he sailed for Shanghai; where, at the adjacent French Jesuit College of Zik-a-wei, he had spent some months in that most discouraging of all studies, the Chinese language, in picking up a few words of English, and in making himself acquainted with the customs and character of the natives.

'And how long do you expect to remain out?' I ask.

'Toute ma vie, Monsieur,' with rather a melancholy smile.

A Missionary Jesuit once in China seldom revisits his own country; he tries to nationalise himself with his flock, with whom, indeed, he lives and dies.

'I have left for ever all who are near and dear to me.'

'What a sacrifice!' I involuntarily exclaim.

'Yes,' he assented, 'and yet I feel perfectly happy and without a vestige of regret. But I admit this is an unnatural kind of happiness, and can only be attained by divine grace.'

'Is not the adoption of Chinese dress and customs very distasteful to you?'

'Well, yes, it is. But to do so is almost one of the conditions of success. Of course a Chinaman would detect my nationality in an instant, and it is very rare that even after a life-long residence we can disguise our origin. Still, our attempts to assimilate ourselves with our flocks dissipate the otherwise never-failing reminder that we belong to the hated race of foreign devils, and is an evidence of sympathy which they appreciate.'

'Have the efforts of your Order at conversion been successful?'

'Oh, yes, conspicuously so,'[1] is his answer. 'You see that, in addition to Christianising them, we civilise and educate them.'

'Ah, yes; education,' say I, with a train of argument roused in my mind, 'i.e. individual reasoning fostered by reading—reading the Bible.' But here I had heedlessly stumbled on a quagmire.

'Not so, Monsieur,' vehemently. 'This indiscriminate reading of the Bible by semi-educated persons is fraught with grievous danger. Besides the Saint Père——'

I try to evade the discussion; my companion fiercely persists—and here, in the poky cabin of a China ship on the Yang-tsze-kiang river, the French Jesuit and the English artillery officer set to work hammer and tongs for hours, arguing on respective tenets, growing hotter and hotter, probably each considering the reasoning of the other to be specious, and each angry that faith—fanatic faith— once wedded fast to some dear error, hugs it to the last.

'Well,' I say after a while, 'let us agree to differ. We are both Christians, we both believe in the same Almighty and same atonement. Let us agree to hope that we may both reach the same goal, though each one thinks his own route the best, the clearest, and the shortest.'

From his aspect and tone of reply, I question if he agreed to hope anything of the sort.

[1] Query, but more anon.

Night had already fallen when we steamed up to the ant-like city of Chinkiang, my Jesuit acquaintance's terminus. He knew not a soul there, but it was possible that a French 'confrère' might have heard of his intended arrival, and might come to the wharf to meet him, and might put him up. Otherwise it was very problematical in what den of horror he might be compelled to pass the night. As this disciple of Xavier and Ignatius Loyola stood on the deck, solitary, in poverty, friendless, without even what Europeans consider a bare necessary of life, a Chinese 'boy,' I could not but say: 'Whatever our differences of opinion, mon Père, permit me to express my reverence for your noble self-sacrifice. Shake hands;' and then thoughtlessly cheery: 'au revoir!'

'Au revoir!' he said gravely, as he took my hand, and then pointing upwards: 'Je l'espère—là haut.'

Chinkiang is one of the treaty ports, and a depôt for tea. A small knot of English, a few tens merely, with a consul to safeguard their rights, and some Protestant missionaries who might learn many a lesson from their more humble Roman Catholic fellow-Christians, have there settled down in a little group of houses, according to custom completely outside the precincts of Chinese filth. One of the mercantile agents who had resided there for twenty-two years without a break had reluctantly resolved, after many a postponement, to revisit his native country. He was an educated gentleman, unmarried, and though deprived of all that we value in civilised life, he had grown into his isolated and, as we should call it, joyless existence so completely, that he quitted it manifestly with a heavy heart. Thousands of crackers rattling off like a *feu'de joie* was the Chinese God-speed at his departure, and he stepped on board our ship with the solemn gravity of the old Westward Ho! emigrants, rather than with the exhilaration of a twenty-two years' exile about to revisit friends and country.

Here I may remark that on my return journey I set to work in a business-like manner to explore the neighbourhood of Chinkiang, as a type of country in contradistinction to town in inland China. Walking through the suburbs, where I notice groups of Chinese children playing at the time-honoured English rustic game of 'tipcat,' I pass under one of the archways of the never-failing walls which here surround all towns at a considerable distance from the main mass of buildings, and make my way to an eminence, from whence I obtain a good bird's-eye view of the curious surrounding country. The shifting vagaries of the Yang-tszye are here strikingly illustrated. 'Golden Island' is a large, high tumulus, now situated well inland. But in 1842 it was an island round which our fleet sailed in their ascent to attack Nankin. There is the usual childish Chinese fort enclosing a large area, its parapet little stronger than pasteboard, on the top of which flaunt innumerable large gaudy standards. There again in a little hollow nook is the small English cemetery. About sixteen or eighteen graves represent the mortality of the tiny European population during as many years. The simple, reverential decency with which it is kept contrasts vividly with the large hideous grave mounds of the natives, and with their repelling coffins placed on the open ground as at Shanghai.

Now we have trudged about three and a half miles into the country, and staring around we become aware that we are in the midst of the largest necropolis on the face of the earth, the radius being about three miles. We are standing in a vast depression, bounded afar by ranges of hills; the whole plane of site is a series of gently undulating turf-covered knolls, and is not unlike Aldershot in its pre-military era, ere the heather had been ground down, and with Cæsar's camp in the distance.

Within this vast perimeter of nearly nineteen miles, and as far as the eye can reach, are packed, rows upon rows in dismal monotony, the grave mounds, without a sign of care or of decoration even according to the depraved ideas of taste of the country. Looking around, I could scarcely see a square yard not thus occupied, except in cases of a few rare patches of rice or other cultivation in swampy spots.

Now in such a monstrous graveyard, which may have extended, for aught we could tell, on the reverse slopes of the encircling hills, is it not probable that the expression 'millions'—a number of which nineteen people out of twenty have not a conception—of graves may be perfectly accurate? Here indeed the whole population of the district, or rather province, must have buried their dead for decades, or even for centuries, of years.

Glad to quit a landscape, the dreariness of which the most ingenious human imagination could not realise, I retrace my steps along the so-called high road. It is about six feet wide, with a thin breadth of paving stones in the centre, sloping towards the sides, which, in dry weather, are ankle-deep in dust, and in wet weather in sticky mud. From time to time bye-roads, really mere sheep tracks, strike in. Along the main route, where ordinary wheeled locomotion could not for one moment be thought of, small gangs of peasants are toiling in the hot sun under heavy burdens of agricultural produce, suspended on bamboo poles, or are struggling with clumsy barrows dragged up the slopes by strings of rope draught, at a maximum expenditure of labour, with a minimum result. And yet this type of Chinese highways is a main artery of communication between enormously populous cities, and through a thickly inhabited country. This consideration, isolated and trifling as it may seem, throws a ray of light on that question of enormous magnitude, the immediate future of one-fourth of the world's inhabitants.

I venture to hazard the suggestion, which I trust may not be considered childish in its simplicity—may not the solution of the above question be contained in the single expression: 'Highways and byeways'? At this moment the entire gigantic empire is, in our sense of the word, destitute of all means of efficient road communication—each city, each district, however populous and important, is virtually isolated. Fuhtais, Taotais, and Mandarins may misgovern, cheat, and oppress with impunity. Those subject to them may, and do have, a general sense of their iniquities; but they entirely lack that nature of educational training which enables men to distinguish between good and evil, to reason on the cause of wrongs, and to devise means for their remedy.

To go a step further: cut off from intercourse with the various fractions of their fellow-countrymen, from a general knowledge of the Chinese world, from the means of collating or disseminating their opinions, they are ignorant of their own powers of combination to procure redress. They acquiesce in the infamous national misgovernment and robbery, and I believe will continue to acquiesce until there arise a mighty simultaneous convulsion of the whole population, combined to annihilate the old order and to set up a new one. Now, of these facts, China's rulers are perfectly well aware. 'No innovations,' they tacitly argue, 'no inventions, no education beyond that of musty, useless fables, and, above all, no communications. Otherwise the people will learn, will combine, and will overthrow us.' Is not the authenticity of this line of argument established beyond all doubt by the destruction of the short line of railway between Shanghai and Wosung, so hated by the mandarins, so warmly appreciated by the populace. Have not the former, with unswerving determination, nipped in the bud the fairest projects for railway lines, which were so easy of construction, and so productive of future wealth, that even bigoted conservatism cannot account upon righteous grounds for their rejection ?

The skilled English engineer, Mr. Morrison, who some years ago came out for the special purpose of laying down the Shanghai railway and carrying out other apparently dawning projects, assured me that there is scarcely any other country in the world where railways could be constructed with greater ease, speed, and cheapness, and with a certainty of a profitable return, equal to those certainties on which we determine the most important transactions of life. But the destruction of the Wosung line, coupled with the general line of action pursued by the imperial authorities, has, he considers, transferred to the remote future the actual construction of a railway system on a large scale, and he has acted up to this opinion by returning to England.

Within the past year the concession of the Pekin Government for the construction of a line from the capital to Tien-tsin has been heralded with much ostentation. It is quite possible that a few miles may be laid down, it is much more than possible that this show of yielding is a fresh illustration of the Chinese

K

method of evading that which they are determined not to perform. 'Highways and byeways,' angrily remarked an English merchant, who dreaded any change, lest it should entail a diminution in the old-fashioned abundant influx of dollars, ' we don't want them. No country in the world is so well provided with natural waterways, and these are far cheaper than roads or railways. They would do us no good. Do leave us alone.' Almost the mere statement of the argument carries with it its own refutation. For instance, it might be infinitely cheaper to pay a half dollar for conveyance by railway in four hours, than to expend four days, without actual disbursement of cash, in struggling in a boat against the tortuous and rapid current of the Yang-tsze-kiang. Of course, as regards expense of transport, rapidity and facility are foremost considerations, and Holland, the best canalled country in Europe, has found it expedient to intersect her area with an infinity of railways.

Now let us draw the converse picture of the principal districts in the Chinese empire efficiently connected with roads and railways. I see before me a magical change effected with startling rapidity. The fertile country is rendered productive because means have been brought into existence to render its productiveness available;[1] commerce instantly receiving a gigantic impetus; communication so extended

[1] Mr. Fawcett, in his *Manual of Political Economy*, shows clearly the striking distinction between the terms 'fertile' and 'productive.'

and increased as to become habitual; then experience, then diffused knowledge and education, and, *pari passu* with the above, Christianity. Meanwhile the nation has been learning *nolens volens* the difference between right and wrong, between a good government and a rascally one; then comes a knowledge of their own power, then combination, and finally the subversion of the old *régime* and the establishment of a righteous administration, happiness and prosperity; not indeed without the calamities of a terrible intestinal convulsion, without which, alas! the subsequent blessings are unattainable.

'But,' it may be rejoined, 'in indicating highways and byeways, you merely indicate an improved condition without the means of effecting it. You do not point out how existing circumstances are to be so reversed as to remove present obstacles; you do not really bring us nearer to the solution of the problem.' Granted, and herein I can only look to the unforeseen, fortuitous concourse of events, or rather, to write more gravely, to the inscrutable workings whereby Providence is wont to remedy the greatest evils. It may take the form of the action of one or more of the great civilised Powers; or the still further decadence of rulers, so corrupt and effete that the slightest further decadence will overwhelm them; or possibly the spontaneous rising of the millions, wearied at last beyond submission by a rule of infamy and misery.

To resume our return walk from Chinkiang necropolis to the steamer. The dwellings of the peasants are little better than mud caverns above-ground, small covered spaces through which the rains must frequently penetrate, only just high enough to admit of the inmates standing upright, without windows or even window openings, chimneys, or doors. The smoke of the small cooking fire rushes out of the entrance aperture, and through it I can discern an accumulation of horrors—crawling imps and crowding harridans in numbers and condition which, together with other nameless filth, can only be paralleled with a carcass decomposing in the sun.

We continue our course up the never-varying calm river, the yellow opaqueness of which has now so much increased as to convey the impression that we are ploughing our way through masses of thick seething mud. At night I still find my ulster a blessing, in pursuance of that experience which travellers are so slow to learn—that we suffer most from cold in warm climates. But the temperature is much higher than at Shanghai, and there is a pleasant sensation of health in the pure atmosphere after the pest-laden air of the native cities. Then the river bank scenery is losing its previous ugliness, dotted with mountainous intervals it is becoming prettier and prettier, is at last almost beautiful, and to sit watching on deck will repay all but those who stupidly close fast their eyes when on their travels.

There is Nankin, famous in the annals of history

for centuries, captured by Lord Gough in 1842, the scene of many a wholesale massacre in later years, a focus of political intrigue, and of rebel plot and outrage. Once it was the capital of the Chinese empire, now it is of contracted importance, with a greatly diminished population of about 130,000 inhabitants. Yet to Europeans it is almost exclusively known by reason of its white cotton fabrics. Perhaps its size can better be appreciated by the extent of its city walls, which start from the river bank, and which we can make out trending for miles inland, tapering and winding among the hills surrounding the main part of the city, which is situated in a vast hollow about three-quarters of a mile from the Yang-tsze. I can quite believe the prevalent assertion that these walls are twenty miles in perimeter. The city is defended by some large straggling earthworks, armed with artillery which is supposed to command the river, but unskilfully constructed and injudiciously placed, inasmuch as they are themselves completely commanded by the adjacent heights. I estimated the breadth of the river at this point to be about 900 yards. About two miles distant on the opposite side is a lower range, not fortified, but occupied as a military station. The ground at the base of the hills is perfectly flat, and in some places marshy.

For some reasons, inscrutable to all but Chinese cabinets, Nankin is not comprised in the comparatively few treaty ports which the Pekin Government in the last extremity of distress has on various occasions consented to throw open to European trade. By such concession some English merchants have made several hundred thousands of pounds, but the towns themselves several millions, plus an increase of prosperity and civilisation which has enabled them to gallop on 100 years ahead of their closed fellows—advantages not to be gauged only by a pecuniary scale. However the fact cannot be got over. Nankin is to all intents and purposes a closed port, though by the Chefoo convention of 1875 steamers are allowed to touch for the purpose of landing or shipping, but in all cases by means of native boats only. There is no European population, jetty, or custom-house, and we steam past it, ignoring and ignored.

Our next point of interest is the ruined city of Tungliu, childhood's Jericho conceived from grotesque old woodcuts which here seem accurately reproduced. There is the enormous square enclosure with perfectly straight walls, there the low, ugly, half-ruined houses, the narrow streets, and above all the conventional battlements ready to topple over at Joshua's blast. Once it had been a flourishing city, but in 1864 it was occupied by the Taeping rebels, who slaughtered indiscriminately and wholesale every inhabitant on whom they could lay hands, and then left it in the condition in which the Prussians left Bazeilles in 1870—there being, by-the-bye, a strong resemblance between the two races in their method of carrying on war.

The number of human beings massacred during the rebellion defies all computation, but it also exceeds all belief excepting where ocular evidence still furnishes a clue. For example, this city, clearly so considerable from the area it covered, is now gaunt and staring in utter desolation. Then, in the rural scenes of the operations of the Taepings, skulls and thigh bones are still sometimes found lying about the fields like flints; they represent hecatombs of untraced human beings slaughtered in these shambles, otherwise the requirements of ancestral worship would have insured their burial. Finally, whatever the variations in the estimates of the population of the empire, all authorities are unanimous in pronouncing it several millions less after than before the rebellion.

It would be difficult to cite a more striking specimen of river scenery than the 'Little Orphan' island, the Ehrenbreitstein of the Chinese Rhine. Standing right in the centre of the river, the ink-dark waters of which here hasten their speed and swirl round it with cataract-like rapidity, it rises with abrupt, almost perpendicular, rocky sides to a towering peaked height, but in proportion as it ascends so does it become less rugged and austere. The lights grow brighter, the dark vegetation of the crags becomes more brilliantly green, the luxuriant creepers of the tropics twine their tendrils in a beautiful maze, patches of colour are represented by patches of bright flowers, small sparkling cascades emerge from mysterious sources, and leap splashing down into half-hidden basins, until at last the contrast between the base and summit is so great that it would seem as though 'eternal sunshine settles on its head.'

Then as regards animated life, there is the national mixture of nature's beauty and man's grotesqueness. Water-fowl, gulls, and cormorants sweep and shriek round the base. Other graceful birds with bright plumage and still sweeter voices flash about the foliage midway up; an occasional butterfly, so painted that highest art is in comparison a mere daub, flutters from the sun above to the gloom below; and, lastly, we have Horace's beautiful woman's head fitted on to a hideous fish; the apex is crowned with ugliest of ugly, childish-looking pagodas, while dotted about the sides are squalid dwellings, whence emerge inhabitants out of keeping in the highest degree with nature's beauties—with pigtails, turn-up shoes, draggle-tailed gowns, and motionless though diabolical countenances.

It really is time that I should say somewhat about the wild-fowl, which at Wuhu, a noted centre of river sport, far exceeded my New Brunswick and Canada experience. Yet people are wont to receive the records of American numbers not merely with incredulity, but with a thinly veiled imputation that you are an impudent liar. Then how can I hope for credence here? Simply by no attempt to deal with numbers, but to quote acreage, and leave the reader to estimate for himself. Well, as we ploughed our way, several acres on either side were crowded with wild geese, teal, and mallard as thickly as in a feeding pond. But what surprised me most was that, whereas their American congeners take flight at the approach of any craft, merely showing as dark patches against the skyline, these Chinese wild-fowl with national sagacity allowed us to steam up to within a few yards of them, tumbling, quacking, and flapping out of our way, making by successive lengths a lane which sometimes extended over a mile. Sorely was I tempted by that brute instinct which, according to foreign ideas, habitually prompts an Englishman 'to go and kill something,' to see how many I could tumble over by firing from deck into the 'black' of them, and was only restrained by remembering that, as I could not stop the steamer to secure the spoil, such an act would constitute animal murder. But had I been in a small noiseless sampan, instead of a huge roaring steamer, these crafty creatures would almost unanimously have flapped an adieu just when I was still a yard or two out of shot, merely leaving a certain number of boy and girl loiterers to be picked up singly.

And here a few words about sport in China generally. It is pre-eminently not the country for big game; certainly there is throughout a sprinkling, thin, but never entirely failing, of tigers, which in proportion to their numbers commit great devastation; there are some leopards, panthers, and a fair amount of small deer and wild pig. But nothing can surpass the excellence of the small game shooting, and this I assert without a shadow of doubt. Of duck and geese I have already spoken; add thereto snipe as often as you choose to fire off your gun, quail so plentiful that you soon cease to take any notice of them, partridges in great abundance, pheasants, and, above all, swans—not isolated shy specimens, but a plurality of those big fellows to be picked up in an ordinary day's shooting, say five swans for two guns. Remember, too, that all this is genuine wild shooting. You make your way up, or drift down, the innumerable large rivers or small streams in that floating shooting-box, a 'house-boat,' land when and where you please, and having tried ground which suits your fancy without the poaching dread of being warned off as trespassers—for the natives view with perfect indifference your trampling even through high standing crops, you can re-embark and do likewise elsewhere. No jealous guardianship of shooting rights.

Probably there is about one sporting Englishman to every hundred square miles, and as for the natives, it certainly is sport, though in another sense, to see them on a shooting excursion. Weapon, a long iron tube without a stock; powder, a handful of what looks like dried black mud; projectiles, a heap of small irregularly shaped iron pellets—lead is beyond their means; firing arrangement, a piece of slow match fastened to the thick end of the iron tube, which is discharged from the thigh. Really they deserve astonishing credit in that sometimes and somehow they do manage to knock over some supremely careless winged creatures crowded together for feeding. Their usual method of destruction is, however, by snaring.

There is no legal close season, but nature has established conditions which limit the shooting period from the beginning of October until the beginning of March. Outside these dates feathered game disappears in the furtherance of their domestic avocations, or if a *père de famille* in the shape of a wild duck or pheasant be criminally slain, his flesh is so exceedingly black and nasty, that after one mouthful you put down your knife and fork and beg his pardon. One freak, however, specially distinguishes the snipe. In early March he grows very lean and disappears; in the middle of April he reappears, crying with unusual shrillness, well plumaged, as fat as a prize bird, and plus two handsome extra tail feathers, viz. seven instead of five. Some that I shot at Shanghai and Foochow were little inferior in size to woodcock. Three weeks later he makes his final adieu. It has, however, been conjectured that these 'spring snipe' represent hatchings from the north of Japan making their way southwards.

No, I unhesitatingly say; do not come 10,000 or 11,000 miles to China to shoot, unless indeed you are one of those who consider that shooting, the tamer the better, constitutes one of the most noble occupations of life, and that a poor shot is a poor-spirited, weak-minded individual, not fit to live. But if you, as a keen sportsman, happen to be in China, remember that you have during the season a certainty of first rate, unlimited small game shooting, first and foremost on the Yang-tsze-kiang river, especially at Wuhu, and then in descending gradations of excellence in the neighbourhoods of Shanghai, Hankow, Foochow, Amoy, and Swatow. As for a little information respecting that inevitable accompaniment the house-boat, you must search for it in a future chapter, or I shall be very happy to reply to any written inquiries, for the general reader would, I fear, become weary of any further shooting talk.

On the Yang-tsze I have an opportunity of verifying the statements concerning the immensity of the Chinese river population. All day and every day we pass through gatherings of small, crazy floating dwellings rather than ordinary boats, each of which represents a family. The occupants always appeared particularly busy, but about what I never could fathom, unless they were endeavouring to secure some of those coarse, small, fresh-water fish which, when cooked, resemble nothing so much as a tallow candle stuck full of pins, but one of which would be held to impart a delicious relish to a whole bucketful of rice.

As for the fields on the margin of the river, they are sprouting riches to the utmost closeness which the area admits—grain of every sort, beans, roots, clover, and grasses. Surely the most ingenious farmer could not grumble here; at a later period large districts will be turned into paddy (rice) fields, and thus the agriculturist manages to get two and even three substantial main crops out of his ground in the year—not merely those impositions in the shape of hastily got in patches of vetches or mustard, whereby the English farmer seeks to cheat himself into the belief that he has made his field do a double tour of duty. As at Shanghai, the cultivation is almost entirely spade. Horses and stock are almost unknown, and hence the enormous value of every conceivable species of manure.

Now we approach another treaty port, Kiukiang, where we take in a further load of Chinese passengers, and stop a few hours for breathing time and exploration. Every leaf of green tea which is imported to England passes through this city, and for a short time, therefore, during the summer the shipping business is here very active and extensive. The requirements of European commerce are met by two large hulks purchased from the P. and O., and formerly among the largest and best of their class. Roofed over on the upper deck, cleared of all masts, gear, and sea-going machinery, they constitute first-rate wharfage buildings, and for many years will float, splendid examples of the strength of our ships of commerce.

Even at remote Kiukiang, where the permanent English residents might almost be counted on one's fingers, they have intuitively set up a lilliputian European administration, with a municipal council of three, which rules the settlement with the regularity of a European principality, and by means of ten Chinese police causes its behests to be obeyed by the swarming natives. And my eyes are gladdened by the small English Bund, in close proximity to horrible surroundings, with its beautiful greensward, its narrow strip of neatly kept marine parade, lined with six or seven handsome European storehouses, and shrouded in a beauty of foliage which only these latitudes can produce.

Of course a European here arrests attention as instantaneously as would a bustard promenading Hyde Park; and, placing myself under the chaperonage of a local agent in the service of those merchant-princes, Jardine and Matheson, I proceed to explore the native town. As usual, it is a type of all that is shocking, filthy, and wonderful, and is utterly unlike anything seen out of China. Then, instead of mere abuse, why do I not tell you something of its details? Because, first of all, I wish that my opinion on these and similar features should be matured by more abundant experience, and because, also, I am keeping the subject in reserve, until we have reached those more complete types—Hankow and Foochow.

Kiukiang, in addition to its monopoly of green tea commerce, is the chief representative of Chinese porcelain manufacture. It seems to be Sèvres, Dresden, and Valloris rolled into one, and then multiplied fourfold. Shops of china, streets of china, acres of china. I turn into one establishment after another; there is no necessity to buy. The European may rummage about for as long as he pleases, the shop people being apparently fully repaid by their curiosity in watching a foreign devil. Each shop is crammed to overflowing with porcelain ware, some of it pretty enough to delight non-connoisseurs, and a great deal of an intensely grotesque ugliness, which raises its value to a proportionate price, and would render a true expert lackadaisical in his depraved admiration. If one could but take some to England! only it would be inconvenient to pack up a pair of six foot, valuable, fragile vases in a field kit bag. I finish my expedition at my cicerone's handsome residence, comfortable with every practicable imported comfort, and where, together with a single comrade of the shipping trade, he will spend—might he not say 'obliterate'—four or five years of his life, with little work, except for a month during the tea season, and fairly happy and contented.

The impression conveyed to me of such an existence of inactive exile was melancholy beyond description. 'Good-bye'—acquaintances of three hours' date here part with as much warmth as those of three years' elsewhere—'Pray come and stay with me whenever, and for as long as, you can;' and I am persuaded the invitation was sincere. He would gladly receive as a guest even a first-class beast.

And now I am becoming conscious that all this time I have been somewhat cavalierly ignoring the most important feature of my journey, the mighty Yang-tsze-kiang itself, concerning which some description may be the less tedious, inasmuch as prior to 1860 scarcely any, if any, Europeans, except the Abbé Huc, had travelled higher up than Nankin, 200 miles from the mouth. Of late years, it is true, a certain number of tea agents have been beforehand with me on the track I am now pursuing; yet the country is to the general public a *terra incognita*. We are approaching Hankow, 600 miles inland from Shanghai, the very heart of China proper, the most remote settlement in the empire, and, with the exception of Ichang, the furthest spot where a European resident is to be found.

What the Amazons are to South America, what Niagara is to Upper Canada, what the Thames is to London, such is the Yang-tsze-kiang—the River of Golden Sand—to China. It runs through a length of over 1,500 miles, it affects the commerce and prosperity of the nation more than all other physical objects put together, and is regarded by them with a veneration exceeding that which they pay to their most cherished divinities. In fine, it is the richest river in the world—richest in navigable waters, in cities, population, tributaries, and in wide margins of inexhaustible fertility.[1] I have already noticed how far out at sea the ocean waters have been thrust out of their bed by the discharging deluge of the Yang-tsze, proclaiming its presence by the masses of thick alluvial soil held in suspension, the particles washed down thousands of miles, some from the Himalayas and Central Asia, where the river takes its source. Then as we ascend one hundred miles after another, how wayward it is in its currents and wanderings! Not stormingly aggressive, but with quiet caprice upsetting, womanlike, all the calculations of experience, and entirely altering the face of its domain. Highest in June, it is lowest in December, and when its waters rise, what freaks they play! Here the margins of the richest fields are crumbling away into the river before our very eyes; in a few months the monster will have shifted her bed several yards laterally; while the plundered soil will have been capriciously heaped up elsewhere, causing a new island to emerge from the waters. At one spot the current, or rather torrent, runs at the rate of six miles an hour; at another, this is reduced to two without any assignable reason. Well may its navi-

[1] See also Mr. Wingrave Cooke's *China*.

gation be considered the acquirement of a lifetime, requiring renovation every year.

We are steaming straight as a line through the midst of an expanse some miles broad. Suddenly we turn off at right angles and almost scrape the bank. 'Why?' I ask in bewilderment. 'Oh, within the last eighteen months the river has been shifting its bed at this spot, and over all yonder square miles of water there is scarcely depth enough to float a sampan.' In certain stretches, indeed, for hours together, the leadsman scarcely quits his post, and carries on day and night the splashing of his lead and his monotonous sing-song chaunt, sufficiently dismal to evoke a legion of blue devils.

Here we are at Hankow—do not confuse it with Hangchow—about one hundred miles south of Shanghai. At a single glance I can picture to myself how enormous must be the population and the commerce of this city, the subject of legendary fame and of that modern curiosity which appertains to the little known. Hankow, together with Hanyan and Wuchan, each situated on the opposite banks of the bifurcating river, extend far into the hazy plains in the distance, and virtually comprise one in the same sense as New York, Brooklyn, and New Jersey make up a single city. Its sharply defined yellow Styx, unbroken by bridges, here crawls with sewer-like sluggishness between the three sections, and over each section extends an acreage of low, level, uniform, thickly crowded roofs, pagodaless, towerless, spireless, and therefore monotonously dreary.

Estimates of population in China are notoriously most difficult of formation, and are habitually inaccurate. At Hankow, one computation fixes the population of the joint city at three millions, which I do not believe; another, with a fair basis for accuracy, at two millions; while a third pronounces it not to exceed 250,000, which is a preposterously low figure, furnished by a preposterously contradictory sub-official, whose chief delight is to differ.

What Hong Kong is to England as regards the pale of civilisation, what Shanghai again is to Hong Kong, that Hankow is to Shanghai. Really on first arrival one may be justified in feeling like Gulliver amongst the Laputians; and oh, how one's heart rises with pleasure at the sight—in juxtaposition with that obscene monster the native city—of our pretty little English concession with the charm of its soft turf, its neat gravel road, its park-like avenue, and its splendid houses! They are about fourteen in number, facing the river, each with its handsome columns, porticos, and verandahs, each semi-embosomed in the shade of its own beautiful trees planted in the adjacent compound, and each sufficiently comfortable with furniture which has been imported from England 11,000 miles distant. Our tiny tract of territory, 800 yards long and 400 yards broad, having been let to us by the Chinese on a lease of 99 years, constitutes a concession with much greater independence than appertains to a settlement, such as Shanghai.

The most prominent physical features in addition to the palatial hongs, which are half residences and half merchant's buildings, are the English and Russian churches, the Italian convent, the Marine Parade or Bund, with three or four wharves, and some ex-P. and O. hulks moored alongside them for the transaction of the tea trade business, two Russian brick-tea factories, a European club, and finally, on the outskirts, the inevitable large, well-kept racecourse. The English population amounts to about fifty, including five or six ladies, and the affairs of the community are managed by a municipal council of five, somewhat after the fashion of Shanghai and Kiukiang. The revenue, of the annual value of about 3,000$l.$, is chiefly raised by a property tax on European residents, and normal public order is maintained by twenty native constables under an English superintendent.

But this resolute little assemblage of Europeans have concerted further measures against the contingency of a popular rising and the rush of a flood of city scoundreldom, for they are by no means prepared to abandon without a struggle their own property and that of their employers, and to take refuge on board tea ships in the river; though with wise foresight they have provided for the instant removal of women and children to the above place of security. A large supply of rifles and ammunition has been stored in one of the central hongs, ready for issue at a moment's notice. Certain residents have been told off to defend special roads, at the corners of which movable chevaux-de-frise are always kept handy as a check to a Chinese mob, which, however, takes good care never to advance a yard under fire; and, finally, a central keep has been designated as the final retreat of the defenders if hard pressed. It is calculated that resistance may thus be prolonged over twenty-four hours, within which period it is hoped some contingency of external aid may occur to their relief.

In the entire demeanour of our Hankow countrymen there is a fine spirit of pride and independence—observable, indeed, throughout China in precise proportion as we are cut off from external aid—which makes us proud of our nation, and not prone to resent at all events the intended sarcasm of the Brahmin, 'You English can do nothing but spin cotton and conquer the world.'

It would have been my own fault had I not in a very short time been on terms of cordial fellowship with nine-tenths of the handful of Englishmen here collected in self-imposed exile. Perhaps their friendliness was involuntarily aroused by the unusual incident of a stray English traveller. Perhaps the words 'Royal Artillery' after my name may have acted as an additional passport. At all events, keen as I was in my Rosa-Dartle-like thirst for information, they were equally keen in even forestalling my wishes.

Their hospitality was unbounded, and I soon discovered that the whole gist of their 'shop' table talk was tea; and no human artifice has yet succeeded in the total suppression of 'shop,' whether among politicians, soldiers, sailors, lawyers, doctors, racing men, or clergymen. *Testa semel imbuta diu servabit odorem.* I quickly catch the epidemic and become persuaded that the one object of surpassing moment in life is tea. What a chance to learn all about it, for Hankow is the largest tea market in the world! Thither, during the season, converge from radii of many miles tons on tons of the newly plucked plant. Thither comes puffing up the yellow waters of the Yang-tsze many a monstrous steamer, with a mixed native crew and one or two charsees (tea-tasters) eager to speed homewards the moment the freight is on board, for in the English market the first arrivals of tea invariably command fractionally higher prices. Foremost among the consignees are Twining and Coope. Then the whole population, European and Chinese, are in the highest ferment of activity, and a day of twenty-four hours is not long enough for their needs. Charsees, compradors (native agents), schroffs (Chinese in the cashier's offices), agents, clerks, and coolies are at work from five A.M. until far into the hours of darkness; they are a proof of the toil of which human beings are capable under sufficient inducement; they concentrate labour which most men spread over a year into a few weeks. For happily for them the tea trade here lasts little more than three weeks. It begins about May 10, is in bulk concluded by June 5, and is completely wound up a fortnight later.

Some kindly, communicative, typical charsees put me through the whole business of tea tasting and tea judging, and in turn thus communicate to me the following facts:—

'Most of the education of a tea-taster, which is a speciality of itself, is carried out in London, though the finishing touch is given in China. Prior to coming out I spent five or six years in the house of one of the great tea merchants in London, Messrs. ———, beginning quite at the bottom of the ladder, learning my business and acquiring the power of discrimination between the shades of tastes of different samples—the faculty can hardly be acquired in a shorter time. Then of late years I have resided here as local agent for one of the China merchants, my sole duty during the tea season being to test and to taste the thousands of samples which then come pouring in. Sometimes I have to taste as many as 150 in a single morning, and at the end of the month's duration my digestive and nervous functions become completely upset by the extra strain on them. On my own responsibility I purchase on behalf of my employers enormous consignments, which are shipped off as fast as possible to Shanghai, and from thence to London.'

Now we enter the charsee's office, spacious and

cool like all apartments for Europeans in China, but differing from them in having a special arrangement of outside shutters whereby an exact degree of light, neither too bright nor too dim, is thrown on the tables.

On them are ranged rows of small white cups and saucers—a coloured pattern would not answer the purpose—little tins of 'musters' or samples of tea, small scales and weights, and on the ground enormous classically shaped, handsome vases, the use of which we shall discover in a few moments. Now we must concentrate our whole attention on the process. Any dawdling would be fatal, and the tests of sight, smell, touch, and taste must be almost instantaneous. It is a cardinal principle that a charsee, to be successful, can allow himself no second judging, but must make up his mind at one stroke on the spot. His first thoughts, like a woman's, will chiefly be valuable.

To proceed to actual business: a preliminary examination is held on the general aspect of each of the samples, which resembles nothing so much as a farmer's scrutiny of a little bag of specimen corn, or a troop officer passing the forage. A small quantity is poured into the hand. Its appearance should be 'neat' and 'level,' with small, even, tightly rolled leaves, free from dust, small pieces of stick, and sweepings, while here and there should be visible little light tips called pekoe points, pieces of tea blossom, which indicate that the plant has been stripped while the leaves were still in a tender state.

Then ensues a great deal of sniffing, for a fragrant leaf will of course produce a fragrant infusion, whereas a sour smell indicates undue fermentation in the early stages of preparation, which will render the product comparatively valueless.

But the one test worth all the others put together is naturally the infusion, and here the charsee seems absolutely absorbed in applying all his senses to this operation. From each muster a small quantity—not more than good-sized pinches—are weighed out with chemical exactitude and placed in respective cups, which are filled up with water just boiling but not overboiled. The cups are covered with the saucers, a five minutes' sand-glass is set running, and the infusion is left to draw. Precisely as the last grain runs out, the charsee begins his tasting, and an exceedingly nasty process it proves. He draws the liquid—of course milkless and sugarless—through his teeth like a horse drinking; he rolls it about his mouth, gurgles, squelches, and finally cascades it out of his mouth into one of those beautiful vases I have already mentioned, and which I should designate by the homely title of spittoon, though it is sought to extenuate the nastiness of their purpose by the classical expression of 'cuspidores.' Then comes the first verdict, or weeding out rejected samples. A tyro can of course easily decide between an exceedingly good and an exceedingly bad sample, but on coming to gradations involving differences of prices amounting perhaps to hundreds of pounds, he will be completely baffled, and the necessity for a six years' education of palate becomes abundantly manifest. If you are penetrated with the conceit of ignorance, you will perhaps hazard an expression of approval of one sample which possibly corresponds to English three-shilling-tea, and will slight another which is possibly four-shilling-tea. The charsee becomes quite vexed with what he suspects must be your obstinacy or stupidity. 'Try again,' and once more you gargle and spit, and if you be honest you will resolutely declare that for your part you cannot detect a pin's difference between the two—but it is more probable that to dispose of the tiresome reproaches you will truckle and fib.

Next we examine the grouts. The colour of the infusion itself is not of any consequence whatever provided it be not suspiciously dark, but that of the soaked unrolled leaves should be light, their smell still fragrant, and each leaf small and unbroken. If large and fragmentary, it may be assumed as a certainty that the sample is of a rough, coarse nature.

Among the specimens shown me were some so fine and valuable that they could not be purchased in England by reason of their prohibitive price, ranging as high as eighteen shillings a pound, and moreover the wealthiest Chinese take jealous care to retain it for home consumption. These sorts are, however, mixed in small quantities of the finest qualities, and the compound is retained at preposterous prices. I was given as a favour about an ounce of twelve-shilling-tea. In appearance totally unlike the usual production, it strongly resembled dried cowslip blossoms, and though delicious in smell and delicate in taste, I must own it likewise reminded me of childhood's cowslip tea. But I should never have dreamed so high a price could be assigned to it. I should add that the tender green leaf of tea can be tasted only in China. It must be dried up ere it is fit for English export.

Without writing a general disquisition on tea, I may venture to add a few additional facts concerning this little-known subject. The various processes are: 'plucking,' as the trade terms stripping the trees; 'withering' the leaves in the sun; rolling them; drying; rolling again; packing, which when required for exportation is performed by the English merchants.

I observed in one of the hongs bars of solid lead piled in large heaps, ready for conversion into tinfoil, the quantity of which used is amazing. There is but one description of tea plant in cultivation, and the various designations are due to varieties in the qualities or to the districts whence they are obtained, or to the method of preparation. For instance, 'Flowery Pekoe' is composed almost entirely of the blossom, and like all other tea has only a faint natural scent. 'Orange Pekoe' has been artificially scented with orange flowers. Congo is not necessarily an inferior tea, but is habitually manufactured out of leaves in an advanced stage of growth, and is therefore large, coarse, and rank. Souchong comes from a particular district. It is curious that there should be some doubt respecting green tea, but according to the majority of authorities it is not stripped from a distinct plant, but derives its peculiarities from a special process of preparation.

Have you ever heard of brick-tea? Not those semi-divided cakes of ordinary pressed tea sometimes sold in England, but the large cakes as hard as stones, consumed exclusively in Siberia and the north of China, and sometimes passing current as money, so well illustrating Professor Fawcett's definition of money as a measure of value and medium of exchange. Hankow is the head-quarters of its manufacture, which is there carried on by two large Russian houses, under the supervision of a couple of Russian agents and a handful of Russian employés—for every other European nation ignores with contempt that article of commerce.

On entering the out-buildings one is struck with the never failing and powerful steaming tea-pot smell, as distinguished from the fragrancy of the simple leaf, as though a thousand English village crones were holding a debauch of 1s. 10d. tea. Then into the manufacturing sheds, where there is a hum of the busiest activity—when indeed are Chinese labourers otherwise than desperately busy?—but there is an entire absence of English order, cleanliness, and method. Crowds of half-naked coolies are shambling about with heavy burdens, getting in each other's way, and claiming 'by leave' in constant discordant cries; and the noise, darkness, dust, steam, and confusion are such that for some time I am quite unable to evolve a clear idea of the system of operations. To take them seriatim: here are rows of barrels containing the raw material—the dust tea as it has been brought in from the country districts. It is partly the result of self-formed powder, partly that of grinding the small broken leaves.

There is no necessary reason why the material should be inferior tea, but as a matter of fact and custom its average goodness is not high. It has been passed through sieves so fine that it is of the minute dustiness of flour. Accurately weighed portions, each of about two pounds, are shovelled into small canvas bags, which are tossed into large perforated metal cylinders, where they remain until impregnated with steam, and without being muddy are of sufficient consistency for manipulation and pressing. From time to time a Chinaman half bends over his naked body into the cylinder and drags forth a dripping bundle of bags, with which he hurries off to the press machine, the whole apparatus and working of which makes up a picture of grotesque absurdity unexampled out of China. The canvas bag is placed in a box without a lid, which in turn is shoved under a press in order to squeeze out the moisture and to jam the tea dough into the properly shaped flat brick.

The pressure is applied, in a most singular sort of nut-cracker fashion, by means of a long bamboo pole, fixed horizontally high up and working on a hinge. A Chinaman, considerably more naked than his fellows, and therefore wearing no clothes worth mention, runs swiftly along a plank fixed close to the bamboo nut-cracker, and with the impetus thus gained springs down a considerable height, accompanying his movement with a piercing yell; but he breaks his fall by catching adroitly at the end of the bamboo, which he thus drags down with him, and by the jerk subjects the tea box under the hinge to a hearty squeeze. Then four or five coolies rush forward, seize the still quivering elastic bamboo, and jerking it down several times the squeezing process is completed. The lever is then released, the box withdrawn, a fresh one substituted, and the whole process repeated. Sometimes pressure is effected by more scientific steam machinery, but the operation I have described is the usual one.

The press-cake, turned out of its mould, proves to be a perfectly flat cube, more like a tile than a brick, about nine inches long, six inches wide, and one inch deep, nearly black, as hard as a brick and with a pleasant tea odour about it. After a slight amount of drying, dusting, glazing and trimming, it is wrapped, packed, and then sent off to Mongolia and Russian Siberia, where alone it is consumed—and consumed in vast quantities—little lumps being sometimes mixed with soup, and sometimes used as ordinary tea. In taste it is not unpleasant, and there is nothing repulsive in the composition, for the statements by various travellers that it is consolidated with bullock's blood and other abominations are, as I have proved by personal experience, pure fiction. The only uncleanly feature is the slovenly manner in which the tea dust is strewed, kicked, and trampled over every square foot of flooring, whence from time to time it is swept up, and with imperfectly pressed bricks worked up into new material. Supervision to prevent pilfering is carried to the highest pitch, but is greatly simplified by the scantiness of clothing of the coolies. For a naked man to smuggle away even a quarter of a brick of tea would be beyond the ingenuity of even the Chinese themselves.

It is evident that the large commercial dealings to which I have referred must involve equally large money transactions; but among the Europeans they are always carried out, both for large and small amounts, by paper bonds, to the almost total exclusion of bank notes and metal currency. I scarcely saw a Mexican dollar or a dollar note during my entire stay. Whist points and 'club drinks' were equally met by 'chits,' I. O. U.'s scrawled on scraps of paper which, clearing-house fashion, are adjusted at the end of the month—a fruitful source of recklessness and extravagance.

But even the better class of Chinese merchants look askance at paper bonds, and to meet their requirements a large amount of 'sycee' silver—silver cast in the shape of shoes—has to be provided, and kept in great heaps in the hongs available for immediate use. Every shoe—rough, glittering white lumps—has to be separately weighed and valued, the majority being worth about $100, and weighing about 7 lbs. They may be divided, subdivided, and even chopped into pieces of the approximate value of one tael, equal to 5s. 2d., but the mere process of subdivision diminishes the value. With the lower orders the medium of payment becomes a great nuisance. They are suspicious of silver—the peasants are even frequently ignorant of its value as a precious metal, and the only coin they favour is the copper 'cash'—clumsily stamped pieces of metal, with a square hole punched out of the centre to admit of string. Each cash is the size of a shilling and about 1,100 of them are equal to a dollar. Imagine the weight of carrying about such a mass of copper required to make up even a few dollars. My expedient was to load my Chinese boy with several strings of 1,000 cash each, which he disbursed according to my directions.

While I was at Hankow, a Chinaman applied to me to purchase for a couple of dollars two live golden pheasants, which he had trapped wild, and which were in such perfect plumage that their crest-feathers alone would have been a mine of wealth to a salmon-fisher.

At the time I saw a specimen of that comparatively rare and recently discovered bird the 'Reeves' pheasant, the habitat of which is in this province. One of its tail-feathers measured five feet one inch, and its size and plumage were of corresponding magnificence. Prompted by the sight of these game birds, I tramped, under the guidance of an experienced sportsman, over miles of the adjacent country in quest of spring snipe, the arrival of which was daily—about April 5—expected. In fields where a week hence they would be as plentiful as sparrows in a rick-yard, not a feather was to be seen, save several specimens of that singular and beautiful bird the hoopoe; but my failure enabled me to verify a singular fact in natural history. The arrival of these snipe *en masse* is preceded by no *avant-couriers*; they suddenly pour in, and with equal magical suddenness they depart. For instance, search at 2 P.M. may be fruitless, and at 4 P.M. the same day may be attended with brilliant results. But if I failed to find game I stumbled across innumerable objects of interest, for the Saul-like experience of going forth to seek an ass and finding a crown is for ever recurring even to a stupid traveller, if he will but train himself to watch and note. What a wealth of wheat! I should almost say six quarters to an acre. What a still more astonishing wealth of garden stuff! Not a weed is to be seen; the entire surface is emerald green with vegetation; every square foot is carefully, laboriously cultivated, irri-

M

gated, and fertilised. Oh, entrancing picture of abundance! But as you value your peace of mind do not touch a leaf, a root, a tuber. It is remarkable that notwithstanding the general deficiency of timber the Chinese peasantry carefully clear the land of all bush and forest, not indeed to facilitate stock breeding, but with a view to drive out of the country all wild beasts.

The soil is saturated with a Gehenna of manure which I dare not particularise; the air, in lieu of being the pure atmosphere of the open country, is charged for miles around with pestiferous emanations which can almost be tasted. Parsimonious ingenuity is exercised to the utmost in turning to account and in accumulating as fertilising agents that which is being now carried about in open buckets, and the consequence is that Europeans will touch no vegetables but those which have been grown under their own supervision. It may, however, be borne in mind as to some extent a set-off that, although there is a total absence of stock and therefore of farmyard manure, a part of the above fertility is due to the widely extending annual overflow of the river Yang-tsze, which on retiring leaves a deposit varying from four to six inches of the richest mud. My companion being a doctor, we pass by a natural transition and successive gradations from the subject of our outraged olfactory nerves to that of Chinese sanitary considerations, medical science and medical missions; but these questions are too comprehensive to be tacked on to the end of a chapter.

CHAPTER IV.

MEDICAL MISSIONS AND THE MISSIONARY QUESTION.

To speak of Chinese medical science would be a parallel to the traditional chapter headed 'The snakes, frogs, and other reptiles in Ireland,' with its descriptive amplification 'There are no snakes, frogs, or other reptiles in Ireland.' There is no medical science among the Chinese. No ignorance could be more profound than the ignorance of their so-called doctors of the first elements of physiology. They have not a notion of the position and function of the chief organs of the body and of the arteries. Their religion, as they are pleased to call their grovelling superstition, imperatively forbids the dissection of human bodies, and even those of animals; and to submit to a surgical operation under the knife of a Chinaman would be almost tantamount to submitting to decapitation. Their doctors, impudent, ignorant quacks, habitually spend about ten minutes on each visit in feeling the left wrist pulse, and then an equal period in testing the right wrist, declaring that there are notable differences between the two, and that, moreover, there are about twenty-four varying pulses in the human body. Among their further ludicrous ideas is a belief that the human eye contains a tiny being—of course this is due to reflection. They also consider that the heart is the seat of the intellect and of the emotions.

Then as to their pharmacopœia, it may be likened to the witches' caldron in 'Macbeth.' I was once shown a very large, rare, and costly collection of their medicinal remedies. It resembled a geological museum, and consisted chiefly of curious coloured stones, various crystals, shells, and pieces of rock, all of which are ground up and administered in small doses. The Chinese also put great faith in ground tiger-bones, macerated puppies, and dried and powdered parts of other animals. In addition were several specimens of roots and herbal medicines, and here 'lateat scintillula forsan.'

My wise and learned informant, Dr. Begg—son of the eminent Scotch Nonconformist divine—had been sufficiently liberal-minded to investigate in a fair spirit of inquiry these vegetable therapeutics, and had come to the conclusion that, though they are mixed with a vast amount of rubbish, and are administered in a preposterously bulky form, they possess valuable curative properties from which civilised practice might learn much. In one department the Chinese doctors are most carefully reticent, though my informant has succeeded in discovering clues which may lead to a more perfect knowledge. I can only allude to it as prophylactics for diminishing the numbers of births. I may remark that the confinements are marvellously easy, that the midwives are singularly skilful, and that newly born males average six pounds.

The prevalence of small-pox is evidenced by the excessive percentage of seamed faces. Of course every consideration of superstition, ignorance, and obstinacy combine to oppose vaccination, but even the Chinese have been more susceptible than the English anti-vaccination society to the convictions of sense and tests, as plain as the postulate that two and two make four. They are now yielding to the preventive system, but, true to their practice of befouling everything they touch, they insist on vaccination being performed up the nostrils.

Cholera and fever are fearfully rife—of course they are. Otherwise it is healthy in tropical climates to live in districts more putrid than sewers, and to breathe an atmosphere so laden with stench as to suggest the possibility of cutting it with a knife. During the hot months the inhabitants of the cities die like flies, while the Europeans in the adjacent settlements continue fairly healthy. In some cases—at Shanghai for example—attempts have been made to cover up one or two open drains, but the consequent outburst of typhoid illustrated the principle that a stifled stench is dangerous, and, paradoxically, that no smells are so dangerous as those which you do not smell.

My doctor-friend dwelt on the incomparable field of practical experience open to the English practitioner in China, especially in surgical cases, which in London would be reserved solely for such eminent surgeons as Sir James Paget, and related to me some characteristic incidents. He once undertook to remove a deep-seated tumour from the favourite wife of a powerful Taotai (governor of a district). Scene: the operating room; crowd of onlookers, wondering at the temerity of the Taotai, prompted by despair in thus trusting a foreign devil; chloroform, and rapid insensibility; exclamations of bystanders, and vehement assertions that the patient is stone dead; rapid manipulation of the knife and instantaneous excision of the tumour. General horror, inasmuch as no Chinese doctor dares even scratch skin deep with a knife; astonishment at the bodily removal of the cause of evidently impending death; awe-stricken expectation as they see that the patient, alleged to be dead, really still breathes; but she is slow in coming round, and the doctor feels his own head sitting somewhat loosely on his shoulders. At last resuscitation, and the patient proclaims—wonder of wonders—that she did not feel so much as a pin prick! Tableau: general outburst of jubilate, and, on the part of the Taotai, transports of delight, accompanied with a handsome cumsha (present) as the doctor's fee.

On another occasion he aroused intense admiration and marvel by the simple operation required to rectify a harelip. Indeed, if it be possible to suppose a Chinaman susceptible under any circumstances of ordinary gratitude, or capable of publicly recognising any point wherein Europeans are superior to themselves, these concessions would apply to English medical practice. In serious cases they will not trust their own doctors one inch, while with a dog-like confidence they will commit themselves unreservedly to an English surgeon. Even in minor current maladies they flock in anxious crowds to the European medical missions. Medical missions—this expression opens up a field for investigation under favourable opportunities of a question which is wrangled over with a malignant acerbity, so frequently the curse of the most beneficent religious enterprises. Hankow is not only one of the centres of the rival missions of rival creeds, but is a focus of that blind hostility to all missionary work on the ground that the undertaking effects no positive good, and is indirectly productive of much harm.

Dr. Begg himself endeavoured to befriend in turn the Protestant and Dissenting institutions, but finally attached himself to the Italian Roman Catholic mission. 'Will I pay a visit to the establishment and, *propriâ manu*, dig out every feature connected with its management?' Yes, please; for if I can first satisfy myself as to results of medical missions, I can subsequently more easily trace the causes of rottenness. The surgery has a friendly look with its familiar rows of reservoirs of black draught, blue pill, and castor oil, accompanied with the medicine smell with which the past generation of childhood was so well acquainted. My doctor-friend eagerly informs me that my arrival is a fortunate coincidence. He is just about to cut out a diseased eye. One glance at the poor Chinese girl stretched on the operating table, another at the array of knives, and I flee like a dog with a tin kettle tied to its tail, and in a cold perspiration, preferring to reverence my friend's undoubted skill upon trust. My Chinese 'boy,' less squeamish and more curious, remains a delighted spectator, and when after all is over the eye is produced in a tea-cup, remarks to me in tones of profound admiration, 'Major, that take-out-eye-pidgin, and that medicine house, number one good pidgin. No hab likee that in China.'

But if I am really bent on forming an independent opinion derived from personal observation, I must brace myself up to witness the painful and the revolting. So I valiantly walk round the wards and visit the patients one by one. Inasmuch as the city population has been variously computed at from 250,000 to two millions, it is evident that only a mere tithe of the applicants can be admitted, and that a careful selection must be made of the cases which are not only the most piteous, but which will best repay treatment.

Surgical cases form the bulk, and tumours, cancerous growths, necrosis, fractures, and local injuries are largely represented. As the doctor approaches each bedside, the occupant gives tongue in good truth. A torrent of eloquence unmarked by commas or full-stops, a detail of symptoms, lamentations, and even tears— so very rare among the Chinese—and passionate appeals to the doctor, as if in his hands indeed were vested the issues of relief or of suffering, of life or of death. He succeeds in soothing each with a few kindly sympathising words in their own language. Without this linguistic accomplishment a doctor could not dispense with an interpreter, and hence he would be much hampered in his labour of love; yet few have emulated Dr. Begg in his industry and humanity, which have prompted him to master that type of intricacy, the Chinese tongue, sufficiently for medical practical purposes.

I had long sought for an opportunity of inspecting the deformed feet of the women, but hitherto without success. With the national inverted ideas of decency, the foot is the one part of the person which more than any other part the Chinese female is reluctant to bare, but here at last is my chance. In my assumed character of a medical friend of the surgeon I visited a female patient, who was directed to strip her legs. To have witnessed the removal of the eye could have been scarcely more revolting. The leg bone near the ankle fleshless and shrivelled, as thin as a chicken's drumstick; the parchment-like, purply skin stretched tightly over it; the four lesser toes stunted and twisted so completely under the foot that they are three parts buried in the flesh; the great toe and the edge of the heel bone forming mere points of tottering support; the other portion of the heel and the instep clubbed into a hideous, shapeless mass of deformity. Never again do I wish to see so ghastly an object as the naked foot of a Chinese woman.

The wards would perhaps have barely met with approbation in England; in China they were a marvel of comfort and cleanliness. The difficulties in enforcing the latter quality, even in the most limited degree, are enormous, and of incessant vexation both to the doctor and the nurses. These are chiefly Italian lay sisters, kind, quiet, pleasing-looking young women, the mention of whom leads me to the main work of the mission, the hospital being merely a sub-section supported by special contributions. Very civilly and readily did the *madre superiore* accede to my request to view the establishment, deputing Sorella Carolina to act as my guide. Loyally and freely did she show me over every corner, answering in detail all my questions, and even encouraging me to seek confirmation of her replies from the other sisters. Their staple language was of course Italian— a few words of French, but not a syllable of English.

The interior arrangements of the convent were of

that severely simple nature characteristic of similar religious seminaries; the sisters had allowed for themselves few comforts and comparatively little extra cubic space, notwithstanding that the plea of the stress of extreme heat is elsewhere universally accepted. Then I am conducted into room after room full of Chinese children, and it is explained to me that one of the functions of the place is that of a foundling hospital.

'Then what are those eighteen or twenty miserable old cripples doing here?'

'Ah, signor, herein we have deviated a little from our rules; out of pure compassion we allow those few poor wretches to linger out their last miserable days here in peace. Their subsistence costs us next to nothing. But we have some 1,000 children on the strength of the mission. About 500 are babies and are put out to nurse, on payment, in the city, subject to the constant supervision of our sisters. I can show you the greater number of the remaining 500.'

And sure enough I walk through several nurseries full of grotesque little Chinese imps, ranging from about two to twelve years old, and in every stage of employment.

'Tell me first where you get your recruits?' I ask.

'They are brought to us, generally as infants, without any particular secrecy, and abandoned without reluctance, inquiry, means of subsequent identification or reclamation. All these children without one single exception are girls, for Chinese regard with indifference, if not with annoyance, the existence of girls, as trumpery vexatious expense. The parents are only too rejoiced to get rid of them. Of their boy children, on the other hand, they are immoderately fond, and we have never yet had a boy-child among the hundreds of babies who have been left here.'

Subsequent inquiries fully confirmed Sorella Carolina's representations. There can be no doubt that infanticide is carried on in a wholesale manner throughout the length and breadth of the empire, with little or no check from the authorities. As soon as the girl-child is born, say No. 2 or 3, and whose existence therefore is held to be a costly superfluity, the father quietly scrags and buries it, and there is an end of the matter.

The mission children are divided into different classes according to their ages. The two-year-old group, strange little imps, grotesque with their infantile Mongolian features, intensely black-haired and bright-eyed, are too young, notwithstanding all their precocity, for much beyond play. Here a class, on an average five years old, is being taught to weave. The habitual cheerfulness of the place seems to be at a strangely low ebb here, and I notice many instances of unhappy expression. After a little inquiry I trace the cause. Many are actually suffering from that terrible national cruelty practised on girls as soon as they approach the age of five : the tying up of childhood's chief beauty, their plump little dimpled feet.

'Imbandite,' says Sister Carolina, pointing to some children whose looks of torture are even more piteous than tears, and then she further explains : 'Their sufferings are dreadful, especially at the first binding up, and never seem entirely to quit them day or night, giving their faces that settled look of pain. By degrees the feet become partially numbed, but even then the old pain sets in acutely whenever the bandages are removed and replaced. This continues, though with diminished severity, until they are sixteen or seventeen. Sometimes festering and consequent effluvium ensues, for which the only remedy is powdered alum. We employ two Chinese women for the sole purpose of bandaging feet. You are shocked, signor, and so are we; we consider the practice barbarous and cruel beyond measure. But it seems a matter of expediency that we should yield to a prejudice far more intense than any other in this country. Were we to run counter to it our repute among the Chinese would be very evil, and our sphere of utility much curtailed.'

My excellent nuns, I demur to your reasoning. The mere stupidity which will render these children crippled, hobbling, practically feetless, I can, though with difficulty, waive. But I do not see that the intense and prolonged suffering involved can be pardoned by any special pleading of expediency or justified by any sophistry of your religion.

On further inquiry I ascertained a few additional particulars concerning a practice which seems to have been introduced about 970 years ago. It appears that the muscles of the legs become strained by contracted feet, and that the calves entirely disappear. The first process is to truss the foot up tightly in such a manner as to bend the four smaller toes under the sole, in the soft part of which they almost disappear; then the foot is bound down like the turned over angle of a jujube until at last the ball of the natural foot fits into the hollow of the sole, and it becomes a shapeless lump. The instep is where the ankle was, and all that is left to tread the ground is the ball of the great toe. Sickly children sometimes die under the process. It is, however, difficult to find a husband for a girl with natural feet. The Chinese admire the distorted gait induced, they consider a full-size to be of masculine ugliness, and urge the advantage that the crippled women are prevented gadding about.

It is sometimes stated that the practice is becoming somewhat less frequent, and I think this is to some extent true in the south. But north of Amoy it continues universal, while among the richer classes throughout there are no exceptions. Here is a point of consideration for the Darwinites. Though the hands and likewise the feet of men and women of all classes in China are conspicuously small, slender, and tapering, the feet are not of that diminutive size which we should be led to expect according to the theory that the artificial usage of many generations at last constitutes a hereditary characteristic.

I inspect room after room full of children, busily, eagerly, and—putting aside the feet abomination—happily employed in all the stages of weaving, spinning, and needlework, from the simple operation of passing the threads from right to left, to the climax of silk embroidery, which even a clumsy man devoid of taste can perceive to be of extraordinary skill and beauty. Then the little creatures are so proud of their work, so eager that I should scrutinise and examine the labours of each separately. Their instructors, about seventeen in number, and all Italian sisters, have furnished another instance of religious zeal surmounting mountainous difficulties. They are fully purposed to devote the whole of their young lives to the most practical and least alluring forms of God's service, so they do not carry out their undertakings by halves—they have actually learned to speak Chinese, and the clatter between mistresses and pupils is of a very amusing description.

'Now,' said practical, cheerful Sorella Carolina, 'I will show you our school. The teaching seldom lasts longer than two hours a day, and is limited to reading and religious instruction.'

'What, no writing, or arithmetic, or geography?'

'No, signor, none whatever. Our limitation, which

at first sight may appear so preposterous, has only been adopted after the fullest consideration. The happiness and prosperity of these children when grown-up will be immensely furthered by their skill in handicrafts, and by an education which shall make them first-rate housewives. Any book-learning beyond reading would be a positive drawback to them. Their friends and their husbands would regard such unwonted knowledge with suspicion and dislike, and the acquirement of writing, for instance, would be to them somewhat worse than a complete inutility.'

My entrance as a visitor is invariably signalised by the little elves springing to their feet, and, in lieu of the traditional curtsey bob, bending down and gleefully banging their foreheads against the floor. Only my conceit, flattered at such an obeisance, is instantly put to flight by their inharmonious peals of mocking laughter at the strangely absurd appearance of this barbarian, and I understand that their comparisons with their own childish experiences are somewhat as follows:—

'How red his cheeks are; how ugly white his face is; what an enormous nose; his eyes are quite round; what a lump of hair he has over his mouth; why, he has got no pigtail, and he *has* just got a big pair of ears!' Then fresh peals, but, apparently prompted by the instructress, they wind up with what was intended for a chorus of song, but which, far from possessing a trace of the melody of childhood's musical voices, remind me of nothing so much as the rasping of dozens of nutmeg-graters. But I do not see a sign of punishment or grief. Here at all events we have 'Reading without tears.'

'And your religious instruction classes?'

'Are held daily, and of course we attach to them a maximum of importance. We find the children intelligent, and readily responding to teaching;' and I am shown a baptism class of eight or ten girls, aged about twelve years, being prepared for the rite. Probably circumstances had interfered with the usual convent custom of baptising the foundlings on first admission. These children seemed to listen attentively, and to answer readily, and the sister assured me that any who were backward or unappreciative were put back for further instruction.

'Now, Madre Superiore and Sorella Carolina, I admit you have given me the fullest latitude to investigate every detail of your foundling establishment. Will you explain to me the outline of your system. In more definite terms, in seeking to spread Christianity, how and where do you start with your task, and what is your subsequent guiding principle?'

Reply. 'How: by taking in hand the pliable twig, i.e. childhood, and ignoring the gnarled, hardened, obstinate old tree. Where: in the very thick of this city, the most populous district in China, of which these numerous twigs are part and parcel, and whose leaven must, in time, leaven the whole lump. On what principle : so to train these children, so to free them from the trammels of their countrymen's abominations, so to render them exemplifications, moral and physical, of the blessings of Christianity, that in grown-up age they may unconsciously become apostles who will turn the folly of vice and superstition to the wisdom of our Saviour's religion.'

'Amen. Thank you; God speed you in your efforts.'

At Hankow, and indeed throughout China generally, European opinion strongly approves the Roman Catholic system of medical missions and strongly condemns the Protestant. 'Oh, there are always two sides to a story,' urge the defenders of the latter. Very true, and habitually one side is the right, and the other the wrong one. That I might judge impartially, I inspected on two separate occasions, with even a more careful scrutiny, the Hankow kindred Wesleyan Medical Mission.

I apply for admission. 'No can come,' says the coolie Cerberus, 'they makee Joss Pidgin.'

'Well, but I Christian, I make Joss Pidgin too,' and half reluctantly I am admitted into a room where Divine service is being performed in the presence of about eighty Chinese, of whom some twenty-five are children.

Great as was the surprise which my entrance created, it fell far short of my own stupefaction when, on the 100th psalm being given out, the congregation sets up the most extraordinary yelping it has ever been my fortune to hear. There is not a single note which is not outrageously discordant, or which does not remind me of cats screaming on the roofs of houses. There is, it is true, a certain approximation to cadence, but this renders the general effect still more burlesque. Higher rises the wooden shouting, half jangle and half yell, and the first sensation of the ridiculous gives way to painful surprise that the missionaries do not seem to be aware of the absurdity of the performance. My neighbour—an English assistant—thrusts into my hand a Chinese hymn-book, with vehement indications that I too should join in this novel harmony. I firmly resist; I do not know a single word or a single character, while the only sound I fancy I can recognise is 'chin-chin.' To attempt to lead the congregation into a more melodious strain by the mere repetition of 'chin-chin' would, I conceive, be both futile and irreverent.

Then follow extempore prayers in Chinese, then a harangue, and then some of the congregation ascend the platform and relate their experiences. One rather hang-dog-looking fellow of about thirty discourses volubly, his subject being, as I was informed, his experience of opium eating. He somewhat reminds me of a temperance lecture by an ex-inebriate, and does not impress me favourably. Another speaker of equal glibness, but more mature years, holds forth to the same effect. At about this stage I am assailed by that frequent concomitant of indeterminate services, a sensation of vacuity and dulness, and, which is more important, I notice that this is fully endorsed by the rest of the audience.

Thus far they had at all events preserved a semblance of attention, but at last nature asserts herself, and the undisguised sighings and naive yawnings are impressively portentous. Then empty medicine bottles and cups are held up to the light, and.say as plainly as spoken words, 'About time to finish your harangue. Let us get on to the salves, the potions, and the boluses. At the conclusion of service the patients flock into the surgery for treatment.

'Do you make attendance at prayers a condition of medical advice?' I inquire.

'Oh, dear no, certainly not; the former is entirely optional.'

Still unsatisfied, I run the matter to ground, and come to the conclusion that, though no record of names is kept, the patients proceed straight and immediately from the chapel to the surgery, and therefore I cannot reverse my opinion that the spirit of compulsion is present.

The Scotch doctor, whose practical Christianity and zealous exercise of skill on a suffering humanity which neither can nor will repay him I hold in high esteem, conducts me round the wards, which under the circumstances were satisfactory, though perhaps not quite equal to those in the Italian mission. The scale of operations appears much smaller, the out-patients are far less numerous, and the inmates do not exceed thirty. As in my former experience, there is the same verbosity of querulous sufferers, and the same revolting sights; but the maladies seem to be of a somewhat different type, surgical cases being greatly in the minority. Skin diseases, fever, cholera, dysentery, and the results of opium eating are most prevalent, the latter vice especially being regarded as a distinct disease, and subject to special medical treatment.

One applicant holds out a string of 900 cash, equal to about three shillings. This is taken possession of by the doctor, and the patient is entitled to residence in the hospital under restraint for fifteen days. Should he demand his freedom at an earlier date, he forfeits a proportion of his deposit. This little incident speaks volumes. Three shillings to a coolie would represent the value of about a pound to an English labourer, and with a people so pre-eminently thrifty, the mere pledging of so large a sum is to them the strongest inducement to submit to restraint for the allotted time, and so to get their full money's worth.

In the school the attendance was thin, and, inasmuch as no handicrafts are taught, there was an absence of that cheerful activity which so much impressed me in the Italian institution. Instruction was given both in reading and writing Chinese, and an amusing effect was produced by the discordant sing-song of the children, accompanied by violently swinging their bodies. Various texts were pasted up in the different wards, but the selection did not appear to me judicious. Instead of typifying the happiness and kindly affection of the beautiful Christian religion, they were the usually adopted Shibboleths of that special section of a party which approximates to the Roman Catholics in meting out the most appalling retribution to all who differ from their own tenets, which, after all, are not always to be found in the Bible; that party which denies that all forms of the Christian religion lead to the same end, though some routes are surer and safer than others; that party which holds other Christian views than their own to be only a shade better than heathenism, and regard workers of Christianity under another flag as more detrimental than open foes; that party, in fine, which is almost hostile to the conversion of 350,000,000 Chinese, unless the conversion be carried out precisely according to their own prescription. A single incident to illustrate the narrow-mindedness of their teaching. In the room of one of the Chinese assistant missionaries was a prayer-book, which called forth some remarks from my conductor evidently of the nature of strictures. On my inquiring their purport, the reply was: 'This prayer-book has, you see, a large cross embossed on the outside. Our Chinese friend here has certainly High Church tendencies, and to this I was taking exception.' High Church tendencies among the natives of Hankow, where among several hundreds of thousands of Chinese heathen there are not probably a score of them who in a religious point of view know their right hand from their left! Can the tithing of pot-herbs go farther?

'Are you satisfied with the results of your missionary labours?' I inquire.

'Very much indeed. I have in this district a total of about 500 converts. For many years I have been labouring, and the good seed is at last springing up and bearing fruit.'

Now the very magnitude of the number quoted first aroused my doubts as to its accuracy, which ripened subsequently into absolute certainty, as opportunities enabled me to prosecute inquiries in authoritative sources, and to compare results. Five hundred converts! Not a single unprejudiced witness among lay authorities ventured to assert that that number could be even approximately correct as applied to the joint results of the huge cities of Hankow, Chinkiang, Kiuchiang, Shanghai, Foochow, and Swatow. And among the ostensible converts how fractionally small is the number of those who are sincere in their convictions, who are not actuated by any considerations of aggrandisement, and who would incur misfortune through adherence to their faith. 'Five hundred converts,' and 'the good seed is bearing fruit!' Fifty honest converts would represent a stupendous success;

and as for the good seed, alas! that that idle, careless, unpractical labourer should have flung it about in so unwise and wanton a manner as to have extinguished in so many cases all hope of its germinating, as to have entailed a dismal desert of failure, and as to have brought down ridicule, discredit, and discouragement on the few more wise and more devoted husbandmen.

Yes; I take indignant exception to the published glowing accounts of results and success, backed up by statistics so fallacious that they only just escape the stigma of being garbled. Indeed, I have before me at this moment a flaming report on China missions—would that I might particularise its title—the statements wherein have been concocted either by a knave or a fool, so grossly false are they. A case came within my knowledge where one of two missionaries who had been journeying together furnished a discouraging report. The head of the mission remonstrating, declined to forward it, and urged him to re-write it in the spirit of his coadjutor, who had expressed himself to the following effect:—

'One Sunday afternoon we landed at ——, and in a very short time the poor natives came crowding round us, thirsting to hear the Word of God.'

The reply was: 'I was present at that moment with my coadjutor, and I assert that his statement is not true in the sense he implies. We landed on a Sunday, and the inhabitants mobbed us—but the remarks of the inquisitive rabble were: "Look at those foreign devils, how oddly they are dressed; and what enormous noses they have!"'

To resume my inquiries at the mission :—

'Yes; the patients are very grateful to us for the spiritual as well as for the physical advantages we afford them.'

Good people in England—the one point in which the most experienced observers in China concur, is that the inhabitants show their strangest deficiency in the lack of gratitude. Gain being their sole motive power, they consider self-interest to be the mainspring of the incomprehensible dominant race. The optimist philanthropist, if he have one grain of the wisdom of the serpent, will be incredulous of the disinterested attachment of his most trusted employé, or his most faithful Chinese friend. Under some circumstances he will put the fullest amount of confidence in their integrity, but he will be equally confident that to gain the slightest shade of personal advantage the kindness of years will be tossed to the winds. Gratitude! No, the plant does not grow at the Hankow mission, or elsewhere in China; and as for 'spiritual advantages,' the phrase ceases to be hypocritical when it obviously can deceive none but those who have stitched up their eyelids.

'I see you do not teach your pupils any handicrafts, any sewing, weaving, or spinning?'

'Oh, no; we omit this on principle, lest the

adoption of the Christian religion should be a mere cloak for worldly advantages.'

The Chinese 'humph,' properly intoned, has the eloquence of pages, and here appears to be the most appropriate reply.

'Why do you not start with "the twig"—with the children without previous convictions to be uprooted; whose untaught minds would be ready receptacles for religious truths, which they would naturally transmit to their children, and who would not be subjected to the same obloquy as adults?'

'Well, we do not approve of that system: firstly, because the right principle is to convince adults of their errors, that they may train up their children in the way they should go; and secondly, on the ground of expediency, because the unconverted parents would oppose us on the ground of detriment to their children's prospects of attaining their *summum bonum*, future civic dignities.'

I reply that the 'right principle' is the one which, provided it be straightforward, attains the greatest success; and I quote the results of the Italian mission to refute this argument, and the equally weak one of 'expediency.'

It is probably quite unnecessary to state my conclusions, whatever little they may be worth, in comparing the Protestant and Roman Catholic mission systems as illustrated at Hankow. But as a counterbalance I gladly point to a brighter picture

THE MISSIONARY QUESTION. 187

of Church of England work at Foochow—brighter because more wise and liberal, and bearing some traces, however faint, of honest results. Here, too, I obtained a good deal of reliable information from an ex-army chaplain, with whom I had served in auld lang syne.

Foochow is the centre of mission work over an enormous district, where the total number of Christians is, according to missionary statistics, about 400 —a number which other authorities attenuate to a fractional part. In the country sub-districts the clergymen in charge adopt to some extent the national costume, live among the people, and learn their dialects, of which there are six variations within a very small area. Although their expatriation is not life-long, as with the Jesuits, their residence is prolonged over a sufficient number of years to familiarise them with the inhabitants.

In fine, I gather that a large proportion of the Foochow workers, in favourable contrast with their brethren in some parts of China, perform useful, genuine, disinterested, though not brilliantly successful, work. Once, when in the native city, I stumbled across a neat plain building, which challenged observation in opposition to the inconceivable dirt and tawdriness of the adjacent dwellings. A few Chinamen were dropping in, and I discovered that it was a sort of native Christian meeting house. A Chinese teacher was addressing a congregation of about thirty, whom he certainly had managed to interest. I may add that the curiosity which my entrance aroused was utilised by the preacher, who pointed me out as an exemplifying moral that, though I was a foreign devil, differing in race, language, aspect, and habits, I, even I, had a soul to be saved, and in this respect was identical with the Chinese.

'How do you set to work in the first stages of conversion?' I asked the ex-army chaplain.

'We address promiscuously gathered assemblages. Perhaps the interest of two or three stray individuals may be thus arrested, and they come to us afterwards to know what this new religion may mean. If teachable, they receive further instruction, and, after a probation which sometimes extends over a year, and tests of sincerity evidenced by minor sacrifices in conformity with the Christian religion, they are admitted to baptism. From time to time we travel about the country, passing the nights in a meeting house where practicable—otherwise reduced to the horrors of a Chinese inn. We find a little knowledge of medicine, even though it be the slightest smattering, invaluable in procuring for us a footing where other means fail. Christian converts are not subjected to any considerable persecution unless they decline to share the expenses of ancestral worship, i.e. prayers and offerings to the spirits of the dead. Deception and insincerity is so all-pervading a spirit among the Chinese, that it is especially expedient to avoid pressure on our converts, and hence I even make attendance at family prayers entirely optional with my own coolies.'

'Are the Roman Catholic missions friendly to you?'

'Fairly so, except the Spanish, whose hatred of Protestants is unbounded. It is necessary to be very suspicious of Roman Catholic statistics. Their sole object seems to be to obtain consent to baptism. That effected, they have done with the individual, who simply goes to swell the number of converts, many of whom are ignorant of their most elementary tenets. This very morning I asked a Roman Catholic convert, who was Jesus Christ? Not only was he unable to answer, but he was totally ignorant of the Virgin Mary.'

'Tell me some of your principal difficulties.'

'Polygamy. For instance, a childless convert, yielding to the sorrowful entreaties of his wife, recently took to himself a second. We considered ourselves compelled to put before him the alternative of repudiation, or of being put out of our congregation. Then there is the open, prevalent licentiousness of the European merchants' (of which more anon).

'Ancestral worship is another difficulty. The Jesuits sanction it, and, at first sight, there may appear certain advantages in tolerating this, almost the sole, feature of softness and reverence in the Chinese character. But were we to concede it, we should be assenting to the worship of another besides

God, and, with such an inconsistency, how could we hope for honest progress?'

Here I may remark that at first sight that ancestral worship which plays so prominent a part in the religion of the Chinese appeals strongly to our sympathies. Homage to the spirits of departed forefathers! it sounds at worst but a weak superstition, and surely it carries with it the brightest of virtues in the veneration it also inculcates of children to parents. The young are even compelled by law to support the aged, who to the last day of their lives can, ostensibly at all events, legally enforce obedience and respect. A father struck by his son is justified in putting the offender to death on the spot, and the most torturing forms of execution are reserved for parricides. On the death of parents sons are compelled, whatever be their occupation and rank, to withdraw from the world for a space of two years. Thus it is a common remark that the career of a great statesman is never ',safe' until both his parents are dead, inasmuch as their decease may suddenly compel him to withdraw from public life at his most critical period, leaving the field free for the machinations of his rivals. Only a special rescript of the Emperor can abrogate this requirement—a favour which was recently extended to Li Hung Chang, the Bismarck of China—and yet this alleged veneration for parents when probed deeply contains in it little which is really virtuous. There is little reverence of heart, little really kindly feeling and less tender affection. It is merely an outward act of superstition, a compliance with 'old-o' custom and law; an obedience to the letter, a total absence of the spirit. Who ever supposes that a Chinaman would incur voluntary genuine self-sacrifice out of true love for his father? Those authorities who are best qualified to judge are unanimous in declaring that the national capacity for personal affection and friendship, for gratitude and generosity, for chivalry and honour, exists in a most limited degree. Even for their simple 'thank you' their language has no equivalent. They have many hyperboles at their command to express grovelling submission and adulation, but no term in acknowledgment of the thousand and one daily amenities which embellish civilised life. Truth indeed is no virtue, and a lie is no vice with them, involving on the perpetrator not a vestige of discredit or shame. As Mr. Cooke aptly remarks in his book on China, to say to a Chinaman ' you are an habitual liar ' would be like saying to an Englishman 'you are a confirmed punster.'

Amongst certain excellent features of the Foochow mission, I must specially cite their system of colporteurs, and in praising this valuable work the most reliable opinions concur. They tramp about all over China, apparently free from sectarian tricks and prejudices, and limiting their attempts at conversion to an annunciation of the first principles of Christianity. They distribute Chinese Bibles at a low price, the sale whereof is considerable, because even a Chinaman of the poorest class considers that the mere possession of a printed work may originate a profitable repute for knowledge. Moreover, these books are secure from destruction, since a special sanctity attaches to all written characters, quite irrespectively of their purport, inasmuch as they form a medium of instruction in the doctrines of Buddha and Confucius. Even printed advertisements, or the merest scrap of a letter, may not be utilised for waste-paper.

'Does the purchaser sit down at once to search his Bible?'

'Oh, dear, no. It is quite a chance if he will open it once to the day of his death. On the other hand there is also an off-chance that their curiosity may some day be stimulated; that they, or perchance their descendants, may turn over the pages to find out for themselves somewhat concerning that Christ Whose teaching they may, or should, have heard will make them so much better and happier. And if, in future, there be among our missions more Christianity and less "Churchianity," this distribution of the only guide, which can never mislead, may be described without the shibboleth of spiteful sectarianism as the "sowing of the good seed."'

I may add that high authorities have informed me that the Chinese translation of the Scriptures is exceedingly incorrect and unsatisfactory, partly owing to the impossibility of finding native words which accurately correspond to certain Bible expressions.

For instance, it is undoubted, however amazing, that there is even now a considerable question as to the Chinese equivalent for 'God.' A revised translation is an urgent desideratum.

My record of missionary evidence would be very incomplete were I to omit my experience of that most celebrated institution in all China—the Jesuit establishment of Zic-a-wei, Europeanised into Sickaway—about six and a half miles from Shanghai. Founded by the French, whose missionaries far preponderate over those of all other nations, it comprises a monastery, convent, schools, and an observatory of such excellence as to supply foreign shipping with valuable astronomical and nautical data. Through the usual foul and tawdry village, over the inevitable stream, with its seething mass of putrid slime, and I find myself before a large block of stone buildings, the architecture and general plan of which bear an indefinable stamp of French origin, in such marked opposition to the English settlement. Baffled in my attempts to penetrate the enceinte of the fortress-looking walls, I address myself in French to a Chinese figure, with a long black pigtail, but with the betraying brown beard, and the brown hair on the top of his head. 'Mon Père' beams with delight at hearing his native language, and eagerly constitutes himself my chaperon and guide.

Within I notice various eagles and strange sea birds in captivity, and a kitchen garden like that of a

French country house, fertile in the production of those salads and pot-herbs which play so prominent a part in a French repast. The chapel bell tolls for the Benediction, and the numerous inmates, all in Chinese costume, are streaming forth to the service. My guide must leave me.

'May I too not attend?'

'Ah, oui, Monsieur, most certainly if you like. But,' askance, 'surely you are not of our faith?'

'I am of the Christian religion, so why should I not be present at Christian worship?' and so, with unconcealed marvel at the laxity of my principles, the Père conducts me through gloomy passages and dark cloisters, replicas of foreign monasteries, into the chapel, extensive and gloomy, but revealing a certain amount of grandeur. Oh, the strange sight, partly solemn, partly burlesque, and, must I add, partly painful through its theatrical insincerity. Of course the central group is about the altar, as brilliant with candles, as gaudy with tinsel and flowers, as richly decorated with heavy gold embroidery and carving, as is the wont of a Church which seeks to touch the heart through the ephemeral impressions of sight and sound. The priest, in all the splendour of his pontifical vestments, chants with sonorous intonation the Latin service; but dignified and devout as he seems, there is something strange about his enunciation, and something still more strange about the cut of his jib. Why—yes—my heart alive! he is a genuine John

Chinaman dressed up in all the simulacra of Roman Catholic prelacy. Around him cluster eight scarlet acolytes, likewise Chinese imps, and an additional imp who rings the bell and whirls the censer. Three assistant priests, however, are Frenchmen, and about twenty French Jesuit Fathers are my fellow occupants of the gallery. They are dressed from top to toe in orthodox Chinese fashion—blue robes, blue trousers, turned up shoes and pigtails. Yet the would-be disguise is too transparent to baffle a moment's scrutiny. The mobility and dignity of expression, the European-cut features, the abundant beard, in opposition to the parchment and almost hairless face of the native; above all, the fine hair, sometimes red, surmounting the coarse, artificial, intensely black pigtail, form the strangest contrast to the original.

From the dark recesses of the chapel peal forth the tones of an organ played with manifest taste and skill, and with familiar strains accompanied by Chinese choristers, who, though not equal to those at St. Margaret's, Westminster, have been tuned out of their wonted national yelping. The rest of the congregation, of which the total is about four hundred, is made up of two hundred native school children, quiet, orderly, and with a supernatural look of impish wickedness about them, and of the employés of the establishment. The service lasts but a few minutes; the congregation streaming outside resume their avocations, reminding me of a pious French village called to vespers, and I resume my investigation with the Jesuit Father. He informs me that the actual residents, exclusive therefore of children and assistants, amount to 500, some of whom are Chinese candidates for priesthood; others, about 100, are European priests, studying the language and making themselves acquainted with their business ere setting forth on the vast scene of their missionary labours, and twenty are permanent resident instructors and priests. Of course he declares the success of the missionary efforts to be great, and indeed his assertion that the recognised Roman Catholics in the vicinity number 400 may be accurate. But this estimate includes the hereditary Christian families, for it is one of the national features that if the head of a household changes his religion his descendants follow the same faith. By-the-bye he never spoke of 'Christian converts,' and evidently regarded all who were not 'Catholic' proselytes as still in a condition of heathendom. Nor were Protestant missionaries, *mutatis mutandis*, one pin more liberal.

The investigations and records of the Zic-a-wei observatory form valuable addenda to modern astronomical science.

'Does your experience confirm the general belief in the scientific knowledge and mathematical acquirements of the Chinese sages?' I inquire of the superintendent.

'Oh, dear me, no! Herein they are as utterly

ignorant as children. I am of opinion that some ages back they may have had some rudimentary glimmering, but that through lapse of time they have quite lost the little they ever knew.'

I would here express my own belief that the much-bepraised Chinese system of universal education, honour paid to learning, and competitive examinations open to the whole empire for public offices of emolument, are all of the purest nature of 'windbag.' There is, it is true, much learning by heart page after page from their preposterously absurd authors, much poring over antiquated writings, which are in the main such a farrago of folly, fable, and falsehood, such a compound of pedantry and puerility, that a knowledge thereof does more harm than good. The names of the proficients in these various grades of rubbish are published all over the kingdom, and they themselves are publicly conducted from city to city with every pomp and circumstance.

It must, moreover, be conceded that a large proportion of the general population can manage to read and write a little of their own appallingly difficult language. But of genuine education in its good sense there is scarcely a trace. Originality they have none. Arts and sciences, modern history, languages and literature, philosophical investigations, mechanics, matters affecting the daily welfare of the community, nay, the most elementary knowledge of the geography of the world—any attempt to diffuse instruction in the above is successively ridiculed, scouted, and then hounded out of existence. Talk to average types, not of the lower but of the middle classes, of the benefits of railways, electric telegraphs, steam machinery and engineering undertakings. They listen with the aggravating stupidity of incredulity, or else will reply: 'Oh, yes. Long ago, many a time and oft, we discovered and essayed in China these railways and telegraphs, and others of your so-called inventions. But we have deliberately abandoned them as either useless or mischievous.'

Point out to them that China on the map represents only a fraction of the world, and their reply is: 'All very fine, but that map is one of your construction. Take a Chinese map and you will see that our country comprises the greater part of the universe.' On the other hand, show them England. 'What, that little remote spot, scarcely so large as a single one of our provinces! Talk no more to us of your wisdom, power, and riches. You are only allowed to exist through the sufferance of China.'

One morning a comparatively highly educated instructor of the Chinese language expressed to his English pupil, with whom I was acquainted, his satisfaction at just having read in a native newspaper that 'the Queen of England had, with her usual accuracy and punctuality, handed over to the Government at Pekin her usual tribute which she pays to the Chinese empire.' Ridicule and argument were completely thrown away. The professor remained unshaken in his belief that England was a tributary, in a sense, of China. The unparalleled and universal ignorance of the Chinese is indeed the mainspring of the power of the mandarins, and were this dissipated, their reign of tyranny would be indeed jeopardised.

Quitting the convent I encountered my first and last experience of a Chinaman showing even a semblance of fight against a European. The coolie holding my horse, dissatisfied with my payment, and evidently regarding me as an easy subject for plunder, especially as the shades of evening were gathering, and the natives of the solitary village were crowding around, snatched hold of my bridle. 'Ah, would you?' said I, merely raising my switch, and in an instant he slunk away like a whipped spaniel.

Having put the reader in possession of certain missionary facts, can we not draw similar deductions?

1. Does China offer a wide and promising field for missionary labour?

Wide? Yes—of unparalleled magnitude in every sense. A nation comprising one-fourth or thereabouts of the population of the world, spread over every vicissitude of climate and soil. Promising? No—discouraging to the highest degree. To consider the Chinese, with so much intelligence and industrious foresight, in the light of untutored savages. whose minds may be easily moulded to a new creed, would clearly be the height of absurdity. But to attribute to them, with their intellects so hemmed in by the restrictions on the diffusion of knowledge, and so stunted by the prejudice and custom of ages, powers of reasoning by analogy and following up a chain of deductive argument would be scarcely less fallacious. The missionary, therefore, has to contend with the anomalous combination of the incredulity of civilisation and the crass stupidity of ignorance.

The religion of the Chinese is comprised in the observance of a few symbolical rites, and in the study of the moral precepts of Confucius and Lao-tse, and is held in contempt by the learned, the indifferent, and the materialist.

I can scarcely be wrong in asserting that the psychological characteristics of the Chinese are scepticism, superstition, and indifference, plus a lingering suspicion that after all religion may turn out, after death, not to be a fraud, and that it will be prudent to provide for this eventuality and to keep an eye on the main chance. In other words, 'Oh, God, if there be a God, save my soul if I have a soul.' A missionary reproached his Chinese convert for invoking the assistance of false gods during the perils of a typhoon. 'What for no have two chancey (chances)?' was his excuse. 'Jesus Christ number one chancey—Buddha number two chancey.' One day, trudging in the interior of China over miles of ancestral graveyards, I impatiently broke forth to my unusually intelligent

China servant: 'Surely, surely, boy, you cannot be so silly as really to believe that this mock paper money and these masses of corrupted provisions, with which the graves are far and wide bestrewn, can be of the slightest use to the spirits of the dead?' Answer: 'Humph, I no savvy (know); perhaps yes, perhaps no. No can tell. Plenty many peoples think joss pidgin (religious business) great foolo. But China oomans talk, and China mans must do.' One touch of nature makes the whole world kin.

2. Has Roman Catholic mission work been hitherto successful, and, if so, to what is due its superiority over ours? Compared with Protestants it has prospered, and even absolutely it has achieved a fair amount of apparent success. But I doubt if the roots have really struck deep, if they would survive the slightest intermission of labour or the slightest tension from persecution. Their teachers have carried the doctrine of expediency too far—they have appealed to superstition and self-interest rather than to reason and righteousness—their teaching has not been founded on a rock; so when the rains descend and the floods come the house falls, and great is the fall of it. But in the first instance their task has been easier than ours, because their tenets can be more easily assimilated to those of Buddhism. The Jesuit priest may say to his flock, 'You invoke the shades of your ancestors. Well, there is no great harm in that under restrictions. We, too, pray to the spirits of the de-

parted just.' By-the-bye the Dominicans will not admit ancestral worship, and hence have been much less successful. 'Your priests profess asceticism. So do we. They are the medium of communication with heavenly powers. So are ours. You love to decorate your temples and shrines. So do we.'

During my travels, I carefully inspected about twelve of the most venerated Buddhist temples,[1] some of them indeed of China-wide celebrity. In every single instance without exception their resemblance internally to Roman Catholic places of worship was most striking. In many cases a couple of hours' labour in transformation, and the likeness would have been complete. There is the same interior architectural decoration, the same gilding and sombre lights, the same richly embroidered altar cloths and draperies, the same guardianship of relics, and the same highly beautified raised shrines with burning tapers, flowers, and clouds of incense. Even the postures and genuflections are not dissimilar. Remove those monstrosities representing Buddha and his wives, and those miniature devils representing the Chinaman's 'number two chancey,' or alternative to a deaf god, affix a few crosses, distribute a few *prie-dieu*, introduce a pot of holy water, and, as I have said before, in the shortest possible space of time the temple will be converted into a gorgeous counterpart of a Roman Catholic place of worship.

[1] Viz. at Shanghai, Hankow, Foochow, Yuen-foo, Kushan and Canton.

When the Jesuits first began their labours in China, they themselves exclaimed that the devil had been allowed to burlesque their rites. *Vice versâ*, at Shanghai, I observed in a chapel for Roman Catholic converts, representations of our Saviour as a Chinaman, and of the Virgin Mary as a Chinawoman, while, minus the idols, the chapel closely approximated to a Buddhist temple. But it is an act of simple justice to acknowledge the self-sacrifice of those Jesuit priests who, for ever abandoning their country and snapping in sunder the dearest earthly ties which can bind a human being, devote the rest of their existence to an unattractive life of cheerless solitude and privation, with the sole and noble object of furthering the welfare of the most odious and ungrateful vermin whom Providence hath ever suffered to crawl on the face of the earth. By so doing, however, their measures, unlike those of many of the Church of England, are of no half-nature. Living and dying amongst their flocks, speaking their language, sharing their vicissitudes, and participating in their interests, they become in course of time one of themselves, and acquire a hold unattainable by any other means.

3. 'You have spoken with scarcely veiled condemnation of the "expediency" system of conversion pursued by the Jesuit missionaries. Can you not, then, express an opinion favourable to their antipodes in every possible respect, the Protestant labourers?'

Oh, no! With the staunchest loyalty to its principles, I cannot conscientiously express an opinion otherwise than that that faith has never shone so feebly or worked so ineffectually as under the present guidance of its, on the whole, idle shepherds and dumb dogs—at least according to my own feeble lights.

'Your lights forsooth. Can the superficial observation of a casual amateur contain at best more light than a flickering phosphorescent iridescence?'

I reply that, in the first place, the casual amateur has greater facilities for hitting blots than the bigoted professional. Secondly, I adduce in support the evidence which I began with prescience to collect as soon as I suspected the rottenness of the tree—the evidence of the most righteous, reflective, and reasonable among our communities at Shanghai, Hankow, Kiukiang, Chinkiang, Foochow and Swatow. In one place only, Foochow, did I hear a single voice raised in defence. Elsewhere there was an absolute unbroken consensus of disapprobation, rising sometimes to reprobation.

Now to substantiate so sweeping a condemnation, I may be fairly required to adduce some specific charges. I charge, then, Protestant missionaries with postponing the interests of their religious calling to the furtherance of their worldly prospects; I charge them with frequent sloth, with an unhumble strife for social status—for which of course their wives are habitually responsible—with an arrogance of *ipse dixi*, and with an absence of conciliation. I charge them with promulgating glowing statements of success which are not borne out by facts; with undue absence from the scenes of their supposed labours; with discreditable readiness in looking back from the plough before making moderate progress in their labours. In fine, I hold them largely responsible for a state of affairs which will be denied by few but those who have stitched up their eyelids and then declare that they cannot see—a state of sloth, nonsuccess, and disrepute. I will quote the evidence of one layman out of much which I garnered in—that of an English official resident at Pekin. After fourteen years of much personal experience among the missionaries, he had only encountered three English whom he could respect.

To use the plain-spoken terms of another official, the missionary business in China is by no means a bad business to run by that class of the clergy who occupy that debatable land which is one grade below gentlemanship, and from which the majority of the Chinese Protestant missions are recruited. Poverty stricken and without prospects at home, out here they are provided by the various missionary societies with an assured and liberal income, to which is added 100*l*. a year should they be married and 50*l*. extra for each child—a practice surely founded upon Mormon principles. The above is supplemented by liberal contributions from the resident English merchants, amongst whom illiberality is an unknown quality even in matters whereof they do not approve. The missionary now lives in a condition of affluence which would be unknown to him elsewhere; a luxurious house with luxurious appliances and table, coolies to carry him about, and an ample margin of dollars. 'Why not?' Granted if he fairly earned it; but the contention is that he metes out labour to himself with an unduly indulgent measure, that he shirks those privations to which the Jesuits so cheerfully assent, and that he even declines a temporary sojourn among his nominal flock—that potent means of acquiring personal influence. In epidemics or during the trying hot season he flies to pleasanter pastures. In fine, he performs his perfunctory duties in a perfunctory fashion. Meanwhile he, and especially his wife, live in a constant state of bicker with the influential European community, who, if approached in a wise, conciliatory manner, could do so much to aid him. On one point, indeed, his zeal rarely flags—his extra incomings of dollars, for which he appeals with a mixture of petulance and the air of a man denied sacred rights.

Well, in the course of a few years the missionary becomes tired of his work, or discovers a more attractive opening elsewhere. Apparently regardless of the fact that during the first part of his sojourn his services can have been little more than of an apprentice nature, he leaves the scene of his labours precisely when, by his indoctrination, he could be most useful, and hies him back to England, probably with a nice little accumulation of dollars wherewith to start in his new clearing. There he holds forth, on all possible public occasions, on the privations and toils, the thrilling adventures and hair-breadth escapes of a missionary's life—the chances are 20 to 1 against any of his audience being in a position to contradict him—and dilates with touching unctuousness on the heathen Chinee 'thirsting to hear the Word,'[1] such is the conventional but preposterously inaccurate expression. He can scarcely fail to gain repute—especially among silly women little apt in weighing evidence—as a noble champion of Christianity, whereby he assumes a social status to which his birth and breeding have by no means entitled him, and in many instances he will in some fashion reap much substantial advantage.

Or, suppose him nominated a missionary bishop or dean, in how many instances do not his residences become discreditably brief and far between? It might be supposed that in this more than in any other calling, the principle of a scrupulous performance of distasteful duties would apply with irresistible force, but the normal condition of missionary dignitaries seems to be that of home leave and handsome salaries, which have been calculated on the assumption that the post has involved expatriation. At last the scandal of absence becomes too grave to be longer

[1] See p. 184.

endured; the dignitary gracefully resigns, and as the ex-bishop of this or the ex-dean of that, holds a high ecclesiastical status in England, probably ultimately eventuating in a sinecure, where he has little or nothing to do and is well paid for doing it.

With such captains, with such rank and file, can we be surprised at our present failure? Can we even hope to hold our own with the Jesuits who, whatever their errors, at all events possess the splendid characteristics of unfaltering perseverance, of undeviating performance of duty, and of unhesitating self-sacrifice. No; we must concede that the best founded evidence, including that of the few really honest, disinterested Protestant workers, admits almost unanimously the failure hitherto of our missionary enterprises in China.

'You know you have my unbounded sympathy and respect,' said an official high in authority to a missionary on his way from Singapore to China, 'but tell me honestly how many sincere conversions you consider you have effected during your twelve years' sojourn,' and the answer, sadly and deliberately given, was, 'Three, only three, who I believe were thorough and honest. I have met with numerous other nominal cases, but after my years of toil I cannot persuade myself that I could reckon more than three staunch Christians.'

At Pekin, one of our missionaries employed as a teacher a native Christian of whose sincerity he had

had, as he believed, seven years' experience. At the end of that period it was discovered that the convert at the conclusion of evening service had been wont habitually to open the chapel as a gambling house. On another occasion, as I learned, a party of English sportsmen came across an English missionary, who offered to conduct them to some good shooting ground. As their intimacy increased he told them his story. With a self-devotion rare amongst Protestants he had buried himself in the midst of a rural population, and yet, after three years of unremitting toil, he had come to the conclusion that during that time he had not made one single honest convert.

May we not deduce from the foregoing evidence that those who assert that thus far missionaries have made numerous sincere Christians are governed by delusion or are guilty of fraud?

I have been sometimes met with the argument that the above statements in no wise apply to the China Inland Mission, which is an entirely distinct organisation. But in the almost unanimous chorus of strictures passed in China itself no exception was made in favour of any one missionary branch, and, moreover, I have before me the publication of this society called 'China's Spiritual Need.' I am persuaded that no impartial resident in China would for one instant deny that it is replete with mis-colourings, and that the whole tenor of their own evidence compels us to bracket this branch with the other Protestant societies.

Of course the Chinese will, for the sake of the smallest temporary gain, assent to many of the forms of Christianity, and this hypocrisy is not unfrequently fostered by the shallow views of their teachers. A religious deputation entreated the Governor of Hong Kong to discontinue employing on the public works on Sundays certain coolies, who, be it noted, were not supervised by Europeans, on the ground that this labour was opposed to the precepts of Christianity. Was this sheer stupidity or sheer duplicity, for it could hardly be maintained as a reasonable conviction? With equal force a Jewish community might entreat that Christians should not be employed to work on Saturdays. Sunday is no more a sacred day in Chinese belief than any other day, and is, in fact, much ess so than their very few semi-religious festivals. But they have worked this mine among the English with considerable acumen and success. 'Chinese Sunday' is a frequent plea for leave of absence, and even 'Chinese Good Friday' is occasionally attempted.

'So you join the chorus that missionary labours are a failure, and a mere subterfuge for clerical hawks; that converts are invariably scoundrels, and that we had much better leave the natives to their heathendom, and in lieu apply the much-needed labour closer at home?'

'God forbid!' is my earnest disclaimer of a threadbare argument, which I suggest is utterly fallacious. Had the principle held good in early days that a work should be perfected in its birthplace ere it is diffused elsewhere, when would Christianity have been introduced into England, or indeed into Europe? Because an enterprise, in itself noble, has failed through causes which can be distinctly traced and remedied, is it, therefore, to be abandoned? Far more; if the clearest injunction: 'Go ye into all the world and preach the Gospel' may be disregarded without guilt, there is an end to the obligation of obedience to the plainest commands of our Saviour. No; let us remodel the enterprise and try again, remembering that a fool, a bigot, or a firebrand can do more harm than ten good men can repair. Perhaps even my indication of defects and remedies may be worth a passing thought.

1. One of the foremost *desiderata*, I consider, is that the heads of missionaries should in all districts be gentlemen, gentlemen in the conventional sense if you choose so to phrase it, who are not only highly educated, but who wear well-cut, well-brushed clothes; who are men of the world, of tact and discrimination; who will say and do the right thing, at the right time and place; whose experience is varied and conversation interesting. 'Oh, my dear sir, do you suppose the apostles were gentlemen?' says Mr. Oily Gammon, and in replying to this irrelevant, irreverent remark, anger becomes a virtue; but the following single argument amongst many available is a sufficient con-

futation. The cases are not analogous. The apostles had received direct teaching from our Saviour, and, as 99 out of 100 Christians believe, were inspired by the Almighty. An ecclesiastical official, connected with missionary administration and in authority second to none, was once warmly refuting the disparaging opinions which he had induced me to express, and he wound up vexedly: 'I cannot admit your charges; but what we really require is a higher class of man, both of gentlemen and scholars. My urgent remonstrances on this point have been quite unheeded.' Exactly herein lies the gist of my contention.[1]

I would point out another grave drawback accompanying a low type of missionaries, with a good deal of 'land' on their own hands, and with a deficiency of clean linen and h's. They are outside the pale of that powerful European interest, the resident merchants or their agents, most of whom possess the externals of gentlemen, while all recognise one when they see him. The missionaries are never by any chance met at their houses in a social capacity. Generally they are antagonistic or unknown to, or despised by, those local potentates and vast employers of labour, who possess in the aggregate an enormous influence over the native population. Now suppose the case reversed, and the clergyman working with the friendly co-operation—to put aside the better

---

[1] Would that I felt myself at liberty to publish the name of this witness and of others equally authoritative. They are, however, at the service of those who may choose to inquire further.

motives—of the merchant. Can the influence of this new factor be over-rated. 'Ah, but the open and prevalent immorality of the English residents compels the missionaries to shun transactions with them,' says the already quoted ecclesiastical dignitary. What! do you deal with a great evil by merely evading its open presence?

2. Let the resident merchants continue their present splendid liberality, but let the contributions be in the first instance transmitted to the central administrations in England for subsequent payment of salaries and other disbursements. Thus the prestige of the local missionary will not be weakened by his sending round the hat.

3. Let residence among their flocks of all the missionaries, whether high or low in office, be actual for a certain specified time—not theoretical. I am far from endorsing the requirement of the Jesuits that the worker should immolate himself in a life-long expatriation, for I believe that the infusion of fresh blood materially strengthens working machinery, and that labour will be more vigorous and successful if maintained only for a limited time. But for the time being let them not be constantly shirking their duties. That which their hands find to do, let them do it with all their might, regardless of privations, weariness, and the disruption of home ties, like duty-doing soldiers, of whom they should be types. 'This is a hard saying.' Yes, indeed. Therefore pledge not your-

self to the task without counting the cost, lest you bring the noble cause to shame.

4. Lastly, let the aspirant for missionary labour in the far East make a point of acquiring in England a considerable proficiency in practical medical art, such as how to deal with fractures, to take up arteries, to treat flesh wounds, abscesses, skin diseases, &c.; how to prescribe for ague, rheumatism, cholera, small-pox, dysentery, and fever. Of course he can merely learn the most elementary principles of treatment, but in the present profound ignorance of the Chinese of the science of physiology and medicine, even a slight knowledge will be many points in his favour, while a moderate, though practical, proficiency will ensure his influence and further his success to an extent greater than all other advantages put together.

And lest I should appear designedly to cast ridicule or discredit on all missionary enterprise, I venture to suggest for the consideration of my readers my own conviction that the disinterested, sincere, hardworking missionary has emulated the deeds of the ancient heroes of the Christian religion, and has excelled the most brilliant exploits recorded in chivalry.

CHAPTER V.

A CHINESE INLAND METROPOLIS.—HANKOW.

I KNOW not if I shall succeed in telling you aught which will interest you, but I can guarantee that what I relate must possess the advantage of novelty. Comparatively few Europeans have visited, far less systematically explored, the huge inland Chinese cities, and our imperfect knowledge of so many millions of these our strange fellow-creatures illustrates indeed the threadbare saying, that one half the world knows not how the other half lives. Said a seasoned Indian general whose life had been spent in Oriental scenes, and who accompanied me on one of my numerous explorations of a large native city, 'No, among the many strange sights I have witnessed in India, I have never seen anything approximating to this, or even in the least resembling it.'

Again, among the few who visit or reside in the littoral settlements, there are still fewer who are not more than satisfied with a single experience of all that is unwholesome, foul, and disgusting. Only those who are bent on sifting the matter to the very bottom will face the ordeal of incessant explorations. Hankow I take as a type of a Chinese city, and I will describe seriatim my wanderings about the city; but inasmuch as Foochow, Shanghai, Kiukiang, Amoy, and Swatow each possesses remarkable characteristics of its own, I will from time to time diverge from my original to call attention to the collateral.

To take one day's experience as a type of several others, accompanied by my Hong Kong 'boy' and by a local Chinese employé of Jardine and Matheson's firm, I set forth from the English concession at Hankow, entirely cut off and distinct from the Chinese locality, to the native city. We pass by the chevaux-de-frise stretched across the entire breadth of the road, and under the custodianship of the native police, dressed like a chimney ornament on a cottage shelf, stiff, dazed, and uneasy in his walk, and altogether the oddest, most childish amalgam of Chinese puerility and the dignity of the British police. His authority over his fellow-countrymen is paramount. His business is to keep the British concession quiet and select; he will not allow it to be desecrated and disturbed by any naked, shambling, talkative coolies, and all such, unless they are mercantile employés, or unless they can produce the inevitable 'squeeze' money, are refused admission by this Cerberus. Immediately on the other side of the barrier runs the never-failing city wall, ditchless, with its gloomy archway and its guard of three or four loungers, ostensibly soldiers, but the very incarnation of disreputable, dirty, hang-dog raggedness.

We pass under the portals, and at the first glimpse the thought occurs to my mind, 'Abandon hope, all ye who enter here.' But for the shame of irresolution. it is not improbable that I should turn round and flee. I scarcely think that the historical hero of the 'Night in a Workhouse' had greater need to clench his teeth, hold his breath for a moment, and vow that he would go through with his self-imposed task.

Now for it; let us go ahead, and in an instant we plunge from decency, order, and civilisation into a crowded throng and surroundings the furthest antipodes to the above characteristics which the wildest fancy could devise. I am in a narrow—not street, not alley, but—labyrinth, eight feet wide measured straight across, but owing to cumbered margins, with not more than three feet of width available. Two cannot walk abreast; single file is indispensable, and even then the jostling is incessant. The path is roughly paved it is true, but with a depression in the centre wherein stagnate the liquid impurities of the city. Then the dwellings which line this labyrinth—they are merely propped-up laths, rickety, shaky as a pack of cards, without windows, doors or chimneys; inside shaded off into a darkness which here is a friendly concealment of all which is best hidden; outside with the single overhanging story stretching across, and nearly cutting off the only pure element in the huge den, heaven's atmosphere.

Let us hurry on, the mere sense of motion is a relief. Are these bustling throngs really our fellow-creatures? Are they not anthropoidal demoniacal baboons? Look at their three-quarter naked bodies, sometimes indeed equipped only with an eight-inch-wide cloth, which covered their dirty, parchment, unnaturally hairless skins. As a matter of fact they must be of extraordinary endurance, but there is not one fine-built fellow amongst them—muscleless, all arms and legs, and far below the average European standard. As for their faces, suffice it to say that their eyes are mere slits, their mouths enormous fissures, noses like flattened pieces of putty, cheek-bones, high, disfiguring knobs, and expression, an evil and malignant leer. Of course their shaven foreheads, and their pigtails trailing down their naked backs, give the final touch to one's disgust. The women are but a shade better in appearance. Clothed with decency, I grant, there is the counter set-off of their hair piled high on the top of their heads, in black glutinous moulds like huge leeches; they are more stunted in appearance, and, worse than all, being almost invariably possessed of the distorted feet, they hobble about in the most ungainly, crippled fashion. As for the children—where is the prettiness which I supposed accompanied the young of all animals on emerging from a condition of callowness; where the smooth, unwrinkled skins, the tender, dimpled limbs, the downy hair, and childhood's laugh and expression? Not a vestige of all this. In lieu they are in every respect of form, feature, and coal-black pigtail merely pigmy, stunted men and women, further conspicuous with scabious heads. No scenic master could picture to himself more perfect representations for the imps of hell in the opera of 'Roberto il Diavolo.'

Hark to the voices and clatter, carried on in one loud unvarying din! Is it mere fancy or prejudice which originates extreme repulsion thereto, which seems to weary the ear and the brain? No; it is susceptible of a reasonable explanation. We usually talk of the pitch, the intonation of the human voice— it is high or low, soft or discordant, and thereby we imply the existence of musical attributes. But the Chinese voice possesses not the faintest trace of melody or resonance. I can only liken it to the noise produced by pieces of bone or lumps of wood knocked against each other. A loud, wooden, expressionless, monotone cackle, without rise, fall, or rhythm —without the burst or even the ripple of laughter, without the minor key of plaintiveness. A single sentence uttered in their midst by a European seems in contrast like music.

Quickly wending my way with my guide and my 'boy,' forming respectively my advance and rear guard, I pass through the outlying labyrinths into a small, square, unbuilt-over place, into the narrow area of which are crowded some of what I may call the incidents of the city. There are four jugglers and acrobats. Their performances are quite childish, with the exception of their sword exercise, executed with a weapon in each hand. The bright, sharp blades flash about high and low in a singular and dexterous network of involutions, their chief joke apparently being to 'wh—ish' them close to the faces of the spectators without inflicting injury. I was immediately singled out as the subject of their skill, and the ridicule of the bystanders, for I own that my nerves were not sufficiently steady to resist the impulse of starting back in avoidance of the flash which seemed almost to scrape my nose.

There again is a horrible cripple, dragging himself along on his knees, for he is footless, and reveals his two dreadful ankle stumps in order to extract subscriptions from passers-by. The injury has been self-inflicted by tying strings tightly round the lower part of the leg, causing the feet to mortify, rot, and drop off. A large proportion, about 70 per cent., die under the mutilation, but those who survive consider themselves amply repaid by ensuring for themselves a source of income which lasts out their lives.

There is a heaving, seething heap of bodies and rags; they too are beggars, filthier than the most filthy apes in the manner they divest each other of vermin. There is another beggar prone on the ground, his head wantonly grabbling in a mass of putrid liquid offal, with concomitants about his mouth and head which I dare not further describe, lest the reader should close the pages in pure nausea. He, too, demands alms, which are put in a basket held by one of those strange, weird, black-tongued, half-wolf, half-Pomeranian, Chinese dogs. Poor, faithful, obedient dog, he too has plunged his head into a heap of mud, in imitation of his master, but with much of the grotesque about him. For notwithstanding his grovelling attitude, which he has patiently maintained when two hours after I find him in the same position, his tail is wagging, his ears are cocked, and his black beads of intelligent eyes are sparkling with a roguish twinkle, as if he were poking sarcastic fun at the imposition.

Now I cross a sort of shallow canal, but in looking over the edge I almost start back in amazement and disgust. It is nothing half so sweet as an open cesspool, or half so clean as an open sewer; it is a large stagnant oblong, winding between the thick masses of dwellings, filled with every organic element of putrefaction, with every object of indescribable horror, exposed to the full rays of the sun; just sufficiently solid to prevent its being trickled away, or desiccated into comparative innocuousness; just sufficiently liquid to aid to the utmost the process of putrefaction and to ensure the liberation of the poisons to the atmosphere. It is safe to assert that no other towns in the entire universe except Chinese towns have in their midst such a Gehenna; because in no other towns are there the same combinations of enormous populations packed in such small areas, the same contradictions of semi-civilisation and bestiality, and the same conditions of climate, soil, temperature, and stagnant sites.

But, with such an accumulation of essence of plague, what becomes of the principles and laws of hygiene which have been dinned into our ears during the last twenty years? The laws of hygiene are thoroughly vindicated, for the dwellers in this neighbourhood die off like flies, especially in the hot weather, and especially of fever, cholera, and dysentery. 'Masquie'—never mind—say the mandarins. It is difficult to imagine any subject held in lighter esteem than human life in China, unless, indeed, when a special form of death, such as suicide or misadventure, becomes the means of extortion from the survivor, who in point of fact may be entirely irresponsible for the catastrophe. Here I may remark that by no Utopian perversion of truth could we call the Chinese brave, and their strange readiness for suicide can only be accounted for as one of their characteristic national contradictions. A man who wishes to spite his enemy will sometimes kill himself with a roundabout view to vengeance. For example, at Hankow, recently, a barber prosecuted his employé for the theft of two or three dollars, whereupon the latter, after a little scheming, committed suicide, not through morbid shame, for theft in China involves not a shadow of discredit, but as a means of involving disastrous consequences on his master. Sure enough, the widow was easily able to prove that her husband's death had been due to the course pursued by the prosecutor, who thereupon was condemned to pay about 120 dollars for the support of the bereaved family.

Having completely mastered all squeamishness, and thoroughly satisfied myself as to the chief constituents of this lake of infamy, I scuttle away as fast as possible from it, and again plunge into the labyrinths of the more central part of the town. And yet, in my capacity of investigator, I must still, with however great reluctance, say somewhat more on this unsavoury subject of the atmosphere of Chinese cities, because of the momentous considerations which hinge on it. This circumstance of pestilence has involved with it ignorance of the great centres of native life, development of commerce, and the most fatal curtailment of missionary action. Neither interest nor duty have thus far in the smallest degree counteracted this evil. Englishmen will pass years in the concessions, and unless under dire stress will not for years enter the precincts of the city; many will not allow their wives to be even carried rapidly through the streets in a chair.

Now let me strenuously repudiate all affectation.

A disagreeable smell, say at Bethnal Green or Bellevue, may be met with a wry face and a salutary spit, and there is an end of the matter. The stench of the Chinese cities, in their worst forms and under a sweltering sun, produce nausea and headache of a severe nature which last throughout the day, with the probability of subsequent indisposition which, if you are fortunate, will only last several days. A case came under my notice at Amoy of a lady who, notwithstanding her husband's prohibition, visited in a sedan-chair the city. In about half an hour she could no longer hold out, and was brought back, having literally fainted. Many Europeans during their progress keep a lump of camphor in their mouths. Others, myself among the number, smoke incessantly and furiously. I can only say that when I could smoke no longer, I used to feel myself perforce compelled to retreat out of the town, and that after my final experience—viz. Amoy, which I believe to be the most loathsome town throughout the length and breadth of China—I was attacked by indisposition which clung to me for many a day after, and the nature of which pointed to malaria.

But, says the sceptic, why should the miasmas be of the altogether exceptional nature which you describe? Well, I cannot and I will not enter into details; they are not fit for publication in such a work as this. I can only hint that garbage of every conceivable nature, including household detritus, is piled not only under one's feet, but under one's very nose in festering masses, fermenting in the sun. Remember, too, that this effluvia is not to Europeans merely an abomination, but a never-ceasing abomination. A French gentleman, asked by a lady to send her an assortment of perfumes, replied, 'Madame, in China there is but one scent, and that is not a perfume.' Their emanations can almost be tasted, and one can only express surprise, where every ounce of manure is prized as though worth its weight say in copper, the smells are not cut into slices and laid for fertilising purposes over the ground.

Numbers of coolies, aye, and even of female bearers, are incessantly staggering through the streets, jostling one with their burdens of fœtor carried in tubs, and evoke the sympathising remark of my compassionating 'boy': 'Major, plenty too much take care of bucket.'

Well, if we cannot away from the smells, let us get away from the discussion of the odious subject for good and all. Choking, exhausted, sweltering with the hot stifling atmosphere, I continue to shuffle rapidly through the everlasting labyrinths, and turn my attention to the strange shops. Special trades and handicrafts are allotted to special localities, and entire streets are occupied with dealers in coffins, very substantial, handsome in carving and strange in form, for the Chinaman attaches great value and will spend large sums of money on his last tenement.

Others are filled with smoking apparatus, with ivory carvings, with silk produce, with provision supplies, or with porcelain ware. Among some of the latter I noticed large collections of old English bottles, which are highly prized, there being a large proportion of Bass' beer bottles, with the familiar red trade-mark and label. These sold for about $4\frac{1}{2}d.$ each, relatively an extremely high sum.

There was perfect freedom to stroll into every shop, to turn over the wares higgledy-piggledy, and yet to make not the smallest purchase. The traders were lost in gaping wonder at the strange aspect of the customers, at their extraordinary dress, their long hair, their, to them, grotesque features, and especially at the stupendous size of their noses. Remember that this organ in the Chinese is represented by a little pat of putty.

When I really meant business and wished to buy, a scene of chaffering and wrangling took place more appropriate to fishwomen at Billingsgate than to the purchase transactions of an English gentleman.

'How much?' I ask.

'Ten tollare' (ten dollars) is the reply.

'Oh,' genuinely moving away, 'that is too much.'

'How much will give?' is the eager inquiry.

'How much?' I say contemptuously; 'why, about three dollars.'

'Can do, can do!' is the joyful assent, and before I can say 'knife' the article is transferred to my possession. Next time I am more crafty, and instead of offering a third of the sum demanded, name a fifth.

But all this chaffering is excessively distasteful. Of course it is all carried on by means of interpreters, and when it comes to paying, my 'boy' takes off some of the heavy necklaces of cash under which he has been staggering, and unstrings a few hundreds of these clumsy coins.

This process of paying is mechanically a troublesome business; as I have already explained, there is no gold coinage whatever, and very little silver. In ordinary cases of minor value, even silver coins are looked at suspiciously—they are little known to the mass of tradesmen here. They are fingered, chattered and disputed over in a tedious manner, until after some experience I adopted the expedient of loading my 'boy' with necklaces of copper cash, of which about 1,100 equal 3s. 8d., or 24 equal 1d. They are small disks of metal with square holes punched out of the centre, as means whereby they may be strung, and clearly a back-breaking weight represents a very small sum.

On one occasion my conductor led me through many a weary maze in search of a particular shop wherewith he assured me I should be enraptured. It proved to contain a collection of Lowther Arcade refuse stock, of every imaginable description, and the ideal of everything that was trumpery—broken accordions, gingerbread ornaments, children's toys, and for all of which were demanded preposterous prices.

It was a subject of incessant interest to watch their manufactures, wherein, although great industry and a quaint sort of ingenuity were displayed, there was a primitiveness and simplicity of the patriarchs. There was no vestige of steam machinery, although one would have supposed that the steam appliances on board the tea ships would have suggested how advantageously they might be utilised for general industries. No, 'old-o custom' again interposes; let us beware of the vicious innovations of those foreigners. Such mechanical, routine processes as silk winding and weaving, for example, are carried on entirely by hand. A dozen naked creatures manipulating threads, warps, woofs, shuttles, and wheels, which could have been worked with double the efficiency, and at a tithe of the cost, by a single steam crank. Even grinding corn is performed in a manner which it may be supposed was pursued by Abraham and Lot. There is the threshing floor, across which a current of air blows and carries off the chaff; there the uncovered mill-stones, and there the Oriental-looking, meek-eyed buffaloes tramping in a circle, in endless monotony. Those meek-eyed buffaloes, by the way, display a good deal of sour Chinese bigotry. Though they are blinded with leather pads, in an instant they discover by their scent the proximity of us Europeans; they sniff, stamp, and evince a raging desire to make for us if they could only ascertain our whereabouts.

As a rule I used to walk for hours through the most crowded parts of the city, without encountering a single specimen of a European, or at most one missionary or official agent, almost undistinguishable in the recesses of a covered sedan-chair, in which he was being hurried rapidly along. My appearance, therefore, leisurely investigating afoot, aroused a considerable amount of curiosity, and young and old quickly gathered around me in unsavoury proximity. So long as I was on the move it was always possible to keep the numbers down to some twelve or fourteen; but the moment I halted or went into a shop they clustered around me unpleasantly close, criticising my appearance and acts evidently in no favourable manner, and when I wished to resume progress my way was for some time actually barred.

I cannot say there was any overt act of hostility against me, but the demeanour of the rabble was habitually distinctly scowling and unfriendly. I was classed as one of the foreign devils, somewhat more unpopular at that time than usual owing to the French transactions at Tonquin; for in the minds of the Chinese all Europeans are bracketed together be they English, French, Germans, or Russians. This covert aversion in every countenance of a surrounding crowd gave a very unpleasant sensation of the necessity of never-failing watchfulness, prudence, and forbearance.

A wrangle, and in an instant the consequences might be serious.

I must own that on more than one occasion there lay ensconced in the bottom of my pocket, but handy for instant use, a small loaded revolver, and a handful of loose cartridges. Of what avail against a crowd of assailants? Of much, if driven by dire necessity to produce it. A totally defenceless European might be instantly kicked or hustled to death, where one armed with a six-shooter might, with resolution, clear a lane for himself through a Chinese rabble, each individual of whom, fearful lest a bullet should find a billet in his particular head, would with national pusillanimity shrink aside from a resolute Englishman, before whom they intuitively cower. It seems almost superfluous to remark that in such contingencies the keynote is instant action and resolution. A faltering moment and the position becomes desperate. I found the demeanour which secured for me the greatest freedom from annoyance was a more masterful one than would be wise or indeed would be tolerated in a civilised city. 'Step aside, idlers and toilers, wayfarers and bucket-carrying coolies; you must needs make way for me. I will not diverge one inch for you,' and without fail was the tacit demand conceded. 'Very boorish and ill-judged,' do you say? No, not here. A Chinaman would regard your mutual give and take of civilised courtesy as an acknowledgment of your inferiority, and quite possibly might next proceed to hustle you. As one old resident once put it to me: if a passer-by in England were to spit in your face you would knock him down. A parallel insult is intended when a Chinaman jostles a European.

After all, however, so far as is practicable deal with every incipient quarrel ere it has developed into aught serious with a laugh and a joke, so far as a joke can be perpetrated by gestures. The rabble will instantly respond, and, under cover of this, you can retire with dignity. But beware, above all things, of sarcasm or scorn. To this ridicule a Chinaman is childishly sensitive, and prone to take desperate and vengeful offence at the slightest indication thereof.

Now that the first feelings of bewilderment and dazedness has worn off, let us watch those minutiæ of street scenery which reveal so much of the national character. At frequent intervals I see men having their pigtails tidied up by professional barbers or by the friendly aid of a neighbour—to perform the operation alone would be quite impracticable. The unplaited queue streams in thick masses four or five feet in length down to the ground. So it really is in most cases your own, and not borrowed. The luxuriance is remarkable, though the quality takes away all admiration; of one intense, uniform black, even in children coarse and straight as wire; slimy, clammy, and unhandsome. One soft, brown English curl, which one would caress as the plumage of a beautiful bird, would be worth a whole sackful of this horsehair. What a careful dry shave over three-fourths of the forepart of the skull, which process has to be repeated about every six days! What a feminine brushing and plaiting and finishing up of the pigtail with ribbon, white when mourning is represented. You nasty creatures! every single one of your actions has an element of dirt in it, and here you wind up with a filthy operation on the ears.

'Boy, why do you submit to such bother with your hair? Why do you not wear it like mine?'

'No savvy. Every Chinaman do same ting; old-o custom.'

'Well, I savvy; 300 years ago, the Tartars conquered you and compelled you to wear the national type of servitude, pigtails, and you have continued the custom without comprehending the meaning.'

The pigtail is valued as dearly as life, and to be without one is the sign of a rebel.

I remember noticing at Foochow a man who, in consequence of his father's participation in rebellion, was under sentence of permanent deprivation of his pigtail. A more abased, shame-stricken wretch it would be difficult to imagine. He had adopted the clothes of a European, and seemed to be constantly in cringing conciliation of the English favour.

Boy-children of scarcely a year old are shaved as to their skulls and equipped with a miniature black pigtail, depending down their yellow little necks. Old men, naturally as bald as coots, carefully twist up their few scanty grey hairs about the nape, into the size and shape of a mouse's tail. On the other hand, if they be grandfathers, custom concedes to them alone the right of wearing moustaches, which at soonest is never worn until forty years have been attained. For some occult reason—certainly not veneration, for they are incapable of that—advanced age is considered a great merit. 'What is your honourable age?' is a frequent form of polite questioning. As a matter of fact, nature seems to deny the whole race of Chinese any hair whatever on the face until they are about fifty years old, and then in very mangy quantities.

What an enormous number of fresh-water fish, chiefly carp and eels, just gasping out their lives, are exposed for sale in tubs! Coarse, innutritious food, no doubt, comparable to a tallow candle stuck thickly full of bristles; but so very little animal food suffices for the needs of the Chinese. I often meet them carrying three or four gudgeon-looking creatures, strung with great care on a rush, according to the method of the fisher-schoolboy. Or look there at woman after woman carrying with elaborate precaution two or three ounces of animal matter, clearly destined to form the accompaniment to the family mid-day meal of rice. I say 'animal matter' advisedly, for to define the nasty morsel more accurately would be perplexing. I should hazard the conjecture that as a rule it consists of the brain and eyeballs of a rat, with a piece of the viscera of a pig in an imperfect state of health and preservation. The mere sight sends a shiver down the back.

Here I come across a street full of eating-houses. Upon the floor is heaped every edible in a Chinese dietary: some hissing hot lumps of roast pork and gelatinous stews, fish rapidly decomposing, livid joints, bean cakes resembling tablets of honey soap; their one civilised eating luxury—roast duck, and various dark treacly masses, which quiver as they are divided. The tea-houses are better. Tea alone is sold there; the 'fixings' are clean, and the occupants are quieter than those of an English beer-house. Look at those everlasting coolies and their bamboo supports and packages, or, ten times worse, buckets. Always at a rapid jog-trot, as being the pace most in conformity with the elastic bendings of the bamboo, always toiling with might and main—one of their few virtues—and always emitting horrible howls, more or less loud in proportion to the weight of their burdens. These groaning apostrophes apparently afford them infinite relief, but the annoying clamour they originate may be gathered from the fact that in most English concessions this coolie-groaning is strictly forbidden, though the enforcement of the prohibition can only be carried out with great difficulty.

These pigs—the in England highly prized, queer-snouted, aboriginal pigs of China—wander about the labyrinths, and are for ever getting in one's way, but they are less objectionable than the aboriginal human beings. They are here largely consumed, but no European would under any compulsion dream of touching a morsel of their foul-fed flesh. A piece of Chinese pork is a synonym for the acme of that which is horrible, and if a native official presents as a 'cumshaw' (complimentary gift) a loin of pork, it is instantly handed over to coolies. Mother-pigs too contribute to the Chinese dairy. Cows, and even goats, are unknown as farm-stock, and therefore milk does not exist as an article of diet, which in some measure may account for the sickness of the children.

Here is a peep-show. Think twice ere you look at it. The first two or three pictures will be singularly pastoral and innocent; the next two or three will be ingeniously and grotesquely obscene. Here again is a fortune-telling bird, an ordinary-looking little creature, cooped up in the narrowest of cages, implicitly believed in by the superstition and the credulity of sceptics to forecaste fate by picking out with its beak a particular card from amongst a pack spread before it.

Now we stumble across a queer description of procession. Everyone looks so extremely cheerful that I should have taken it for a wedding, were it not for the handsome, substantial, dark wooden coffin, not at all like the English conventional skull and crossbones pattern, in rear. Behind us is borne a paper image of a white cock, symbol of the creature into the body of which it is believed the soul of the deceased passes at the moment of dissolution. The *cortège* winds up with various sorts of provisions, a small baked pig being especially noticeable. These funeral feasts are carried out on a most rationally economical principle. The ghosts of the departed, it is argued, can feast only on the spiritual essences of the food, and therefore, after it has done duty in dumb show at the grave, it is devoured with a great deal of relish by the mourners. Mourners indeed! I have seldom seen a more grinning, jovial, talkative lot; not a vestige of a tear or a sigh from the nearest relations close to the corpse. A Chinaman laughs when he tells you of the death of a friend, even though he be dear to him. Nor can I think this was merely the concealment of real deep feelings, for I believe that a less affectionate race of creatures than the Chinese do not exist on the face of the earth.

Carefully on the look-out for the expression of the emotions, I have never yet seen a Chinese mother kiss her baby, or any interchange of caresses between any two individuals. I have never even witnessed a tear, a sigh, or a sob, except indeed on two occasions—at Hong Kong,[1] and near Foochow—where I came across a woman making a formal set lamentation over a hillside grave, with gestures, invocations, and discordant yelps, suggestive of the most perfunctory of performances. It is singular, moreover, that the Chinese nod

[1] See p. 14.

the head in token of affirmative, but that the negative shake is unknown amongst them.

Here comes a religious show; it is as well to get under a doorway while it passes, for it sweeps along the entire width of the alley, and, like many another religious show, is arrogant in claiming for itself exclusive rights of mummer deference and egotistical space. Tomtoms and cymbals, rabble and priests, precede it and follow it. In the centre is a grotesque idol, nearly shrouded in canopies, and bedizened with abundance of tawdry insignia. I have seen shows not unlike it, though less of a burlesque, in Roman Catholic countries. In rear of the procession are conveyed two little demon idols, with a distinct though carefully restricted amount of honour. The Chinese, in the midst of honour done to their gods, almost invariably pay a little simultaneous court to their devils, on the principle of making sure of both powers.

From this procession I turn by a natural transition to a joss-house, a general description of which I have given elsewhere,[1] but many possess special characteristics of their own. For example, one at Shanghai contained a greater multiplicity of inferior idols: I counted about thirty-six of them. Rather larger than human size, tawdry in decoration, of course of grotesque ugliness, and ranged along both sides of the temple. One idol was especially efficacious in answering the prayers of the sorrowful childless.

[1] See p. 202.

A repulsive-looking priest rushed up to me, and with many gesticulations set going a 'chin-chin' (worship), tomtoms banging, lights burning, and incense smouldering, finally violently claiming high payment for the display.

At another joss-house I was invited to pry into my futurity by the casting of lots. A vase full of rolled up spills, on each of which was marked a number, was put into my hand, and by a jerk of the wrist I shook a single one out. Its corresponding number was then sought out of some sacred ciphered sentences on separate slips, and from it I was supposed to be able to deduce my future good or evil fortune. I may remark that the Chinese have a philosophical principle that each one can absorb a certain limited amount of good fortune, and that any superfluity does harm. The only individuals who regarded the process with greater unconcealed contempt than myself were the joss-house functionaries themselves.

I suppose there are few countries in the world where there is a more elaborate and ostentatious machinery for upholding the action of the law, as certainly there are none where such action is distorted into the most barefaced iniquity and oppression. Maladministration and an absence of public probity are universal, the mandarins being chiefly occupied in raising money by outrageously nefarious means. The Yamen (native court-house) is a constant place of reference in all official transactions, whether with the

Chinese or with Europeans, and a Yamen next enlists my attention. On its outside archways are stone figures of fanciful monsters, or rudely executed pictures in flaring colours of savage beasts, dragons spitting flames, tigers with appalling fangs and claws, in grinning rage, and apparently intended to warn the population not to come within the grasp of the law.

As an instance of bullying being defeated by a swagger, which was justified by success, I may mention that in one Yamen at Foochow, I and my companions asked to see the interior of the court-house. 'No can, Mandarin [magistrate] not there.' We resume our progress through the streets, and in a few minutes are overtaken by breathless myrmidons of the law. 'Mandarin say he must savvy who you are —what your names—what you want here'—through an interpreter. 'You impudent fellows!' we angrily reply. 'How dare you speak to us in that way? Just go back and tell the mandarin to mind his own business, and not to send insolent messages to Englishmen.' Now the result quite excused the arrogant answer. Had we submitted ourselves to the authority, we might probably have been subjected to serious inconvenience, whereas, as a matter of fact, the emissaries shrank away cowed, and, though we lingered about the place for a considerable time, we were not subjected to any further annoyance.

To resume. In the vicinity of the Yamens were disposed several cages constructed of bamboo, with gaps between the poles. Each cage was full of prisoners, and each set of prisoners represented a sight distressing to humanity. The passing throng cast glances at them of feeble curiosity, but I could only marvel with painful interest at a scene so thoroughly typical of this strange, cruel, little-known people and of their backward civilisation, one of the features of which is a stolid inhumanity to man and beast, and a total indifference to sufferings however piteous. One day at Foochow the struggles of a drowning man absorbed the interest of a crowd, who nevertheless made not the slightest effort to rescue him. A bystander, unable to obtain a clear view, expressed a doubt whether the man had really perished, whereupon the irritated mob immediately tossed the sceptic into the river with the remark, 'You had better go and look after him yourself.' He, too, perished. Their wanton torture of their domestic animals is a daily sight in the streets. To rescue human life even at a minimum amount of personal risk never enters their heads. Compassion is an unknown factor in their unamiable hearts, and how then should they display any pity for those on whom the law has laid its hands. Men and women, boys and girls, young and old, there they were huddled indiscriminately together; the entirely innocent—for there are always many such incarcerated, victims of mandarin extortion—with the indisputably guilty, unless nature has told a malignant falsehood respecting their scoundrelly physiognomies; a few are cheery, more look miserable, and still more stolid and indifferent. But all without exception, inured and acclimatised as they are, cannot fail to suffer dreadfully from the heat, the stifling atmosphere, and the swarms of musquitoes and other insects. In some cases their friends have come to supply them with food and drink, and are talking to them through the bars.

I look a little more closely and I see that a certain proportion of the captives are being subjected to the torture of the cangue, or heavy wooden collar —not, remember, as in our infliction at Shanghai on Chinese criminals, a mere advertisement of their offence and restriction of their freedom, but downright severe torture, bearing some resemblance similar in its nature to the rack, the boot, and the thumbscrew. The sufferers' hands are bound, the collar projects far outwards all around, the grievous weight is pressing heavily on their shoulder blades, and in course of time swelling of the bones and festering ensues. With expressions of patiently borne yet extreme pain the miserable creatures seek for a little alleviation by jamming the edges of the cangue against the sides of their prison, and in this attitude they stand for hours, tortured with ever-increasing bodily anguish, with fever, weariness, and thirst. My thoughts travel back to the middle ages at the sight of these terrible cages, with their animal-like captives, who are treated with much less humanity than civilised nations would treat trapped vermin.

Of course a few cash induce the nondescript ruffian-looking prison officials to answer all my inquiries, and to show me over some of the precincts. These triangular wooden frameworks, like our rough paling round single trees, are strangling machines, and are in frequent requisition. The prisoner's neck is screwed up within so that his toes can just touch the ground. Very slowly he chokes, and becomes insensible. Then he is cast loose and revived; then choked again; and so backwards and forwards until, at the discretion of the head functionary, his life is finally extinguished. 'To-day is an unfortunate day,' says my guide. 'No executions happen to be on hand, but if you will come two or three days hence you may see plenty. Meanwhile I can show you several murderers awaiting their turn for disposal,' and before I can realise what I am to behold, I am ushered into a separate prison yard. In an instant ten or twelve frenzied-looking creatures shuffle up to me, some men, some women. Forbidden to wear pigtails, their long black hair is flying in Medusa-locks about their heads; the heavy fetters of remote tradition clank on their arms and legs; wild, ragged, maniacal-looking, they address themselves to me with furious gesture and raging speech. I can only suppose they have become distraught with suffering and terror. They are every one of them atrocious murderers, and every one of them qualified for the next batch of executions, though the actual date of the punishment of each is rendered cruelly uncertain. What do they want of me? Oh, money to buy food and opium. Well, there are thirty cash ($1\frac{1}{4}d$.) for you, dreadful woman, who poisoned your grown-up daughter, and one hundred and twenty (about $5d$.) for you, comparatively light offender, who murdered your friend. The recipients are quite satisfied.

While on the subject of murderers I will retail the account given me by an English resident at Pekin of a scene of execution which he witnessed. A criminal, tightly bound and in a miserable condition through ill-treatment and terror, was dragged to the place of public execution and brought before the presiding mandarin. Knocked over, prostrate, his captors banged his head against the ground, in imitation of the habitual voluntary gesture of obedience. Now it is a fundamental principle of Chinese jurisprudence that a prisoner before he can be executed must not only make a public confession and written acknowledgment of his guilt, but must entreat that capital punishment may be inflicted on him. Should he prove unaccommodating in the matter of this formality, he is taken back to prison and subjected to a little further torture and ill-treatment, until at last he will recognise that death is the least of the two evils. In this instance the prisoner was perfectly amenable. 'Yeow'—or some similar word signifying 'Pray do!' shouts the executioner in his ear suggestively. 'Yeow,' howls the wretch. 'Ah, hearken, people,' says the mandarin. 'He acknowledges his crime, and begs to be allowed to expiate it. Go on, executioner.' Whereupon that functionary, with a grotesque affectation of scrupulous precaution against the substitution of a scapegoat, with a piece of red chalk ruddles a line down the prisoner's neck, who is then dragged back a short distance. An assistant seizing his pigtail drags it until the neck is in a state of tension, the sword descends, and decapitation is easily and neatly effected. The bleeding remains are then dragged up to the mandarin's chair, and head and trunk are placed in juxtaposition, so that the ruddled marks may correspond, in fact just as we test the accuracy of a cheque by the counterfoil. The total number of criminals paraded was twenty, but of these only fifteen were executed. A certain number are habitually reprieved just as the sword is about to descend, sent back to prison for about a year, and then brought out again. So that the miserable prisoner is kept in all the horrors of uncertainty until the blade is raised. But if reprieved three times his life is finally spared.

There are three degrees of capital punishment: 'To be cut into one thousand pieces'—the most severe sentence reserved for the crime of parricide or matricide, and I have no particular quarrel with its being regarded in this country of ancestral worship as the most horrible wickedness which it is possible to commit. The criminal is stabbed and slashed in non-vital parts for such a length of time as may seem fit to the presiding mandarin ere he receives his *coup de grâce*. Next comes simple decapitation; and last of all strangulation, which is held in higher favour than the other two methods, inasmuch as the criminals are then sure that in the next world there is no prospect of the wrong head being fitted on to the body.

Well, we have had enough of this native prison, with its spectacles of misery and bodily torture; but, though we may hasten from the precincts of the enclosures, I cannot, as a faithful narrator, so far as lies in my power, of native city sights and characteristics, let you off from the consideration of one of the most prominent features of Chinese life—the never-ceasing action and tyrannical meddling of the civil power. Here comes a mandarin's procession, swaggering along, before which the quaking natives give way in shrinking submission. All authorities in China are surrounded by satellites, such as bodyguards and police agents. The mandarin we now meet is preceded by two lictors, with rods, in black caps, and two executioners in red caps. Next walks his aide-de-camp, his head protected from the sun by an enormous gay umbrella, carried by two men; then the great man himself in a handsomely decorated, closed sedan-chair, borne by six coolies. After all, the terror with which they are regarded is perfectly reasonable, considering the enormous extent of their power of life or death.

A short time ago the countless mobs of the poorest classes in Hankow showed signs of getting a little out of hand, of becoming somewhat disorderly, and the Taotai considered that a little mild but practical admonition would be salutary to the mass. Accordingly his underling executives gathered up, more or less haphazard, sixty low class inhabitants, chopped off their heads, and affixed them over sixty gateways. Why the precise number of sixty heads? Because there were precisely sixty gateways which required this decoration. These ghastly grinning headpieces retained their position for so long that the sight and effluvium became unendurable even to the Europeans in the settlement, and the Taotai at last consented to their removal. To gratify my wish, to confirm this undoubted statement, my guide searches for 'one, two piecey head,' if by chance I may thereby still obtain ' good look-see.' No, they have all been removed.

Semi-officially perpetrated horrors are, indeed, of incessant occurrence in these remote cities, for which the head mandarins have always ready some excuse equally plausible and hypocritical. Quite recently a man was publicly strangled, with prolonged tortures, in one of the above described wooden frameworks. Said the British Consul remonstratingly: 'It is no part of my business to take exception to the capital punishment. But why did you not carry it out in a manner less revolting to humanity and civilisation?' 'Oh,' replied, in substance, the Taotai, 'you are under a misconception; we were without the necessary authority from Pekin, and we had no intention of inflicting death at all. We merely put him in the strangling machine to punish him a little, and while there he happened to die.'

Again, a short time previously, Dr. Begg, the skilled English official doctor, a most trustworthy and enlightened source of information, witnessed, he told me, a large crowd gathered round a flaming pile. He ascertained that a Buddhist nun was being burned to death. His allegation of a fact, which really virtually occurred then and there before his eyes, was pooh-poohed and hushed up. But how can we doubt its actual occurrence?

Will you next accompany me, reader, in my visit to some 'guilds,' as the Europeans designate certain traditionally celebrated institutions of all important Chinese cities? The two selected for inspection were the Shangsi and Tchangsi corporations, perhaps the most celebrated in the Chinese Empire. The buildings alone cost over 75,000*l.* each, an enormous sum when the abundance of costly material at hand, and the nominal price even of skilled labour, are considered. They have been completed within the last five years, and permission to view them was only obtained after preconcerted arrangements with the mandarins. These guilds, which greatly resembled one another, strongly illustrated the absence of combination in Chinese architecture, as in every Chinese undertaking. For example, we were shown over a series of halls until we lost entire count of their numbers, each individually a wonder of beauty and magnificence, and yet bearing not the slightest relation to its neighbour as regards builder's plans, purposes for which designed, or style of decoration. Elaborate galleries could only be reached by pigeon-house ladders, magnificent halls through coal-hole-like staircases. However, this haycock of wealth, and, in a vitiated sense, of beauty and art, when examined in detail was of extreme interest, and probably constitutes objects without any sort of parallel throughout the world.

Their banqueting halls were enormous in area. The centre space was unroofed, as is quite permissible in such a climate, and thereby greatly added to the sense of vastness. A fountain played in the centre, and around the sides the space was arranged in wide covered archways. Here again is evinced the absence of co-operation. The hall contains no central table whereat, according to Western notions, a president may exhibit his pompous disposition, and the members bore one another with orations which are but self-glorifications in ambush. Instead, innumerable small tables to accommodate six or eight are scattered about, and here the company unstring their tongues in the ceaseless talk so dear to a Chinaman, because as no one requires an audience, each man is at liberty to speak simultaneously. At one end stands the inevitable stage, destitute of scenery, but an endless amount of wonderful, intricate carving, which is carefully protected by wire gauze, about the flies and margins of raised platforms. There is throughout a considerable amount of decoration on a large scale in the way of arches, pillars, and gateways, and on a small scale in gilding and minute carving. But the all-pervading impression of dirt and dust mars the general effect terribly.

Now I crawl up many a flight of ladder steps to the galleries, and in an instant I am struck dumb with astonishment, and—rare sensation in China— with admiration. Assuming that one acre measures about seventy yards each way, several acres of guild roofing and ceiling are exposed to my view, and every square inch inside and out is covered with porcelain ware of surpassing brilliancy, delicacy, and beauty. Imagine the treasures of a dozen Mortlocks in the shape of the most valuable breakfast, dinner, and dessert services spread out before you most neatly and artistically affixed to the roofs of Regent Street in a bright July sun. There is not a scrap of coarse work; the yellows, the purples, the blues, and the reds are of the most delicately blended colours, and these superb, elliptically shaped tiles slope gently up to the topmost ridges where at home we should look for chimney-pots, and wind down to the eaves where we should expect gutters, finishing off with twists which are rather Chinese-ish and pagoda-ish, but which certainly cannot be called out of place. Really a few dozen of these tiles turned into a dessert service would constitute a magnificent wedding present. And the final finish to this splendour of decoration is given by some beautiful dark-wooden fretwork lining the porcelain inside and out.

Next I go over several joss temples. Will you come too? No—better not. I have already spoken so much about them, and have still so much more to say concerning certain remote and unknown shrines, that repetition will place me in additional imminent danger of being cast aside as an intolerable bore. I will only mention that they deviate in no respect from the usual type of every combination of Roman Catholic magnificence and meaninglessness, of subdued light and stifling incense, of the richest tawdriness and the most repulsive priests, plus some monstrous figures of Buddha, his wives, and several small devils.

But if you will accompany me to one of several halls of audience or ceremonies, we can survey that which is scarcely less wonderful and beautiful than the porcelain roofs, and which is most favourably illustrative of painstaking industry and undeveloped wealth of this strange country. The roof of the large hall, lofty and heavy with sombre arches like a typical baronial hall, is supported not only by immense dark-wooden cross-beams, but by the most stupendous pillars of the same material—in aspect it resembled walnut—which it has ever been my fortune to behold. Of these pillars, eight or ten in number, each is composed of a single trunk which cost 1,000*l*. Beautifully varnished or lacquered over, they glow in various shades of the richest dark mahogany. A collection of seats, compromises between thrones and arm-chairs, are canopied and shrouded by innumerable folds of lovely silk drapery, the original texture of which is half concealed by a marvel of gold embroidery. Walnut-wood carvings are ranged on every available space, and is strikingly relieved by gilding of that gold, not brassy, look which only China can produce.

The ugliest objects in the hall are innumerable carved and gilt dragons, with protruding goggle eyes, indicating ubiquitous vision, and five appalling claws, tokens which represent the Imperial crest, in contradistinction to the four clawed dragon, and as such are supposed to confer extreme honour on the guild. Around the walls are ranged twenty or thirty gigantic gilded implements which are the insignia of the guild, and are carried in procession on State occasions, such as enormous spears, axes, swords, halberds, and, most strange of all, a long pole surmounted by a huge hand holding a pen in the attitude of writing.

Perhaps those who in England vex our souls with swaggering or with selfishly mysterious scrawls—

selfish because to decipher them necessitates an unpardonable amount of trouble—might condescend to learn a lesson from the value which the Chinese attach to caligraphy. Numerous carefully preserved manuscripts, some of them two hundred or three hundred years old, are disposed all over the walls, prized not by reason of the purport of what is written, but solely as specimens of perfect handwriting.

Altogether the general aspect of these audience halls strikes me as imposing and handsome, the sole occasion when to my mind aught that I witnessed in China merited these epithets; and, moreover, there is an air of Eastern golden magnificence and solemnity about them which reminds me incessantly of the descriptions of the old temple in Jerusalem. To carry out the parallel, this courtyard might be the outer precincts; immense ironwork railings, heavily gilded and stretching half-way towards the roof, separate it from yon outside court of the Gentiles, the illusion being further heightened by a few grotesque, squalid-looking figures who bask in the sun, and watch with never-ending curiosity the progress of us, the strange-looking visitors.

Those who performed the part of cicerones are gratified beyond measure at our wonder and admiration. 'Come,' say they, hurrying us away eagerly, 'we show you what belong to number one good look-see,' is their pidgin expressed promise. What an anti-climax! We are conducted to a Chinese garden, the acme of all that is finicking, trumpery, and ridiculous.

The miniature trees, however, are wonderful. Oaks, chestnuts, pines, peach, orange, and cedars growing in flower plots, some of them sixty, some of them thirty years old, but not one of them thirty inches high. To effect this, the tap-root of the seedling is in the first instance cut off. Subsequently the suckers are constantly removed, the young shoots pinched back, and the soil continually stirred. The leaves of these dwarfs become by degrees smaller, and their trunks and branches ridiculously gnarled like miniature patriarchs of the forest.

I can only liken their gardens to the little plots of ground appertaining to some of the earliest built Wandsworth villas. It is a duplicate of the scene represented on the domestic willow pattern plates. There is a miniature puddle into which trickles a miniature gutter; there are some miniature goldfish, there a miniature arch-bridge and temple, miniature trees artificially stunted, pathways wriggling about like worms all over the poky cramped area, and miniature rock-work. Every inch is economised, but the whole is childish beyond description. I need scarcely say that even on the assumption that one trace of prettiness could have been discernible, it would have been entirely marred by the inevitable accompaniment of a heap of extreme nastiness in a corner, and the normal overpowering stench.

Our Mandarin entertainer winds up his civilities

with a repast wherein he has evidently flattered himself he has combined the luxuries of China with the coarse tastes of Europeans. Champagne, introduced with much circumstance, like tepid gooseberry; the new season's tea in China cups, each of which contains a pinch of the sweet-smelling leaves, sugarless, milkless, pale, and oh! so good; melon seeds like little chips of wood; raw water-chestnuts like elder-pith steeped in sugar; Chinese pears, yellow and russet like the finest jargonels, but dig your teeth in one and you will find it inferior to an inferior swede; cigars, always good out here; and, to finish up, five or six very stale sweet biscuits out of a genuine Reading Huntley and Palmer's box. My eyes are riveted during the meal on my host's astonishing finger nails; nails! they are talons, projecting literally about three-quarters of an inch from the quick. He is elaborately careful in displaying these beauties of which the Chinese are very proud, as they consider them characteristics of high rank and of exalted avocations which have exempted them from manual work. We part with much ceremony, 'Chin-chin' we incessantly reciprocate, and press together the palms of the hands, by way of intimating 'I have the honour to be, sir, your most obedient servant.' Do what I would a European bow or two on my part would slip in, but I fancy he attributed it to a sort of St. Vitus's dance, and replied in Chinese according to the usual form: 'Do not walk fast,' to which the proper response would have been to the effect, 'Pray sit down and take your rest.' Handshaking is here unknown.

But ere I quitted these famed guilds, I crawl up to one of the loftiest of its pinnacles, from whence I obtain a complete bird's-eye view of the conjoint cities of Hankow, Hanyan, and Wuchau, and then I realised into how very small an area a vast Chinese population is crammed. The entire expanse is a vast sheet of the curved, traditional Chinese roofs, more dismally black except where porcelain tiles intervene, through exposure to the weather than the dingiest purlieus of Westminster; perfectly level because all the houses are of the same height, unbroken by chimneys, and unmarked by those columns of smoke and factory towers without which, or some such conspicuous marks, it is almost impossible to estimate the area of a town. Besides I cannot discover a single opening, I cannot even trace a single street. Ah! yes, those almost illegible lines indicate the lengths of their narrow labyrinths, with their eight feet of breadth. They argue, 'If room to pass with bucket, what for use of largee road which take up ground?' and in a purely utilitarian point of view their reasoning is tenable, for throughout my entire experience of Chinese cities, and indeed country districts, I have never encountered a single wheeled vehicle of any sort or description, except occasionally a kind of wheelbarrow.

Perhaps the reader will now understand why the extent of population is so uncertain a factor. That it is enormous in comparison with the number of and area occupied by dwellings is self-evident. But in the absence of a properly organised census this mere huddling together presents an insuperable obstacle to even an approximately accurate calculation. A fire, one would suppose, would be as instantaneously and wholesale destructive as a lump of smoking sulphur thrown into a wasp's nest. Well, a conflagration here is a terrible calamity; but, on the other hand, the sketchy construction of the houses renders their demolition, and consequently the interposition of a vacant space between the flames, a rapid process; and see, the masses of wooden houses are intersected at wide intervals by lines of fire-proof brick walls, which limit the effects of destruction.

We pass an immense number of opium shops; let us go into some of them, and witness for ourselves the alleged terrible effects of opium smoking, apparently habitually admitted without question as an incontrovertible fact. There is the long, dark, low opium room, down which are arranged numerous divans of dirty, tawdry, scarlet drapery, on which are stretched the smokers. There are rows of opium pipes, lamps, and various apparatus, together with little jars of about the capacity of a good-sized ink bottle, containing the treacly-looking drug. The atmosphere is sickly and heavy, and perhaps one-third of the inmates are stretched in a condition of coma, one-third are smoking, and one-third are lounging vacuously about. Yes, I must own that the occupants are, as a whole, in a miserable condition of stupefaction, and present the aspect of emaciated but perfectly quiet, sluggish drunkards. The silence and stupor are painful, and are only broken by the rare sound of a child's squalling, who is reduced to silent terror by the threat of being given to that foreign devil, which is equivalent to any English menaces of old bogey.

Now on many occasions I repeated my visits to the opium shops, and always with the same result. I found that these so-called dens by no means reveal any patent amount of evil, except the wasting of money, and as I investigated more and more the whole question of opium, I became more and more persuaded that the wholesale denunciation of our national wickedness, apparently ignoring the fact that an enormous amount of opium is grown in China itself, contains a good deal of catchpenny claptrap. It would not be listened to by any reasonably wise man for five minutes consecutively if the matter were argumentatively represented and fairly weighed, and if instead of the begging-the-question title-page, ' our iniquitous traffic in opium,' were substituted ' British commerce and the exportation of papaver juice.'

To classify the abuse of opium with that of alcohol is clearly preposterous, inasmuch as the influence of opium does not in the smallest degree tend to mania and violence—indeed, its promptings are precisely in the contrary direction. The Chinaman detests beer, wine, and spirits; he will not get drunk, but consumes opium instead, and it has been estimated that one-fourth of the population are opium-smokers. Opium represents in fact that nature of stimulant which, however disguised, is used in some form by almost every nation in the world. That opium hinders conversion is absurd; but, say the missionaries who declaim, but cannot reason, in antagonism to wiser men who can reason, but for want of practice cannot declaim, 'Nothing shall persuade me but that to further the commerce of, and to profit by large revenues raised on, an article the use of which is attended with such appalling evils, must be a national crime.' No—'nothing will convince you,' if you start with that preface; do not let us waste thirty seconds in trying. It would be more hopeful to endeavour to persuade the total abstainers that to drink a spoonful of alcohol is not an evil equal to prostitution, or a High Church person that to wear peas in his boots and a hair cloth next his skin is not a transcendently pious action. But if it can be established that the use of opium is not an abuse *per se*; that indulgence in small quantities does not necessarily lead to excess; that moderation herein, like moderation in wine, is the rule, and excess the exception; that opium in small quantities like wine, which 'maketh glad the heart of man,' may be regarded as in many cases beneficial and in others as one of those enjoyments bountifully bestowed to increase our enjoyment in life—if this be established, is it necessary to add one single word in refutation of the alleged crime of opium commerce? And those who are best qualified to judge have answered thus to my inquiries :—

'Do you know many consumers of opium, and are the effects always evil?'

'I know an immense number of people who have consumed opium for twenty years without injury to their health. The practice is almost as common here as tobacco-smoking is in England. Vast numbers have practised it for years and without any ill effects whatever. Some, but a comparatively small minority, have become the slaves of it, and have declined rapidly in mind, body, and general prosperity.'

'Then I deduce that you consider temptation to excess is not so overpowering; that a single iota of enjoyment does not irresistibly lure a man to destruction?'

'Most emphatically not. The seductiveness is far less than that of alcohol, its results are far less fatal, and its dominion is far more easily broken through.'

'Does the practice meet with the condemnation that it is fraught with much general evil of the mass of the reasoning population?'

'By no means. If indulged in moderately it is held a harmless enjoyment, and deprivation would be like depriving the poor labouring man of his pipe in England.'

But I can adduce far better evidence than my own cursorily gathered information. Dr. Ayres, the eminent prison medical officer at Hong Kong, in consequence of the bigoted action taken by the local anti-opium league, felt compelled to set forth the results of his vast practical experience and carefully registered observations concerning the alleged evils of the use of opium. Briefly stated, they are that

1. Opium smoking neither emaciates the body nor enervates the mind if indulged in moderately. Of course a man may starve his stomach by it as by tobacco, if to indulge in the luxury he applies money which should be spent in the purchase of food.

2. Prisoners who are old and confirmed opium smokers when deprived of their opium suffer no greater inconvenience than is experienced by the deprivation of any luxury to which a man is habituated. Neither their weight or their health is affected by opium smoking being prescribed or withheld as a medical measure. On liberation from imprisonment its resumption is attended with no ill results.

3. The great proportion of opium is consumed in the form of smoking, and not in chewing or drinking. But when the two latter practices are resorted to, the evils are great and unmitigated, and can be vindicated by none of the arguments which apply to smoking.

May not this latter point be the solution of all

the contradictions and misapprehensions? May it not be that the opium eater, who is comparatively seldom met with, but who invariably offers a pitiable object of physical and mental decadence, is indiscriminately taken as a representative of the opium smoker, and that the sins of the vice of excess have been laid on the moderate gratification of an innocent indulgence. As for the opium tax, it rests on the same foundation as that on spirits. It renders dear an article which is harmless if used temperately, but injurious if indulged in to excess.

I was once present at the receipt and examining by a mercantile firm of a large and valuable consignment of opium. The precious treasure was carefully packed in ordinary casks. The hard earthy-looking balls, almost in the condition in which they had been scraped from the poppies in Persia, were of the size and weight of a cricket ball; cut open they presented a laudanum look and smell, and needed but little melting and purifying to transform them into the thick glutinous mass ready for immediate use.

I induced a wealthy Compradore—Chinese agent of an English mercantile establishment—to invite me to his house that I might experience to some small extent the sensations of an opium smoker's gratification. There was the still, cool, quiet room with its subdued light, its handsome scarlet luxurious divan, and its necessary apparatus of pipes, lamps, and implements, and there were the cups of tea. By direction of my host I stretch myself at full length and place the amber mouthpiece in my mouth, while he manipulates the appliances. A lump about the size of a pea of the semi-viscous opium is drawn out with a small silver sort of skewer; the substance is for a few seconds frizzed in the lamp, then placed in a hollow in the pipe stem, rather than in a bowl, then frizzed again with the red-hot point of the skewer, and I am told to inhale. About four whiffs of rather sickly, sleepy, but pleasant smoke are the result, when the small spluttering pea goes out, and the fidgeting with more opium is resumed. 'Well,' said I at last, tired of the apparent preliminaries, 'but when is the real smoking going to begin?' 'Begin, why you are hard at it.' And after a few more inhalations, which produce rather giddy, Dover and Calais sensations, I arrive at the conclusion that to derive the slightest gratification from opium smoking, a long apprenticeship is indispensable.

But we have now been toiling through Hankow from eleven till two, on foot the whole time, for though a sedan-chair is possible, it is not under the circumstances pleasant, through miles of alleys in the closest contact with everything which to a European is odious. I may fairly urge that I have had enough of it. So passing through a waterside population living in the most fragile of rush pens, called 'mat-houses,' such as might be suitable cover in England for a few chickens, I make my way to the river's edge, and quickly jumping into a sampan I escaped from the curiosity crowd following me in numbers at this moment, as I counted, exactly forty.

The river Yang-tsze Kiang is at this point about a mile broad, and crowded with every description of boat, from mandarin junks to the ordinary sampan, as densely as the city streets of London at three o'clock in the afternoon. But our boatmen thread their rapid way with the most remarkable dexterity, cutting in and out with the nice calculation of a London coachman, and at the very last moment avoiding even a graze where a violent collision seemed inevitable.

My flagging interest is once more roused by this remarkable water highway. There is a junk laden to its gunwales with copper cash, and yet the amount estimated does not in value exceed 5*l*., or about 29,000 coins. Money in this instance scarcely seems to fulfil its function of being a convenient means of exchange. There are a large number of war junks armed with a single swivel gun, probably a S.B. 6-pounder, altogether beneath contempt for warfare against civilised nations, but possibly serviceable in keeping down those pestilential vermin of Chinese waters, the murderous creek pirates. There is a Chinese gunboat, built under European direction, and in general bearing all the dignified aspect of a perfect capacity for the give and take of the hard blows of work and war. But at this moment she is employed in some pompous ceremonial connected with the conveyance of city magnates. Ridiculous flags, with burlesque sprawling five-clawed dragons, are fluttering from every yardarm; bright canopies on deck are extended over figures which look inappropriate out of a pantomime; tomtoms and cymbals bang and crash, and the stern vessel of war is transformed into a burlesque of a Lord Mayor's barge. Those miles of hulks, those forests of junk masts, I know not whether to calculate them by thousands or by the hundred thousand, they represent the greater part of the trade of midland China with England, and therefore with the world. Without this foreign export trade Hankow and its hundreds of thousands of population would be decimated by famine, for nearly all the city revenues and industries are derived from it or supported by customs dues.

Here, too, are the wonderful . . . No, I will tell you nothing more as yet about the river life because I wish to narrate it to you under the still more interesting form which I witnessed at Foochow, and because, according to the practice of a judicious visitor, I would wish to say 'Good-bye' when you would desire that I should yet linger a few minutes. And yet I must add a postscript.

My departure from Hankow was marked by an incident which will illustrate better than many pages of writing the anomalies of the Chinese character. One evening, on April 10, at about 9.30, when pacing the deck of the steamer which was to convey me back to Shanghai, I was amazed by the sudden simultaneous sound of tomtoming all over the city, rising every moment and increasing in violence to such an extent as to render it evident that some momentous event was occurring. I scan the horizon in vain for a fire; the only light is that of the soft moonbeams, unusually bright this evening. But there is rather a queer aspect about the moon itself, the upper limb is disappearing. Here is a clue to the sudden commotion—an eclipse of the moon, always regarded by the Chinese with awe and terror. They had sufficient wit to forecast the event to within a few minutes of accuracy, but not sufficient wisdom to divest themselves of an idiotic superstition at a phenomenon which they could both prophesy and explain. No; for ages they have decided that an eclipse of the moon is caused by an attempt of the dragon, or devil, to devour that luminary, and that it is necessary to frighten him away from his repast.

A further portion of the limb disappears. The uproar of the tomtoms and the crashing of the most inharmonious cymbals increase until it might be imagined that every tin kettle in the place had been called into requisition, and at the same time fussy moving lights appear in the usually dark town in every direction, betokening universal agitation. Remember this is not carried on in a few slums merely, but throughout the entire city, with its stupendously large population. And when an occasional deep-toned bell, tocsin-like, mingles with the hubbub, I think that now surely the disturbance has reached its acme. No; part of the moon is still disappearing; the devil is still devouring her. The most desperate measures must be adopted, at all costs he must be driven off, and from the Chinese forts bang, bang, thunder at constant intervals their heavy seven-inch guns with appalling effect, with startling reverberations over the muddy waters of the broad Yang-tsze Kiang. The moon is no longer diminishing, the devil has been arrested in his meal. Bang, bang; the moon is recovering her shape, she is once more perfect; the devil has been frightened away. Sudden cessation of guns, tomtoms, and cymbals; the lights are extinguished, the city sinks into profound repose, and their fears for the existence of the moon are lulled to rest until the occasion of the next eclipse, when the whole folly will inevitably be repeated.

CHAPTER VI.

CHINESE RIVER AND TOWN LIFE.—FOOCHOW.

AFTER having travelled many hundreds of miles through China, I have come to the conclusion that as regards its city and country districts, its population and its products, it is a source of immeasurable interest and amazement, though accompanied with little admiration and much disgust. 'Is there not a charming aspect or a beautiful view throughout this enormous empire?' 'Yes,' I am told, 'unsurpassed, at Foochow.' So I embark at Shanghai in the 'Hae-Shin,' 750 tons burden, belonging to the ex-'China Merchants Company.' The captain, Petersen, is a Dane, there are four or five English ship officers, as many English passengers, a crew of about eight Chinese, and, as usual, an indefinite number of Chinese passengers.

The reality of how completely the mere handful of Europeans is at the absolute mercy of the overwhelming numbers of the Chinese is brought home by the sight of rifles, eighteen in number, for which abundant ammunition is handy, and bayonets ostentatiously ranged under our very noses around our saloon. The precaution is most salutary. The slight moral force which keeps the rabble in order is most remarkable, and usually perfectly efficacious, but it may snap—occasions have arisen when it has snapped—and weapons in the hands of even a handful of Europeans may then with prompt, resolute action suffice to stifle the further progress of easy butchery and piracy.

Really these coasting steamers, so far from furnishing a traditional example of dirt and discomfort, are models of luxury and liberality. Perfect cookery, first-rate wines and cigars, the utmost civility—the Peninsular and Oriental Steam Navigation Company may borrow many a hint from them. For twenty-four hours we plough through the muddy outpour of the Yang-tsze Kiang, the volume of whose waters is so considerable as to tinge even the ocean for many miles. Then gradually we merge into the bluest, clearest water of the China Sea, which is almost without a ripple at this time of the year; the sun is bright, the temperature only just not too hot, the scenery of the rocky coast and rugged volcanic islands between Shanghai and Foochow is becoming more beautiful each mile; to watch the aspect, the doings, and the chatterings of our Chinese cargo is a source of never ending amusement, and the voyage really proves lazily enjoyable. Now we enter the river Min, the mouth of which is guarded by two Chinese gunboats of European construction and armament, and designated 'alphabetical' gunboats in distinction from the trumpery native junks armed with a single swivel small smooth-bore gun. They are in close proximity to several pasteboard-looking, childishly constructed forts, traced on the supposition that the enemy will attack on the strongest side, and will not attempt any flank movement; their armament is manifestly very weak, they possess no flanking defence, they are painted white, probably to afford a better mark to the enemy's guns, and are decorated with a mass of flags.[1]

Between the forts and the alphabetical gunboats are little groups of gaily bedizened junks, whereon are gathered crowds of ragged soldiers, ready, although there is not a vestige of hostilities, to convey garrisons at a moment's notice to defences which are only separated from each other by a few hundred yards. Can puerility possibly go further?

Now we are steaming up the beautiful Min, and I am reminded of the scenery of the Italian lakes in the vicinity of Ancona, especially from the feature of the carefully cultivated terraces which descend in endless steps almost from the summits of the mountains to the water's edge. Look at yon Chinese hamlet nestling in an adjacent hollow, its low uniformly level, chimneyless, smokeless, streetless mass of buildings is crowded into a small area; it is much

[1] Written just before the French attack of 1884.

too tiny to be marked on any map. But look again more carefully into details; count the houses in one small slice only, estimate therefrom the total population. You will find it amounts to several thousands, and in England would probably send a representative to Parliament. Here it is quite beneath notice, in exemplification of the deceptive and overwhelming numbers of the Chinese population.

Pagoda Anchorage, formerly a roadstead for a large fleet of sailing merchantmen of all nations, is now being rapidly silted up, and is little more than a rendezvous for a few coasting vessels. It takes its name from the adjacent pagoda-topped hills, at the base of which is a large China town and an arsenal, which turns out a considerable number of smoothbore small-arms and guns of about the same relative value as the mangonels, petards, and arquebuses of the time of Queen Elizabeth. We are transhipped to a small launch, cross the bar of the three-quarters of a mile broad tributary river Yuen Fuh, and steam towards the capital city Foochow, with its acres of shipping, its forests of masts, its square miles of buildings, and its 750,000 of population, but which shares the habitual comparative obscurity of similar Chinese towns. There are so many of them, they are so remote, and really to Europeans they are scarcely known even by name, unless rendered prominent by historical circumstances.

Arrived at the wharf opposite the handsome,

prosperous-looking establishment and godowns of those English merchant-princes, Messrs. Jardine and Matheson, I am considerably baffled as to my next step. 'Why, put up at an hotel, of course.' Hotel, in the European sense of the word, does not exist in China. You perhaps might, though with difficulty, obtain, in what corresponds to our inn, the shelter of a roof, and of course food can always be purchased. But the associations and accessories would go far beyond the terms privation or hardship; they would involve contact with such disgusting horrors, that no European would willingly face them save for preservation of existence.

I have, however, a letter of introduction to the representative of Messrs. Jardine and Matheson, and I put to the strongest test the traditional hospitality of China merchants of which I had already heard, and indeed personally experienced so much. What! an utter stranger, with a reasonable amount of baggage, with an attendant, swagger into an equally utter stranger's house, summon the head servant, and finding the master absent, state your intention to reside there some days; desire a room, or rather suite of rooms, to be prepared, take possession of them, order tea, and direct that the master be informed on his return that you would appear at the dinner-hour at eight o'clock! Why in England the head of the house would very naturally be dumb with astonishment, and white with rage. Ah, but then in England circumstances do not foster Anglo-Chinese hospitality until it becomes a true virtue which welcomes a stranger with eager kindness; which makes the host honestly solicitous to retain his guest as long as possible, cater for his amusement, and regret his departure; and for all this he is more than repaid—of course assuming that he is a first-class good fellow, and that the guest be not a first-class beast—by temporary association with a fellow representative of the old country, who with him will compare recollections of the general race here known as the ' old folks at home.'

So when, at the dinner-hour, I presented myself in the drawing-room, furnished with all English taste and every English comfort, having arrived by this time at a proper self-consciousness of the insolence with which I had taken my host *nolens volens* by storm, he barely and deprecatingly glanced at my few lines of introduction for the purpose of ascertaining my name, and then made me as welcome as the flowers in May. Indeed, but for his unwearied efforts to interest me during my residence at Foochow, I should have gathered but little there about which the reader would care to be told.

Early the next morning I was aroused by sounds and sights which for novelty could be paralleled in no other part of the universe. Immediately outside my window flowed the Yuen Fuh river of pea soup muddiness, which I have come to the conclusion is the normal condition of most Chinese rivers, about a mile broad, shallow, oily, and apparently almost boiling under the fierce glare of the sun. Over its area are packed, as thickly as herrings in a barrel, ships of every size and sort, from the little British gunboat the 'Foxhound,' with its English ensign, dear familiar token of our country's empire even in these antipodes, to the unwieldy, grotesque junks and the toy sampans, inhabited by a race which philanthropy only can call human. What a snapping of crackers and what a banging of tomtoms far and near. It is the 'chin-chin,' that fetish which stupid superstition designates worship on board ships which have just come in, or are on the point of weighing anchor, in praise of propitious deities, or to deprecate the spite of malignant powers who in this country certainly receive a very large share of adulation.

Loud as is this din, that of human voices rises still higher; the struggling, sweltering, naked coolies are not merely shouting, they are yelling, screaming in incessant chorus, as though subjected to incessant torments. Oh, let us quickly hurry through breakfast, and examine more in detail and in closer proximity that which will amaze everyone who is not a fool. Every sort of cargo, from opium to birds' nests and melon seeds, is being shipped or discharged. Let us step on board some of those sampans. Each is about the capacity of an average-sized Thames punt, but as light and flimsy as papier maché, and is covered with a gipsy-shaped awning, beneath which an entire family, consisting of, say, father, mother, and three children, cooks, eats, sleeps, and has its being; I will not say dresses, because they wear no clothes worth mention, and I have an opportunity of observing that the funny little stomachs of the child imps are swollen to amazing protuberance. And then, oh wonder of wonders, the sampan is as clean and tidy as a new fourpenny bit—the only clean Chinese object I have seen in China. Sometimes, it is true, this virtue is rather marred by the presence of a pig on board, but he is a small, quiet, tidy, dog-like pig, and is unobtrusive, as though ashamed of his own existence. Quack! Why here is a duck tied up in the corner, so sleek and fat. Some day he will furnish a feast for the entire family in this little flesh-eating community.

Look at the bright hothouse plants ranged around the extreme edge of the sampan, they alone give an aspect of prettiness to the craft, each of which is thus decorated. And the mother sits, busy with some feminine nothingness, on boards so clean that you might eat dinner off them. Every vestige of bedding, cooking, and household apparatus is stowed neatly away in a hollow in the bows. The women's pillows are curious wooden blocks, rivalling in comfort, it may be supposed, the stones or sword-hilt which is recommended in the 'Soldier's Pocket-book.' But the Chinese female's pillow merely acts as a support to the small of the neck. She dares not rest her head on it lest she should thereby disarrange that tower of starched hair which she has spent hours in erecting, and which she contrives to keep unrumpled for many days.

The children of tender age skip about as securely as though in a large nursery. They shriek with childhood's terror of Old Bogey when I try to coax one of these hideous little baboons to sit upon my knee. Surely, with all the care in the world, they must sometimes topple over, or be jerked into the water? Ah, I see, you have provided for that contingency by fastening round the child's waist a long, light cord, to which a float is attached, and which, bobbing about as though a huge salmon were at the end, enables you to lug out the little amphibious animal. But only one float is provided? To be sure. There is but one boy. The others are girls. Let them drown and welcome.

Here I must explain that the importance of male offspring can scarcely be expressed in words. Childless Chinese will adopt a nephew, or buy or even kidnap a boy, notwithstanding that capital punishment is inflicted for the theft of a male child. It is the duty of the adopted son to perform funeral ceremonies at his father's tomb. This fetish, and the mysterious honour shed on the possession of boys, rather than pure parental affection, causes the utmost anguish at an illness threatening life; and should the son be at the point of death, it is customary for the mother to go outside the house and entreatingly to cry aloud its name several times, hoping to bring back its wandering spirit. All this honour and consideration is not conceded to girls. Their existence is considered an expensive nuisance; infanticide, though theoretically criminal, is universal, the victims being scragged at the instant of birth, and without any concealment tossed into the nearest hole. A large convenient ditch just outside Foochow was so incessantly used for the purpose that it was found necessary to post up a notice, 'Female infants may not be thrown' here.'

I hire one of these sampans in search of snipe, which swarm here. The man acts as *chasseur*, the woman rows, and the four-year-old imp boy is in a frenzy of excitement, crouching at the sight of wild fowl, gesticulating and shouting with delight when his quick little beads of eyes mark down game. Afterwards I explore a large, muddy, back river, running between a large, dense mass of houses. In my progress I make close acquaintance with what I have come to the conclusion are the most comical and the most interesting animate objects on the face of the earth: the ducks of China. Horses, dogs—pooh, they do not possess a tithe of the intelligence and sense of fun of these most ridiculous creatures. In flocks varying from fifty to one hundred, they are taken into the country under the care of boys, or even of men, for air and exercise, and to pick up their living, and there they behave like a gang of mischievous school children : at one time they march in long lines as evenly as soldiers across the cleared rice or corn fields, greedily gobbling up gleanings; a boy with a long bamboo rod 'dresses' them, and plenty of trouble do they give him. Now play fair, do not slip out of your ranks to seize hold of what does not fall to your share, but every now and then some cunning flankers or some headstrong young duckling makes a greedy dash aside to gobble up some irresistible morsel. The keeper swears, abuses him, and down comes the bamboo with smart smacks on their fat glossy backs. The duck screams out that he will 'never do so any more,' and bustles in his place again.

Here we come to a ford which is so crowded with sampans that young ducks must cross carefully lest they be run over. They collect in a heap, ready at a signal from their keepers to make a rush, like children passing from one side to the other in Regent Street. There is that tiresome duckling again, always giddy and behindhand. You are past bearing. The boy takes him up in his hand, gives him a good birching, and passes on him the sentence of being shut up supperless in chokee for the night. You may bet fifty to one that duck will be exceedingly crestfallen, and will take care not to be late again.

In steaming up the Yuen Fuh, our launch suddenly drives between two or three flocks gravely and compactly swimming across, with a man in a canoe paddling behind and indicating to them the required direction. They are terrified at the inroad, but instead of wildly flapping and scattering like English ducks, they set up a chorus of frightened quacks, and, huddling together, they crowd under the canoe of their master until the danger be over.

This back river becomes wider, shallower, and so thick that we seem to be floating on the top of ill-savouring treacle. At last we come to a regular block of traffic, and in common with dozens of junks and sampans are aground. Out jumps the man into the water and drags us, but, this proving insufficient, the woman tucks up her—shall we say trousers?—remarkably high, and follows suit. 'Really, you might have a little more natural modesty!' *Honi soit qui mal y pense.* It is purely a matter of custom. These Chinese women would hoot in disgust, my English young lady, at your low-necked dresses and bare arms. I must say this jostling crowd are perfect models of good temper; and here again I exhort that, whatever be the irritation or emergency, make a point of laughing and do not be irritable, and the mob will seldom be surly or abusive or spiteful. They, too, will grin, and be rather pleased at the pantomime-chaff of the foreign devil.

At last we extricate ourselves from our quagmire, and shoot into the middle of the swiftly running main river, which spins the crowds of light shipping about with the rapidity of a Niagara current. It is worth something to see the dexterity with which collisions are avoided, the violence of the current circumvented, and the goal of the opposite shore reached, though so far from at right angles to our starting point.

And now I begin to be aware that my informant's admiration of Foochow was fully justified. Close at hand we have the animation of a large river sweeping through a large town. Yet a little further off are the steep, green turf slopes, whereon are dotted the decent church which topped the neighbouring hill, kindly emblem of a kindly humanity unknown in this country, the club with its imposing Italian architecture, and the few European residences, some ten or twelve in number. How charming do these handsome edifices look, with their English gardens, flourishing in all the splendour of colour and luxuriance of tropical growth! Yet a further stretch and we view the fertility of a country, the natural productiveness of which is such that, if the ground be scratched a little and a handful of seed thrown on the top, in a few weeks a splendid crop will be ready for harvesting. Afar off are the 'distant hills,' alternately turfed, wooded, and rugged with rocks. Then over the whole is that bright blue canopy, without which even the best beauties of nature seem to be deprived of half their charm.

Perhaps Foochow more than any other city in China calls forth those qualities in moral superiority, resolution, and dogged laboriousness which alone can enable Englishmen to maintain their position in the face of the overwhelmingly swamping superiority of the natives in point of numbers and wealth. Here we have no concession, not even a distinct band to form a nucleus of action and influence of the tiny community—the European residences are scattered about the hills overlooking the city. We are comparatively fewer in number—about thirty-five in all—here than in most other settlements, though the aggregate of wealth at stake is inferior to none. Of course we have a consul, but our rights formally conceded or tacitly acquiesced in by the Chinese are unusually limited. Finally—and this is a point which can only be fully appreciated by those who have experienced tropical countries—the climate is more hot, stifling, enervating, and sickly than at Hankow, Kiukiang or Shanghai. Hence it is not surprising that intimacy is close, that hospitality is unsurpassed, and that even a casual stranger has opportunities of becoming acquainted in the shortest possible period with the ins and outs of the lives of the Anglo-Chinese merchants and their employés, with their points of excellence and with their shortcomings.

You may dine out as often as you please. Of course you meet the same guests over and over again. You will find them almost exclusively composed of men—clear-headed in action, and energetic both in business and pleasure. Their conversation is apt to drift unduly into trade and dollars, but they are liberality personified. Their gambling is considerable both in cards and racing, their immorality in many cases more than considerable, and it would be well if that homage which vice pays to virtue, sometimes falsely termed hypocrisy, were exercised to throw a cloak over their dealings with Chinese women which at home would cause the transgressors to be rigidly relegated to Coventry. Their houses are furnished with every luxury, comfort, and taste; that endless resource and amusement of Asiatic life, billiards, being represented by eleven tables in a community of about thirty-five Englishmen; wine and cooking quite perfect, coolies and servants preposterously numerous. A lively debating society, a club house, and racing association are maintained, the only drawback to which is the paucity of members. Yet, after all, there is a sufficiency of highly educated, conscientious, well-principled gentlemen in this miniature society to render the average standard of excellence high.

On several occasions at Foochow and elsewhere I have addressed to the English employés the following questions:—'I can perfectly understand your resolution to exile yourselves from England for a definite period, to wipe out of your existence a certain number of valuable years so far as the advantages of civilisation and the enjoyments of a public life are concerned, for the purpose of amassing such a fortune as may enable you to pass the rest of your days free from the cares of poverty. But this limit attained—and one would suppose that to gain it every self-denial would be cheerfully encountered—why do you not relinquish what must surely be a life of sacrifice, why do you not then return in content to England, and pick up the threads of friendship and interest which, for the time being, you have consented to drop? Instead of which I observe that a large proportion linger on to middle age, even to old age, in profuse expenditure of that which they have earned, as though they were content to live and die in China.'

The answer has invariably been the same: 'Nearly all of us come out with the project you have indicated, and nearly all fail to put it into execution. At first we put by money; but example, and the universal principle that only by the indulgence of certain luxuries and the participation in certain expensive amusements can life here be rendered endurable, gradually lead us into extravagance; dollars in China are scarcely more than equivalent to shillings in England, and our annual savings steadily diminish in amount. Then at the end of about five years we return home on leave, and our previously contracted habits, coupled with a resolution to enjoy our holiday, cause us to fling away our accumulations recklessly, and we resume our business in China precisely as poor as when we started, and so the story is repeated *da capo*, until we grow to acquiesce in a life-long residence. Besides the country is no longer a Golconda, and a young fellow must be exceedingly prosperous in his first start, self-denying in incessant economy, and fortunate in speculative investments, if at the end of fifteen years he have piled together 15,000*l*.'

A position in a flourishing merchant's house in China offers, indeed, an opening which many an industrious, steady young fellow might think himself fortunate in securing. Even the junior clerks receive a salary of about 300*l*. a year, plus an allowance in lieu of messing and lodging, or provision for the same in the 'hong,' which enables them to save and invest with high profit the greater part of their income; while if capable and laborious they are almost certain of rapid advancement. But the career must not be regarded as a last resource of a failure scapegrace, who has to be shipped out of England. Good antecedents are exacted, and the *mauvais sujet* spendthrift will not for one moment be countenanced. At the end of five years he is usually allowed a year's leave, with half income provided he return. But should the firm wish to get rid of him, advantage is taken of the conclusion of this recognised cycle of five years to intimate to him that he will do well to seek employment elsewhere.

During my stay at Foochow I obtained, not without difficulty, an invitation to a Chinese dinner party. Our hosts were four eminent Chinese merchants, and it was a clearly understood arrangement that the entertainment was to be in every respect exclusively national, and without the almost invariable alloy under such circumstances of the English element. At about 6.30 P.M. our party of four Englishmen proceeded in four sedan-chairs, borne by coolies, through many a maze of alley to the Foochow 'Philippe's,' or 'Trois Frères,' at the doorway of which we were received with a great deal of ceremonious politeness by our entertainers, whose evening costume varied almost imperceptibly from their habitual morning dress. Indeed throughout China the clothing of the highest and lowest classes differs apparently in little but in fineness of texture.

We were at once ushered into a good-sized dining-room, handsomely furnished, according to Chinese custom, with much heavy grotesque carving, with gilding and silk hangings, the close, heavy atmosphere and the subdued light imparting a sense of oppression. In one part of the room was an elaborately spread round dinner table, in another one of smaller dimensions as a drawing-room table. Buffet, divans, and chairs occupied the remaining space. We were forthwith introduced to four young Chinese ladies of about twenty years old. Now, to make matters clear, I will at once explicitly state that in England their reputations would be considered decidedly ragged, or, to speak more accurately, would have been considered such before the female franchise had received its present wide extension. But they were by no means Pink Dominoes, and in China polygamy and the generally liberal views of morality would accord to them a social status very different from that which they would occupy in respectable European society. Any semblance of a free and easy or disrespectful demeanour towards them was instantly quietly and indignantly resented. I have been thus minute in explanation in order that my subsequent account may not lose its value from the supposition that I am indiscriminately mixing up *demi-monde* and family life. Indeed, for an Englishman to obtain any personal knowledge of the *penetralia* of the feminine home would be quite out of the question, their daughters and wives being invariably retained in the strictest seclusion.

Well, what is the general appearance of these young ladies? Their dress is certainly of the finest texture, well blended, brilliant colours, expensive and peculiar to the country, consisting of the national turned-up Chinese shoes, loose trousers scarcely beyond the pattern of a divided skirt, and a loosely fitting robe tied up close to the neck. They certainly do not follow the habitual English principle that as few beauties as possible should be hidden in ambush, for their costume is the *ne plus ultra* of modesty.

Here my encomiums must cease; they wear a few trumpery ornaments, among which some ugly jade-stone is conspicuous, and their head-dress is that marvel of ingenious ugliness which we have already described. Complexion disagreeably, almost leprous, white with enamel and powder, eyebrows a thin high-arched line almost approaching a semicircle, the result of the incessant use of the tweezers, and two flaring, inartistic rouge splotches on the upper part of the cheeks. Now, what physical beauties has nature bestowed on you? Few indeed. Undersized, thoroughly stumpy, and ungraceful in figure; with long slits for eyes and mouth, and a pat of putty for a nose, a thick bull-dog neck and prominent cheekbones, your hands are your only pretty features, and these indeed are extraordinarily small, not bigger than those of children of thirteen or fourteen, but without any tapering prettiness. In fine, I can only call you distortions of nature; in detail not wholly ugly, but when there seems to be some approach to prettiness, the favourable item is so little set off by, is so inharmonious with, the rest, that the general effect is one of distaste. Admiration, pshaw! It would be more natural to be enamoured with a beetle because of its bronzed wings, or of a cockroach by reason of its delicate legs.

So much for externals. Let us make ourselves acquainted with the mental attributes of our Chinese company, and although the ladies and ourselves cannot speak one single syllable of our respective languages, yet by means of interpreters and gestures we are quickly in the midst of an animated though scarcely loquacious conversation. Their opening sentences are clatter and pout. Why, wherein have I done wrong already?. Kept you waiting for dinner, and you look as if you knew how to scold and to scratch. Well, we sit down to what I may call the *hors d'œuvre* table, whereon are arranged dishes of melon seeds, almonds, sweetmeats, tea, and cigars, at all of which we nibble or sip, and endeavour to set up a thaw by that running fire of vacuous drivel euphemistically called small talk.

'May I venture to inquire if you have had any previous acquaintance with foreign devils similar to ourselves?'

Translated reply. 'Te hee' (what a nutmeg-grater laugh!) 'What an odd devil you are! You have not got a pigtail, and how big your nose and ears are!'

(No doubt, but your remarks are free and your voice is like the crackling of thorns.)

'That bracelet is very pretty. Will you permit me to examine it somewhat more in detail?'

'There' (suddenly chucks it into my lap; then gabble clatter, gabble clatter).

'I want the pin you have got on your neck' (and she makes a grab at my pearl scarf-pin, on which the curious eyes of all the women are fixed). I (trying to soften my refusal with a deprecatory bow), 'Really, really,' and then seeing a corporeal struggle impending, 'Well, then, I tell you fairly, I won't.' Scoffing mimicry of me and much anger.

'Do you ever read? can you write? are you fond of music?' and so on. But, in truth, to retail our conversation would be a sheer waste of ink and paper. Their minds are in a condition of complete blankness and imbecility, but little removed from idiocy. During the entire evening from seven to eleven, and with an incessant chatter, there is not one single sentence or the vestige of an idea worth record. After dallying for exactly three-quarters of an hour with our melon seeds and almonds, we proceed to the dinner table, and enter on the serious business of the evening.

Now I must do the Chinese the justice to admit that, as a rule, they are remarkably moderate eaters, except when it is a question of coolies or children thrusting quarts of watery rice down their flaccid stomachs, and in the present instance the main feature of the table was, that it was crowded with innumerable small dishes of unsubstantial trifles which would scarcely furnish a good mouthful apiece. Little shreds of cold chicken, ham, pickles, cakes, preserved fruits, sweetmeat messes, and dried fish were placed *pro bono publico*, and each individual, stretching towards the centre, helped himself at intervals to such morsels as his fancy might dictate.

But in this case 'help yourself' was to me a cruel sarcasm. There was not a vestige of knife or fork, and in great perplexity I helplessly twiddled my two chopsticks, not unlike thin lead pencils cut square at the end. Their manipulation, a mere knack, consists in pivoting both sticks between the fingers of one hand, and after a little practice it is not difficult to grasp a small object with the tenacity of a pair of pincers; but at the first essay it would appear far easier to eat peas with a two-pronged fork than to catch hold of slippery little jelly fragments with the ends of two slippery sticks, in using which you are not allowed the services of both hands. Of course the table resounds with jackdaw-like laughter at my failures, and the women find endless diversion in applying their own chopsticks to shoving various selections down my throat.

In course of time relays of hot dishes are brought steaming from the kitchen, and set down in the centre of the table. Bird's-nest soup, of course—an expensive luxury which is never wanting in really *recherché* dinners. It is not a mass of twigs, moss, and feathers, but a clean, clear fluid with a yellow tinge, a slightly gelatinous consistency, and about as insipid to the palate as dissolved isinglass. Nothing except in thought to disgust one here, and as we are supplied with little scoops like porcelain medicine spoons, I am not behindhand in the swallowing race. Shark's fins— humph!—pulpy and viscous, one need be hungry to enjoy them. Toadstools—they look spotted and deadly poisonous, but Sir James Paget assures me that they are nutritious as beef steak. Fishes' maws, that is, the lower lips stewed into a snail-looking broth. Ugh! all this mixture of unwonted food in however small quantities, together with the heat, the charged atmosphere, and the 'bouquet de Chinois,' is beginning to make me feel thoroughly squeamish. Still the women, who by the way annoy me by hawking, hemming, and expectorating as incessantly as a forty-year-old Frenchwoman, in keen amusement ply their chopsticks in my behalf. Shark-fin, toadstool, fish's maw. 'Stop, please' (half choking), 'I cannot eat any more.' But as I open my mouth in enunciation of despairing remonstrance, one last tit-bit is thrust in—a pigeon's egg, and a pigeon's egg which, according to Chinese ideas of dainty dishes, had acquired a peculiar relish by having been preserved for twenty years. I hesitate no longer. An alleged inconvenience in my boot enables me to stoop my head under the table. There I spit out my accumulated mouthful of filthiness, and to a similar receptacle I frequently relegate during the course of the evening individual mouthfuls which even my anxiety to be civil could not persuade me to swallow.

Our drink is of extreme simplicity: samshu, raw and cold, and saki diluted and warm, both distilled from rice, naturally fiery strong, and with a horrible rotten rice-straw flavour. A small quantity would render one helplessly drunk, and the Chinese deliberately set to work to produce that effect on their English guests. But the thimble size of the glasses renders the preservation of tolerable sobriety perfectly practicable.

After the incident of the pigeon's egg, the host considerately suggests that we should 'rest a little from eating,' and adjourn to an adjacent table for tea, smoking, and music. What a relief! The tea is like nectar, and the cigars dispel that pertinacious impression on my palate made by the decomposed egg. How delightful will be the music, for these ladies have acquired some celebrity by their acquirements; yet evil suspicion is beginning to dawn on me. Two slave girls hand their mistresses a rude, ominous-looking guitar and fiddle; the Chinese host takes possession of a wooden drum with a look of placid enjoyment, and, ah! spirit of music, which should awaken kindly tranquillising emotions and drive away vexed thoughts, what a terrible yowl is uplifted! The Shanghai opera all over again, only in closer proximity. The women yell with a discord remarkable in its piercing effects; the stringed instruments shriek like a concord of field gun axles deficient in oil, and the tom-toms bang out a dropping fire of wooden shots. Loud is the applause bestowed on, great is the pride of performance evinced by, these *prime donne*, stimulated thereby to still more deafening results. Their flagging energies are from time to time sustained by the services of the slave girls who hold tea to their lips, sipped without any break in the melody, or the amber mouth-pieces of long pipes from which whiffs are continually drawn.

After about three-quarters of an hour of this pastime: 'Let us resume dinner,' says our host, and we solemnly, formally reseat ourselves at the replenished board. 'Gentlemen,' I announce in a ceremonious set speech, 'believe me how thoroughly I value the hospitality manifested by China towards England. But take it not amiss if I frankly confess that the deglutition of a single additional mouthful is utterly beyond my capacity,' and my plea for mercy is recognised though with manifest reluctance. But if I cannot eat, I can be compelled to drink, and the mirth waxes somewhat fast.

A childish game is played, consisting in passing from hand to hand a smouldering paper spill, and he in whose hands the last spark is extinguished pays forfeit by drinking a certain extra amount of samshu.

As some relief to the horror of great dulness which is now beginning to steal upon me, I make friends with the two little slave girls who are never tired of supplying me with little water-pipes, out of which exactly three delightful inhalations may be drawn, when the bowl must be replenished. Poor little creatures, twelve years old, bright eyes, intelligent, free from deformed feet, and of a type of feature probably from the north of China, and differing from the ordinary repulsive Chinese, they interest me further from the melancholy outlook of their lives. In this part of the world the vast inferiority of women is acted on in a practical, systematical manner, and though theoretically slavery only exists in a very modified form, virtually the lives of these children will be one of cruel and degraded bondage.

Eleven o'clock.—I can't, and I won't stop any longer. So after a hand shaking all round, which is regarded with extreme wonder and amusement, for the habit is unknown to the Chinese, we betake ourselves to our sedan-chairs, and each of us borne by two or more coolies, our procession wends its way homewards. This part is by no means the least interesting in the evening's amusement. Our puffing, scuffling coolies hurry us across many a muddy canal with its antiquated high-arched span, through many miles of street labyrinth, destitute of wayfarers, silent as death, dark as Erebus. Then over the broad rapid Yuen Fuh river, with its wonderful bridge of fifty arches, all of which have been constructed without the aid of a trowel full of cement; then through the Foochow Belgravia, where a few swinging dark red Chinese lanterns seem to render the surrounding obscurity still more profound.

In this business quarter there are still some passengers, and they are warned out of our path by the waving of our lanterns by our coolie-bearers and by their loud 'Hyah,' with which, proud of the procession they constitute, they imperiously intimate 'Get out of the road.' Then, as Mr. Pepys would express himself, ' So home to bed, mightily content thereat. But to think how our repast made us not one whit ill the next day.' The secret of this was that about half a mouthful of each dish more than satisfied our appetites, and that thus the aggregate of food consumed was so small that practically we went to bed dinnerless. The whole experience was one to be eagerly sought out for once, but to be resolutely avoided on a second occasion.

Yuen Fuh monastery in this district has the fame of a local Lourdes or Loretto, though personally known to an infinitesimally small number of Europeans, and hence is wrapped up in the dreadful awe of mystery. That I may make an expedition thereto, my host with typical magnificent hospitality places at my disposal the indispensable house-boat with its equipment of coolies.

In order that I might avoid the tedious windings of the river about Foochow, the house-boat, with my chinese servant and baggage, started at an early hour for a preconcerted rendezvous at Yuenki, to which place I betook myself by cutting across country. Setting forth in the cool of the afternoon, I was carried by three coolies in a chair for over six miles through a country entirely novel in my experience of China, up high hills, down into deep valleys, across turfy declivities, weird indeed with thousands of closely-packed graves, and pine-covered summits, and through fields in the highest state of tillage. The aspect possesses all the combined charms of beauty and variety. Suddenly we reach a solitary little hill-top hamlet, and ere I can divine the purpose of my coolies, they flop me down on the ground, scuttle off without even a grunt of apology or explanation, and leave me baffled, bewildered, and helpless in the midst of a knot of wondering villagers who quickly gather round their strange visitor. Unlike the city people, they look pretty friendly and very good tempered, and ready for a joke.

So I encourage those nearest to me, who nevertheless half shrink back, as from something uncanny, by showing them the dozen little trifles which every traveller carries in his pocket—bunch of keys, many-bladed knife, pencil, chain, and, above all, a little box of wax matches. When I explain that each vesta represents a miniature wax candle, and with much ceremony make a present of five to them, they break out into a cackle of pleasure, and seek to propitiate me by bringing me various edibles.

As I shake my head at each successive nastiness, they hold a consultation. 'What does this strange animal feed on?' 'Ha, I think I have it!' and off bolts a man, reappearing quickly with a pot of boiling water, and a cup, into which he puts a pinch of roughly rolled but sweetly-smelling home made tea leaves. Oh, how good was that five o'clock tea at the Chinese hamlet above Yuenki, and how the now familiarised villagers watch with laughing observation my every motion as I make signs to pour fresh water on the tea leaves, many of which I splutter out as they slip through the superposed saucer which admits of the tea-cup performing likewise the functions of a teapot. In my anxiety to establish further friendship, I give one of them a cigar—a mistake, like Columbus's gift of fire-water to the Indians; they begin to crowd round and clamour for presents. 'Coolie,

coolie!' I shout in angry desperation, and forthwith my bearers slink out of a shed where they had been having a debauch of tea.

The extraordinary habitual abstinence of the Chinese from alcohol certainly is a great point in their favour. Their sobriety is unimpeachable, it cannot be exceeded. At rare intervals some of them drink a little of their horrible rice spirit, called samshu, diluted with abundance of hot water. But throughout the whole of my experience never did I behold one single Chinaman the worse for liquor. Virtually they are a nation of abstainers. I address a volley of abuse to the truants which, from their utter ignorance of English, may have been assumed by them as a shower of encomiums, disengage myself from the now troublesome crowd, seat myself in my canopied chair, which, with a chorus of 'ugh's' the coolies hoist on their bruised, swollen, naked shoulders, and at a rapid pace resume the journey. We have now reached the highest point of our route. Afar off I can make out the winding river, we descend the slopes, and henceforth our road lies through low marshy ground.

The shades of evening are closing in, the scenery has become extremely ugly and uninteresting, and I am growing pretty sick of my monotonous journey, and watching my three-quarters naked coolies as they patter along with the measured cadence of their naked feet. We have completely penetrated into the region of rice swamps; for miles the fields are one perfectly unbroken level of slush and water, through which run slightly raised paths, but so narrow that there is only just room to advance in single file. Now, coolies, pray do not swing me and my chair over the edges in that jaunty manner, and do pick your way a little more carefully. A single false step and I shall be floundering in that slosh alongside.

There are some buffaloes struggling with light native ploughs through the rice swamps, wherein the water just rises to the junction of their legs and their bodies. Extraordinarily sagacious animals! When a European approaches in an instant they detect a change of scent, and these mild creatures, once roused, more savage than many an honestly swaggering British bull, act accordingly.

My *cortège* passes alongside many of them as they are released from plough-work at nightfall; they take no notice of my coolies, but suddenly they wind me; they sniff suspiciously, stamp angrily with every appearance of fury, they lower their heads, and, good gracious, there is no doubt about it, they are on the point of 'making for me;' five seconds more and I shall be rolled over in the two feet of slush adjacent. Their driver holds on by the nose ring with all his might, the coolies quicken their pace a little, and the prejudiced, narrow-minded creature is induced to forego for the present his malignant intention. This little pantomime is repeated about every ten minutes, the darkness has become blackness. When shall we have passed these unutterably dreary rice swamps. Hurrah, here is a straggling village, where the oil lamps flickering in Chinese lanterns, and torches flaring fitfully through volumes of smoke, just give enough light to reveal any number of naked, dusky forms, young and old, men and women, shuffling hastily forward to get a glimpse of the barbarian and his chair. We thread through scattered streets made of rickety tumble-down mat-sheds; and here again I am assailed by enemies in the shape of dogs, not the Pomeranian shaped, fur-coated, black-tongued, thoroughbred Chinese gentleman, such as the well-known pet of the Princess of Wales, but the ubiquitous cur, the mangy, lank, black, pariah which, in servile imitation of the buffaloes, instantly scents the Englishman, and in numbers almost a pack pursue him in yelping chorus for about three-quarters of a mile. Here we reach some rocks and cliffs. Our path, picturesque, so far as the rising moon now gives sufficient light, in the highest degree with the large-trunked banyans and the overhanging bamboos, wriggles about in winding descent, such as might be burlesqued in the rock scenery of Fra Diavolo.

Now we are at the river side. I see our houseboat floating motionless alongside. I hear through the darkness one interrogative English word 'Major?' in the quite exceptionally soft tones of my Chinese boy. Wearied out with a long and laborious day, and unhinged with indisposition I had contracted in the slums of Foochow, I scramble on board in delight. No more rice swamps, buffaloes, or yelping pursuers. Here, indeed, I am in the midst of enervating luxury. The boat is pushed off; with the combined aids of tide, oars, and sail we are carried rapidly along the winding river, past villages, past scattered hamlets, past all sign of human habitations, into the profoundest depths of solitude and silence.

The sense of isolation when coupled with illness is extreme. One Englishman completely cut adrift in a country of not over friendly natives, dependent on a Chinese servant for the bungling translation of the simplest directions, the tempting and easiest imaginable prey of the innumerable depredators. On the other hand this is far more than counterbalanced by the charm of novelty and independence, the romance of the scenery, and the little, if ever so little, element of the adventurous infused therein. Let me explore my present domain, the house-boat, which in China plays so essential a part in the sport, amusements, and comfort of English residents. From my previous experience of their proficiency in the art of 'No. One, and how to take care of him,' I am quite confident that laborious ingenuity will have been exercised in providing for luxury. Our crew, I find, consists of six men and a cook, in addition to my own native servant. Below, they and the whole of their apparatus are stowed away in a recess of the size approximately of a Newfoundland's kennel, the whole of the remaining available space being reserved for Europeans, that dominant race who in this country ever claim the best and foremost, and ever as a matter of course have those claims allowed. Speed and appearance in the ship have been made entirely subordinate to roominess and comfort.

There is a most delightful, however tiny, dining-cabin, with every ship's contrivances in the way of cellaret, sideboard, table, rack, and couch. There is my own cabin equally ingeniously arranged. Dinner, cooking materials, and every description of drinkable were here set forth with a perfection very rarely to be found in the average English establishment, with all the appliances and means to boot.

The drawback to the night was that the stamping and shouting of the rowers, the heat and fever, chased far away sleep. Those were miserable hours, of which we have all had experience, and which we mark in our memory with a black stone.

At last the shallowness of the Yuen Fuh prevents my large house-boat ascending any further; by daybreak we anchor in what I can best describe as an amphitheatre of waters overhung with bamboos and topped with perpendicular, rugged, red granite rocks. Several 'Rapid-boats,' flat bottomed, very light, and specially constructed for travelling up the higher branches, crowd round, to one of which I transfer myself and two house-boat coolies for the purpose of carrying my gun and other equipment. We then begin our ascent of the Twenty-rapid course. Two boatmen labour at the bows, two at the stern, my coolies stretch themselves flat, and in ten seconds are asleep—these wise economisers of time are invariably able to drop off at a moment's notice—and bestowing myself under the large central canopy am kept at such tension of admiration and surprise that for no consideration would I miss a single glance. Once more portions recall to me vividly Lago Maggiore, in the blueness and brightness and warmth of the sky especially.

Yet the parallel is scarcely appropriate on the whole, for what lake, however attractive, can compare with the ever-varying, never-ceasing charms of this beautiful mountainous river. Here we are in a dark melancholy river gorge; the water is sombre, thick, and torpid; it is tepid in its warmth to my hand plashing over the boat. Here we suddenly emerge into radiantly bright clear water, dashing along with the foamy speed of a Scotch stream. Here are Aberdeenshire-looking mountains with a carpet of what I am able to persuade myself is Chinese heather, and with bright patches of red granite. Mountain pines run up to the very apex of the slopes, on the sky line of which I scan, with the delusion of association, for the majestic forms of the red deer. Here, overhanging the waters, is a mass of foliage and flowers, of which the largest conservatories in Kew would represent but a sickly and stunted transplanting. Those bamboos, some very tall, perfectly straight, and uncompromising, and bedecked all over with a foliage more lovely in form and colour which no artist in his most high-flown reveries could have pictured to himself—those bamboos prove that the perfection of grace and beauty is not invariably represented by a curve, but sometimes by a perfectly straight line.

Then there are the feathery bamboos, a somewhat different variety as regards leaf, more pliant and drooping, less independent and vigorous in growth, almost coquettishly dipping their tapering branches into the rushing current at their feet. There are azaleas in full bloom with masses of red blossom; there roses in festoons of white; there orange flowers in carelessly wild profusion, loading the air with their scent; there banyan trees, marvel of all trees, with roots starting downwards from branches twenty feet high, the tendrils swinging towards the ground, in which ultimately reached inheritance they will firmly establish themselves, enlarge to an enormous trunk, and found a new generation. Then one's attention and admiration are diverted to living nature. That concert of songsters are they skylarks, thrushes, blackbirds, or nightingales, for I seem to be able to pick out some notes of each? The dictum that tropical birds do not sing is falsified here, for the chorus rivals that of the Bagshot rhododendron groves. Hark to those cock pheasants challenging and crowing as though in Norfolk farmyards. Which are brightest, orioles or kingfishers ? both species flash in vast numbers out of every bamboo thicket. Butterflies so beautifully and brilliantly enamelled that a jewelled setting would seem appropriate to them, flutter along the margin of the river. And what a mighty fish leaps out of that foam and swirl; but he is not a salmon, he is only an overgrown yellow, ugly, vulgar carp, an appropriate denizen of waters owned by yellow, ugly Chinese.

Now the difficulties and interests of navigation engross our attention. We have been sailing, rowing, and even poling thus far, but the river is becoming capriciously and alternately deep and shallow, and at length we reach one of those long stretches of rapids of which we have to surmount about twenty ere we reach our highest point. New tactics must be adopted. At one time we shoot off suddenly at right angles to our original course, and crossing over to the opposite bank avoid a cataract which no boat could oppose. At another we are fairly aground. Out jump the nearly naked boatmen into the water, lash their long oars to the boat so as to form a sort of yoke, attach themselves thereto, and with many a groan, grunt, and struggle plough the craft through the sand bank. At another the swiftness of the rapid would carry the men off their feet, so they are obliged to wade ashore and haul at a long tow line, gaining ground inch by inch, and sometimes straining with such desperate contention against the tumbling rapids, that I am in doubt whether the tumbling rapids will not gain the day.

Though this is one of the district highways, we have few companion craft in our upward voyage, nearly all the traffic is drifting down the river. It is of a multitudinous nature, and is largely composed of those enormous rafts of timber whereon a temporary village has been constructed, reminding one of similar acres floating on Lake Ontario. As if in picturesque contrast, a little five-year-old elfin of the woods darts out from a thicket, springs on to an adjacent floating trunk, thrusts out into the midst of the hurrying torrent, and managing his raft with wonderful sangfroid and dexterity, is borne swiftly round a bend of the river out of view. Such a child in England would be taking his mid-day sleep in his cradle, and a mother would grow sick with terror if he were to toddle within ten yards of the Round Pond in Kensington Gardens.

For nearly four hours do my boatmen toil with that surprising Chinese endurance which knows no diminution, chatter and laugh incessantly, and exchange chaff with the down-river passengers, to whom I am unquestionably an object of amazement and ridicule. Then we reach a point beyond which no boat can ascend; I must disembark and trust to my own legs. Order of march: Coolie carrying my gun. I scarcely know to what use I can apply it—to shoot these bright-plumaged birds, or any posssible game out of season, would be wanton slaughter. However, it adds to my dignity, and I think it just as well to retain the cartridges in my own possession. Twenty yards behind I march with umbrella and puggery in mitigation of the fierce sun, while the rear is brought up by my head boatman, bearing provisions and abundance of soda water.

We strike straight into the country towards those mountains where is situated the object of my pilgrimage, the China-famed monastery of Yuen Fuh, through a native village, where the everlasting yelping pariah curs pursue me as persistently as a pack of draghounds after a red herring dipped in aniseed, and where I cause the same amazement among the inhabitants as a Life Guardsman among the yokels of Devonshire. Come, the miasma of this Chinese slushy-cum-slime is actually thrown into the shade by the fragrance of the orange trees which thickly crowd the ground in careless wild profusion, charming in their covering of snow-white blossom.

Then up the most fertile of valleys, up a glen rather, with a burn which, cleverly dammed at intervals, covers wide steppes of rice fields with exactly the required depth of water. The sluices are adjusted to the nicety of an inch, and the water is further regulated by tread-wheels which the inhabitants work with never varying labour. Here, however, are the usual narrow raised footpaths running between swamps, and the same odiously clever buffaloes, irritated by the scent of a European, doing their very best to bowl me over. Elsewhere the road is bordered with heavy crops of corn, with sweet potatoes so extraordinarily prolific as to throw into the shade the productive powers of all other potatoes, and with acres of luxuriant tobacco plant. The ground is growing very rugged, and precipitous, and steep, and the toil of climbing under this tropical sun is far more severe than ascending the steepest moor on the hottest twelfth of August.

'Coolie' (by signs), 'are we near the monastery?' and he points to a far, far-off crag, suitable for an eagle's eyrie. 'Well' (in extreme dismay), 'I must go till I drop, but I shall never reach it.' Then for the next three-quarters of an hour there is a struggling forward a few hundred yards at a time, varied by the coolie constantly administering to me pick-me-ups of brandy and soda; then panting up fresh crags until in a lather of perspiration, nape of neck and skull aglow, with flanks sobbing like an over-ridden broken-winded hunter, I giddily stagger up to the threshold of the Yuen Fuh Monastery, the Mecca of my pilgrimage.

Why, this is like the most picturesque of Swiss chalets, with its light-coloured pine planks, airy construction, and fretwork roof. And what an astonishing site has been selected—a gigantic three-quarter arched natural cavern, through the immensely lofty dome of which is seen the brightest and bluest of skies, but with its heat tempered by the deep descent of the rays. Arch and precipitous rock-walls are dripping with innumerable rills, which, in some spots, form stalactites and stalagmites; in others, induce the growth of many a tuft of clinging, large, bright-leaved vegetation ; while at the swampy base, or rather open front terrace, is an impenetrable tangled mass of jungle, with every tree from pine to banyan and bamboo, thick enough to shelter fifty tigers, or a herd of buffalo. Chinese are insatiable in their curiosity concerning aught that appertains to the human being, but are as insensible as blocks to all the wonders and beauties of nature.

My coolies impatiently beckon to me to follow them up the outside ladder staircase, and, according to the wont of the country, without a knock, and with your leave or by your leave, we march into the domicile of these holy recluses. There they are, about ten of them, industriously pottering about household trifles. They wear no specially characteristic dress, they are undersized, skinny, grotesque-looking baboons of any age between eighteen and eighty, rather like an average set of coolies, with nothing extraordinary about them except the absence of a pigtail, and the whole of their scalps being shaved as smooth as marble, which makes them extraordinarily ugly. Without surprise or resentment at my intrusion they instantly cluster about me with their habitual buzz of curiosity, and I, in my turn, am bound to admit that I extracted far more amusement out of these creatures than had yet been my hap during my travels in China.

Noticing my prostration as I unceremoniously

flopped down on a bench, they bolt off for the usual sugarless, milkless, teapotless tea; the home-prepared leaf as fragrant as flowers, and the infusion far more renovating than my former therapeutic of brandy and soda. But that pot of nearly boiling water about which you are dancing in gesticulation, you surely do not expect me to swallow that likewise? Oh, I see. I am to mop my scorched streaming face with it; quite right, far more refreshing than the coolest of baths. Then, as I rest and set to work at my sandwiches, the whole ten come near and scrutinise intently my every gesture and mouthful, evidently exchanging between themselves the freest comments.

By way of retaining my prestige, I repeat yesterday's experiment and show off to them, as I would to a set of infants, the various traveller's items I carry about me, with the same brilliant success. Match-box, many-bladed knife, pencil-case, compass, are each examined in careful detail, and when with dumb pantomime, appropriate to a Christmas mummery, I explain the various uses of each, their admiration and delight are boundless. My sixpenny self-closing tobacco pouch sends them off into peals of laughter, but they are fearful and awed at my manipulation of my small leather haversack; concealing the spring-lock with my hand, and simultaneously pressing and blowing on the aperture, I make it fly open in the manner with which most of us have at times attempted to amuse children in arms. But my monk spectators shrink back scared and discomfited: 'This is magic, and we certainly have got the evil one amongst us.'

Yet one of the brethren, I fear of a dangerously latitudinarian turn of mind, resolved to get to the bottom of the mystery, surreptitiously twitches the bag aside, and I watch him, unperceived as he fancies, creep into a corner and puff away at the bag, with cheeks distended ready to bursting. No result. 'There, that white devil clearly is a necromancer,' and he quavers with unconcealed dread.

Come, let us change the subject. They are handling my gun, and, though familiar enough with matchlocks, they are puzzled at the breech-loading apparatus. They eagerly entreat of me to fire it off, and two rapidly successive shots awaken echoes over the hills and far away in a descending gamut of softness inexpressibly striking, I might almost say, beautiful. Over and over again am I entreated to renew this amusement, and keen is the competition for the possession of the empty cartridges; what they want them for I cannot surmise.

'Come, old fellows,' say I, with all the hilarity of recent brandy and soda, 'let us be friends—have a sandwich.'

They shrink back.

' No—well, do try a nip of brandy.

Violent dissent.

' At least join me in a bottle of soda,' making the

cork fly out with a bang, which once more renews their quaking.

'Ah, that white demon is actually pouring his smoking, hissing liquid down his throat!' Dead silence, pause, and one of the monks is apparently seized with an idea. Catching hold of my sleeve and signing to me to follow him, he hastily drags me into an adjacent shrine, and, ignoring the Buddha, eagerly directs my attention to two images of demons which the Chinese habitually worship to avert malignant influences. Clearly he is introducing me to some evil spirits of whom he supposes I must have special cognisance.

But now I have an opportunity of examining every detail of this most sacred idol temple. As regards the mere aspect, such sights have lost nearly all their interest for me from previous frequent observation. There is the usual carving, and gold and silk decoration, half tawdry, half magnificent; the flowers, the subdued light, the candles and tapers, incense, and highly adorned altar—such melancholy counterparts of Roman Catholic ornamentation. There is a mammoth gilt Buddha, sitting cross-legged, with the luring expression to be traced in a fat elderly gentleman or a sensuous satyr. His long slit eyes are of Mongolian type, but his other features, strangely enough, are distinctly European and not Chinese. Still more remarkable, the idols are invariably without pigtails. 'You see we dress our hair like your gods,' said a European to a Buddhist. 'Yes, I see, and is your bodily frame of the same material, brass?' was the ready retort. Ranged alongside of him are his three wives, smaller gilt monstrosities, but their features again revert to the Mongolian form. In a modest recess are the two devils to which I have alluded, and whence comes the strange fact that the tradition of their appurtenances is identical in the far East as in the West? for they are represented with horns, and forked tails tucked in semi-concealment under them, but not with hoofs. They are dressed in conventional Chinese fashion, and hold a horrible-looking hammer and nail as implements of torture. Some clumsy pictures close by represent, as far as I can make out, the future sufferings of the damned.

Now, my friends, I want to find out, but with every possible care to avoid wounding your susceptibilities, what are your genuine sentiments of respect or religion towards these ostensibly most holy objects, not symbols merely, of your worship. I carelessly finger the sacred vessels, I turn over the incense and joss-sticks, I stroll close up to the altar, and at last I smack Buddha's fat ugly thigh contemptuously. I believe I might almost have spat upon him, but the monks evince not a vestige of withholding me, of vexation, or even of disapproval. On the contrary, their careless cackle and laughter is not for a moment intermitted, and with increasing merriment they actually comply with my request for a bundle of the sacred fragrant joss-sticks placed in a corner of the shrine.

The familiarity and contempt with which they treat their idols relieves us from the consideration for feelings which one would otherwise show to the professors of even a degraded folly. 'Buddha smokes his incense and is glad to get it,' replies a priest charged with irreverence; 'why should not I smoke my tobacco?' During a drought it is common to drag the rain-god into the sun, to make him feel how parched the ground is.

Then the priests show me over their domestic arrangements, rather in a spirit of pride than asceticism, but were the practice of this latter quality their object, nothing could be more frugal and rough. The item of their provisions which struck me was an enormous accumulation of ginger roots, identical with those which we transform into preserve, but which they eat simply boiled in their natural condition. Their source of water supply is unique. High overhead the thick root of a bamboo has wriggled its way through a cleft in the solid arched rocks, and, acting as a depending conduit to a subterranean stream, sends a silver thread of the purest, coldest water into a reservoir below.

Once more the brethren drag me off to another temple and triumphantly exhibit to me seven more golden idols and two modestly retiring demons. But

I have had enough of so much which, taken on the whole, is hideously, revoltingly grotesque, with the occasional trace of that which is handsome. Well, monks, good-bye! I thank you much for your civility and hospitality, and I beg to present you with these two empty soda-water bottles (received with extreme delight), and with this pecuniary donation for the good of your monkery (eagerly clutched at, demon though I be). You greedy creatures—more—you don't often get such a windfall as this, and are trying your tricks on a traveller. So, you admit this, and grin thanks, and 'chin-chin,' and away I start to regain my Rapid-boat.

My downhill return journey, freed from the scorching and overwhelming toil of the ascent, gives me opportunities to note many objects previously overlooked. The many thousands of cut-out steps, the narrow path with incessant winding, now skirting the edge of a precipice, now enlarging and running through giant archways or beautiful natural grottoes; above all, the mountainously diversified and tropically rich scenery, a vast garden, and the only one I could call beautiful which I had seen in China—here, indeed, if anywhere, 'every prospect pleases, and only man is vile.'

Suddenly there emerges round a corner a regular type of the disreputable, ill-looking, country loafer and semi-scoundrel. In England he would be a poacher by occupation. Here he hangs about with one of those absurd matchlocks, a tube of iron, stockless, and fired from the thigh by a piece of slow-match—ready to pick up prey in the shape of bird, beast, or human being. After all it is just as well to go about always armed in this country. Some of these rice-fields are used as small fish stews, from which inhabitants are even now taking out the occupants, and are carrying two or three coarse little carp, or a loathsome eel already semi-festering in the hot sun, as a relish to their meal of rice and pickles. I re-embark in my Rapid-boat, in which I am speedily steered down the little cataracts, which remind me of a miniature 'Lachine' on the St. Lawrence, and regain that comparative colossus, my house-boat. Then I cause myself to be conveyed to the vicinity of another riverside object, a waterfall, of which I had picked up a tradition, land on a desolate-looking shore, and again with two coolies strike straight into country. But the sun is now hidden by clouds which are rapidly piling up into inky masses, and my head coolie, partly by signs, partly by a few words of argot which he has picked up, and calls pidgin-English, intimates that we are about to have a deluge—will I not turn back? No, begun, half ended. I may never have another chance; press on.

What began with a thin forest now thickens into an almost impenetrable jungle, with bamboo poles in places as close as stockade work, and a tangled undergrowth; through them, however, rushes a mountain torrent, and by following its rocky course, and working tooth and nail, we make fair progress. True, I am often obliged to wade ankle-deep, even over stepping stones and shallows, but this wetting below matters nothing in prospect of our drenching from above; for now the enormous thunder-drops are splashing down, they come faster and faster, until they assume the proportions of sheets of water. Heaven's artillery crashes as if it would rend these solid rocks, the lightning seems to blind one, and, straining every muscle, I struggle forward through the jungle under the fury of a tropical thunderstorm, the violence of which it is impossible could be exceeded. And yet, and yet, who could close their eyes to the beauties of our path? Those beautiful red masses of hothouse azaleas—I cannot but sometimes snatch at a dripping spray, still more lovely in its bath—those orange blossoms, wild and white among the tangled foliage, imperiously claim my homage by the reminder of the fragrance with which they load even the water-charged air; and those jewelled butterflies lend themselves more readily to admiration from the fact that, beaten down by the storm, they can flutter but slowly aside.

Higher we scramble, until among the crash of the storm and the swi—shing of the torrents a fresh roar arises—ah! the waterfall—but I can only discern it dimly as I stand on the precipitous path, midway between the stream below and the crags above.

'Walkee down,' imperiously shouts in my ear my head coolie. All very well, but that means walkee up again. However, sliding, slipping, and scraping I find myself at the base. Yes, the waterfall is very magnificent, as it leaps down in volumes of white foam, hundreds of feet from the crags above to the boiling cauldron below; but, after all, I have seen similar beauties in beautiful Scotland, and the surrounding tropical adjuncts constitute to me the real charm, so, friend coolie, 'walkee back again,' if you please, to the path above, which is only reached by pulling ourselves up, hand over hand, with the aid of the friendly bamboos.

Back again as fast as possible; as we retrace our steps the torrent is no longer wade-able in many places. On hands and knees do I crawl along the slippery ledges, the firm grasp only of my sure-footed coolies saving me from sliding into the angry rushing deep stream, which would sweep me away as though I were a leaf on the surface. Not a dry thread have I on me, but this is not so much due to the streams overhead as to the streams of perspiration which trickle from me in the midst of the stiflingly hot atmosphere of this steaming jungle. There, in a small clearing, is a wood and rush structure; is it a sort of lair or a human habitation? Human, but it will be hardly wise to seek refuge among these wild Chinese men of the woods.

On, on; but the coolies have lost their way, and

the blackness of the storm is growing into the darkness of night. At last there is a gleam from our houseboat. I may without sentiment mutter, 'Lead, kindly light, amidst the encircling gloom,' and in a few moments I have reached my haven, a dripping, prostrate specimen of thoroughly exhausted humanity.

If I expend even half a dozen lines on a matter of such profound indifference to the reader as my personal indisposition, it is only to explain the sudden termination of a journey whereof the interest was far from exhausted. Fever and other indisposition, materially increased by recent exposure in the sun and the jungle, at last prostrated me so completely, that all my recourse to opium and to an invaluable little medicine chest furnished by Squire failed to bring me to time, and after a mental struggle I decided that my only expedient was to issue the word of command 'Back to Foochow.'

The heat and the rain had reduced all my garments to such a state as to be unwearable until they had been subjected to the stove. So a fire is lighted in the saloon, and I am compelled to sit on deck in what I may describe as coolie costume. Partly drifting with the current, partly aided by the struggling efforts of six rowers, partly wafted along by the light breeze, we speed quickly down the river. The storm has cleared away, the moon gives enough light to tempt us to look, and enough shadow to mystify.

Jagged mountain crests and wooded hill slopes

stand out clearly, and the normal silence is rendered more striking by incidental sounds. Nightingales, or their Chinese representatives, burst forth with their entrancing 'jug-jug;' a startled night bird gives a sudden shriek; hark to that shrill whistle from the bank, human without doubt. It is quickly responded to, and followed by the signalling flashes of a lantern and a certain scuffling on the shore as we pass. The creek pirates, or rather river marauders, are as plentiful as blackberries in these regions. At all events we have been carried quickly beyond those night birds. My coolies work like galley slaves, and pull away at their heavy oars with an unwearied energy which is astounding; and they now begin to lift up their voices in a chorus of unearthly yells, which apparently affords them immeasurable ease and delight, accompanied with stamps of their naked feet which cause to quiver every timber in the boat. Sleep to the fever-tossed unfortunate—pooh!— not a wink till long after daylight. Then I awake about twenty-six miles from yesterday's starting point, and disembarking, buckle to for my six miles' walk across country ere I can regain Foochow. Of course the blazing sun nearly prostrates a European, but the natives heed it no more than we should heed a couple of degrees of frost. Oddly sheltered as to their heads by bamboo-plaited hats, literally of the same expanse as an average umbrella, and with their naked bronzed skins free from perspiration, they dig and harrow, and sow and gather, they drive pigs, ducks, geese, and buffalo, and, above all, they dig-in manure. The children run about as naked as the day they were born; the women, decently clothed, however, performing more than a fair share of work; and I witness busy scenes of suburban industry which I had missed during my previous eventide journey over the same district. The anachronism of sowing and reaping, simultaneously, identical crops attests the fertility of the soil, the industry of the workers, and the favourable nature of the climate. Here are rice, beans, sweet potatoes, barley and wheat, but no oats; not a sign of a horse, a few buffaloes, and no machinery whatever; the labour is entirely manual—even in some cases to the extent of ploughing.

The narrow slippery paths running through the rice swamps are constantly choked with passenger traffic. The wayfarers stop to stare, but make way for me with perfect good temper, and without any attempt at hustling. Group after group do I pass of the most jovial processions of coffin-bearers, singing and splitting their sides with laughter. They are conveying bodies to yonder hill burying grounds, and these spread over an extent equal to that which I have described at Chinkiang, but the graves are far more elaborate and carefully tended. The only qualification for site is that the surface should slope and drain off the rain—no exigencies as to the head and feet lying east and west. Every little tumulus is crowded with irregularly placed mounds, and every mound is besprinkled with joss paper money, on which is stamped in gilt characters a fancy value, destined for the service of the ghosts. There are few inscriptions and still fewer stone or masonry vaults, though here and there is a large semicircular wall enclosing a family resting-place. The space inside has been utilised by the practical agriculturists as thrashing floors, and I see many labourers, like Bible Gideons, beating out the grain with a stick, or causing the buffaloes to trample over the bundles, and effecting the winnowing by exposing the products to the wind of the open air. Foochow at last,

Moderate diet,
A snug loose box, and perfect quiet,

is the best prescription in these climes.

Shall I tell you aught about Kuh Shan, a monastery in the immediate vicinity of Foochow, of almost equal repute and sanctity with Yuen Fuh, but larger and richer? Very little, because there would be a wearisome monotony of description, although in actual experience there was considerable difference between the two. Let me, therefore, dwell only on these points of divergence. Once more I toil up a mountain of the same characteristics as at Yuen Fuh, and as we approach an outlying shrine the deep tolling of a bell, at exactly equal intervals of about thirty seconds, sounds solemn beyond measure, almost weird, as it re-echoes over the rocks and dark, solitary, wooded hills. Here is its origin—a burn turning an 'overshot' waterwheel constitutes a never-ceasing automatic bell-striker.

We dispose of our luncheon within the sacred precincts to the perfect content of the ragged priests, and pick up a little waif and stray experience of the spiritual exercises of the agricultural population. A few wayfarers prostrate themselves before the idol of Buddha, grovelling on the earth, and banging their heads frequently against the hard ground. One inquirer into his impending fortune first knocks his forehead and begs that the divination may be a true one, then he applies himself to a priest, who shakes haphazard out of a vase one of a heap of rolled up papers, each of which bears a sentence which may be twisted into almost any sort of prophecy, and the seeker departs, apparently quite contented. Then to the cluster of wooden châlets constituting the head-quarters of the monastery.

There we see an oblong pond tenanted by sacred carp, which as curiosities surpass their historical fellows at Versailles. The moment we tossed a crust of bread a few feet from the edge, the coarse creatures, about forty in number, varying in size from one to eight pounds, rushed to the spot, crowded as, but far less fearless than, a flock of sheep. These naturally shyest of all shy fish showed not a vestige of timidity. In struggling for the morsels they dragged themselves over the backs of their competitors, half thrusting their own bodies out of the water; they fought, they set up a chorus of loud sucking with their hideous leathery mouths, and they afforded us a full opportunity, for which anglers might vainly seek during a lifetime, of observing their ways. Their existence is carefully guarded over, and they bore many marks of an age which their comparatively small size seemed to negative. One, a six-pounder, was distinguished above his fellows as being of a golden colour, closely approximating that of the ornamental gold fish.

In the temple was a relic, the object of immeasurable reverence—a tooth of Buddha. For long our endeavours to see it were fruitless. The priests declare they do not understand us—they have no relics here—certainly none so holy. But our ascending bids of backsheesh reach at last a point which induces compliance. We are led with trembling awe to a temple, to its altar, to the small shrine thereon; a casket is unlocked, and there we see set, in the precise fashion of a Roman Catholic relic, an ugly, dirty, yellow, gigantic tooth, which an amateur physiologist would pronounce to have belonged to a mammoth horse. Probably the priest judges from our anxiety to inspect the object that we are inspired with a reverential belief in the doctrines of his religion, and, anxious to transact a little more profitable business, he offers for a dollar to convoke a chin-chin, or orison of monks, which shall produce a shower of rain. But we at once close negotiations herein by explaining that our present wish is for a continuance of the cloudless sky.

Quitting the large crowd of dirty, lounging, despicable, degraded monks—the universal contempt with which the ministers of superstition in China are regarded is indeed fully justified—we retrace our steps by a fresh route to our point of re-embarkation. The road leads us through an infinity of stone archways, down a multiplicity of some thousands of steps, and past rocks carved with the strangest and most elaborate devices and curious inscriptions; then through villages scattered about the hot steaming marshes.

In all cases clumps of trees are planted, apparently with the view of absorbing some of the noxious miasmas. But the Chinese seem to possess a talent for giving an air of squalor to all their towns and villages, and here too there is an entire absence of all sanitary arrangements, the usual accumulation of decomposing organic matter, and the consequent terrible stenches.

Before I quitted Foochow I came across a German, from whom I obtained some photographs of the adjacent localities. He assured me that the suspicion and dislike with which Chinese of all classes regard his art is invincible. On one occasion he offered thirteen dollars to clear away some obstructing bamboos which were only worth three dollars, but the proprietor spitefully refused. Ten dollars is the lowest bribe which will induce even a coolie to allow himself to be included in a group, as he considers that by having his portrait taken he brings down on his head the probability of a great calamity within twelve months.

I have repeatedly referred to the serious and incessant inconvenience I experienced, owing to my total ignorance of the Chinese language. Why had I not picked up a few sentences, either by dint of constant association with it or by methodical study? I only abandoned this common sense intention after the most mature deliberation. As for pronunciation and grammar, the books dealing with these intricacies are such as to strike dismay even into those who have made European languages their study, for the Chinese have not so much as a parallel to our alphabet. Certain symbols, derived from sign writing, represent certain root words, which when combined, expanded, and added to, make up their whole vocabulary. Practically, therefore, there is no such thing as spelling; there are as many symbols as there are words—and these are variously computed by different students from 40,000 to 50,000, though for ordinary purposes as few as about 4,000 characters will suffice. It is evident what a prodigious exercise of memory is involved in acquiring the mere rudiments of the written language. Nor can even a slight colloquial knowledge be acquired without immoderate study. An approximately literal translation of an English sentence is constantly impracticable owing to the entire absence of many corresponding terms, and a roundabout paraphrase only is attainable.[1] Translators of the Bible have been beset by a yet unsolved difficulty in adequately rendering the word 'God.' Terms specially applicable to civilisation, such as steamer, railway, telegraph, artillery, can only be rendered by a childish periphrasis. It is worth notice, as an illustration of national churlishness, that they possess no corresponding terms whatever for 'please' and 'thank you;' they ignore all kindly recognition for small services. Again, the same word frequently expresses different meanings according as it is pronounced in a low or high key, there being four different tones in the language. Thus 'shan' may mean a mountain, or virtuous; 'yen' salt, tobacco, or an eye; according as the pitch of the voice is base or treble. The graduated inflections are to a foreigner almost imperceptible. Great as is the difficulty of adults in acquiring Chinese, greater still is the difficulty in preventing English children in picking it up from their amas. The most stringent rules on the part of exceedingly silly mothers fail to prevent gabbling with fluency a language which learned men toil in vain to acquire.

But the most serious drawback of all is the difference of dialects, almost amounting to a difference of language, within very narrow zones. Supposing the student after much patient labour to have vanquished the difficulties of paraphrase and of rapid, inharmonious slurred-over pronunciation, and to be able to

[1] See p. 47.

convey his meaning at Canton; he travels a hundred miles northwards, towards Swatow or Amoy, and the former vernacular is totally unrecognisable. My Hong Kong 'boy' in such a case was as incapable of making himself understood as was I, and he declared with much anger his inability to comprehend one word which his countrymen were saying. At last I discover him talking briskly with some local native servants—but they are actually conversing in pidgin-English. You would search far indeed ere you would overhear a more ludicrous jargon.

In fine, is it worth spending a single week in a labour where the results are so infinitesimally small? Or will it repay one to devote years in acquiring a language so illimitable and ill-defined that erudite scholars never feel they have mastered it, but are for ever compelled to 'keep it up'—a language destitute of the literature of science and art, possessing only compilations of so-called philosophy, which have been palmed off on an uninvestigating world as marvels of sagacity, but which a closer scrutiny reveals as in the main a farrago of folly? I submit, No—waste not an hour in a study as a general rule so useless. There are clearly certain exceptional occupations, such as missionaries and doctors, where a certain colloquial knowledge is absolutely indispensable. Nay more—I cannot but think that such a knowledge would be valuable to the permanently resident English employés. Yet it is a remarkable fact that practically scarcely an individual among these educated gentlemen who have spent ten, fifteen, twenty years in the country can speak a single syllable of the language. But beware how you tread on this ticklish ground, lest you produce a dynamite explosion, the effects of which are altogether disproportionate to the bulk. 'A knowledge of Chinese would be worse than useless— it would be pernicious to us,' is the angry outburst. 'Our transactions are all conducted through the native compradores, who invariably know English, and were it even suspected that we understand the vernacular, the Chinese traders would defeat us with their own facile weapons of linguistic chicane and fraud, and in the long run our business would suffer.' These arguments are so superficial that it will surely suffice to reply that every knowledge must be power, and that the optional exercise of that power cannot be otherwise than a potential element of prosperity. Of course the real reason is that the task of acquisition would be intolerably laborious, with which arguments I heartily concur.

Of the peculiarities, good and bad, of the Chinese intellect in respect of instruction, I once had experience—perhaps rather a favourable one—in one of my 'boys' of about twenty-three, who after two or three unsuccessful attempts at persuasion, at least induced me to undertake to teach him to read and write our language, of which acquirement he was entirely ignorant. He was, however, fairly versed in a colloquial knowledge, and was of an intelligence considerably above the average. At first his progress in reading was startlingly quick—at last it was portentously slow. He exhibited wonderful powers of memory, but a singular absence of powers of deduction. I could easily teach him the spelling and pronunciation of chrononhotonthologos and latitudinarianism, but if with patient endeavour I explained to him that b-o-o-t must spell 'boot,' and then asked for the reading of r-o-o-t, the chances were that the reply would be 'great coat' or 'umbrella.' Similarly in writing, in an inconceivably short time he picked up the knack of caligraphy; so much so, that I was disconcerted at his reproduction of his master's handwriting to an absurd extent of accuracy. Often was I compelled to inquire of him, 'Where does my copy end and where does your exercise begin?' But when we advanced to intelligent dictation, still more to the construction of simple original sentences, he was as much at sea as a child of seven years old. His laboriousness was beyond praise, his artfulness in inveigling me to give him a few extra minutes of instruction was touching —and yet at the end of three months' regular persistent teaching, my feeling was one of disappointment. A dull European scholar would in my opinion be more encouraging in the long run.

Here, for the present, ends the narrative of my experiences of the Far East. I am confident that my facts and deductions will be flatly contradicted by at least one class of individuals—the 'twenty-years-in-the-country-and-speak-the-language' men, who resent the most evident propositions enunciated by unprejudiced newcomers. Forgetful or ignorant of the Western world, and ignorant of their own ignorance, they insist that we should disbelieve all we have actually seen and heard. And though I have laboured to write truly and impartially, how, as Mr. W. Cooke says in 'China,' can I hope to escape inaccuracies in speaking of a country which represents one mass of contradictions—of a country where roses have no fragrance, the women no petticoats, and the magistrates no honour; where old men fly kites, and puzzled people scratch their backs instead of their heads; where the seat of honour is on the left, and the abode of intellect is in the stomach; where to take off your hat is insolent, and to wear white is to wear mourning; where, finally, there is a literature without an alphabet, and a language without a grammar?

INDEX.

ABO

ABORIGINES near Foochow, 295
Agriculture, 102, 141, 161, 319
Ancestral worship, 189, 190, 201
Anglo-Chinese, 30, 280
Animosity towards Europeans, 229
Anomalies, national, 329

BANK at Hong Kong, 7
Barbers, 231
Bargaining, system of, 227
Bell, automatic, 321
Bird's-nest soup, 289
Boat. *See* Rapid-boat and House-boat
'Boys,' Chinese, 44, 327
Brick tea, 156
Buddhist monks, 307, 322
Buffaloes, animosity towards Europeans, 228, 297, 305

CANGUE, 241
Carp, 321
Children, importance of male, 275
Chinese submissiveness, 67, 230; inability to comprehend English character, 101; suppression of knowledge, 128; incapacity for gratitude, 185, 191; courage, deficiency of, 222; beauty, low type of, 286; conversation, 286; temperance, 296
Chinkiang, 124
Cholera, 165
Chopsticks, 288

FOO

Climate, Chinese dread of wet, 21; tropical downpour, 22; heat of, 23; health of, 28; unsuitable for children, 28
Compradores, 327

DEVIL-WORSHIP, 311
Dinner-party at Hong Kong, 31
— Chinese, 284
Doctors, 163
Dogs, pariah, 298
Dragon-devouring moon, 264
Drainage, neglect of, 222
Dress, native, 16, 21
Ducks, extraordinary numbers of, 136
Ducks, sagacity of, 277

EATING, Chinese method of, 119
Eggs, decomposed, a luxury, 291
Emotions, expression of, 236
Employé, career of English, 283
Executions, 243
Extravagance of Anglo-Chinese, 281
Eye, extraction of, 168

FEET, deformed, 169, 173
Fever, 165
Firewalls, 256
Fish, coarseness of, 233
Foliage, 301
Foochow, arrival at, 270; scenery, 279; social life in, 280
Foochow Mission, 187
Food, Chinese, 73, 254, 289

INDEX

FRE

French administration at Shanghai, 75–78
Funeral, Chinese, 14, 235
— military, 53

GARDENS, botanical, 27; private, 253
Gateways decorated with heads, 246
Graves, at Shanghai, 105; at Chinkiang, 126; at Yuenki, 309
Groaning of coolies, 234
Guilds, 247

HANKOW, 146; precautions against revolt, 149; exploration of city, 216; streets, 217; guilds, 247
Hanyan, 146
Happy Valley, 18
Health, 19
Hong Kong, ignorance concerning, 1; harbour, 3; hospitality, 4; houses, 6; population, 16; cemetery, 18; Sunday at, 41; native quarter, 48; Queen's birthday parade, 51; defences, 58; financial statistics, 62; acquisition of, 63
Honkiew, 74
Hospitality, 272
Hospitals, 169, 180
House-boat, 299
Hwangpoo River, 66–69

IDOLS, 236, 310
Ignorance respecting Europe, 198
Imitative powers, 328
Infanticide, 276
Inland Mission, 209
Innovations, aversion to, 128
Insects, 37
Instruction, religious, 177, 186

JINRICKSHA. *See* Ricksha
Joss-houses, 237
Jungle, 315

PEE

KIUKIANG, 1
Kowloon, 60
Kuh Shan, 320

LADIES, Chinese, 285
Language, knowledge of Chinese, 324
Lascars, gun, 57

MACHINERY, absence of, 228
Mail, arrival of, 42
Mandarin pageantry, 245, 263
Medical Missions, 167, 178
Medicines, 164
Min, River, forts at mouth of, 269
Missionaries, Père Gannier, 121; ill success of, 185; Foochow labours, 187; difficulties, 189; at Zic-a-wei, 193; opening for, 200; success of Roman Catholics, 201; failure of Protestants, 203; their indifference, 205; remedies of defects, 211
Money, nature of currency, 159, 227, 263
Music, 110, 291
Musquitoes, 40

NANKIN, 132
Navigation, difficulties of river, 303
Night scenery, 347

OPIUM-HOUSES, 256; opium, exaggeration of evil, 257; examination of samples, 261; experience of smoking, 262
'Orphan' Island, 135

PAGODA anchorage, 270
Passengers, mixed nationalities of, 116
'Peak,' 34
Peep-shows, 235

INDEX

PER

Perfumes, 225
Pheasants, gold, 160; Reeves', 161
Photography, 323
Pidgin-English, 46, 326
Piracy, 61, 347
Police court at Shanghai, 85
Ponies, 97
Population on rivers, 140
Porcelain tiles, 249
Portuguese in China, 49
Prisons, 239
Procession, religious, 237

QUARRELS, street, 230

RACING, 97
Railways, 129
Rapid-boat, 300, 314
Ricksha, 12
River life, 273
Roads, 126
Robbers, 33
Roofs, decoration of, 249
Routine of a hot day, 22

SAMSHU, 290
Schools, 171, 181
Science, Chinese, a delusion, 196
Sedan-chairs, 12
Shanghai, river approach, 66; general aspect, 68-70; boundaries, 72; French concession, 74; history, 78; form of government, 80; statistics, 82; social life, 93; Sunday at, 95, 98; gambling, 96; suburbs, 99
Ships, facilities for rising of native passengers, 117
Sickaway. *See* Zic-a-wei
Singing, 110, 291
Slaves, 262
Smells, foul, 223
Snipe, 16

ZIC

Soldiers' daily routine, 56
Sport, 104, 136
Stanley village, 61
Street sights, 220
Surgical operations, 166

TEA, brick, 156
— judging, 154
— tasting, 150
Temples, 202, 310, 322
Theatre at Shanghai, 108
Thunderstorms, 26, 315
Toadstools, 289
Torture, 241
Trees, miniature, 253
Tungliu, 134

UNEDUCATED Chinese women, 286

VICTORIA, town of, 11
Villages, Chinese, 107, 132
Voices, inharmonious, 219

WATERFALL, 316
Writing, excellence of, 252
Wuchau, 146
Wuhu, 136

YAMENS, 238
Yang-tsze-kiang River, 116; shifting of bed, 125, 145; scenery, 132; unknown to travellers, 144; magnitude and riches, 145; a crowded highway, 263
Yuen Fuh Monastery, 306
— River, 272, 301
Yuenki, 296

ZIC-A-WEI, Missionary station at, 193

PRINTED BY
SPOTTISWOODE AND CO., NEW-STREET SQUARE
LONDON

www.ingramcontent.com/pod-product-compliance
Lightning Source LLC
Chambersburg PA
CBHW032047220426
43664CB00008B/899